Jesus and the Essenes

By
Dolores Cannon

Originally published by Gateway Books, The Hollies, Wellow, Bath, BA2-8QJ, United Kingdom. First Printing 1992, Reprinted: 1993, 1994, 1997, 1998; First American Publication 2000 Ozark Mountain Publishing, Inc., 2nd Printing 2001, 3rd 2006, 4th 2009, 5th 6th 2010, 7th 2011, 8th 2012, 9th 2013, 10th 2014, 11th & 12th 2015, 13th & 14th 2016, 15th 2017, 16th-19th 2018, 20th & 21st 2019, 22th-24th 2020, 25th – 28th 2021, 29th - 31st 2023

For permission, or serialization, condensation, adaptions, or for our catalog, please write to: Ozark Mountain Publishing, Inc., P.O. Box 754, Huntsville, AR 72740, Attn: Permissions Dept.

Library of Congress Cataloging-in-Publication Data
Cannon, Dolores, 1931 - 2014
  Jesus and the Essenes by Dolores Cannon

  Eyewitness accounts of the missing years of Jesus, the portions that have been removed from the Bible, and the community of the Essenes at Qumran. The information was gained through regressive hypnosis, conducted by Dolores Cannon. Includes Bibliography and Index.

1. Jesus 2. Essenes 3. Dead Sea Scrolls 4. Hypnosis 5. Reincarnation
I. Cannon, Dolores, 1931 - 2014 II. Essenes III. Title

Library of Congress Catalog Card Number: 99-076754
ISBN# 1-886940-08-8

Cover Design by Drawing Board Studio
Illustrations by Joe Alexander
Book set in Times New Roman
Book Design: Tab Pillar
Published by:

P.O. Box 754
Huntsville, AR 72740

WWW.OZARKMT.COM
American Edition printed in the United States of America

Contents

Preface

Who am I to think that I dare to write a book which will upset or at least shake the foundation of the beliefs of many, Jew and Christian alike? I respect beliefs. Man must *believe in something,* even if he believes there is nothing.

This is the story of a people who dedicated their lives to the protection and preservation of knowledge. I can relate to that. To me the destruction of knowledge is a very terrible thing. These people seem to have passed the proverbial torch to me through the eons of space and time. This information was not given to me to lie gathering dust on a shelf It was meant to be revealed once again to others hungry for knowledge. It is as though the Essenes almost speak in whispers in my ears. "Write", they say to me, "the knowledge has been hidden too long. Write, do not let the knowledge be lost again." So, I feel I must pass along what I have learned. If this upsets some, I hope it is understood that I am not setting out to do so. If it makes some think, this is my intention.

I cannot claim that what I have presented in this book is the absolute truth, facts beyond dispute. I don't know, and I doubt seriously whether anyone alive has the answers. But maybe, for the first time, break loose from the mold that has held you prisoner since childhood. Open the windows of your mind and allow curiosity and the quest for knowledge to enter like a fresh spring breeze and sweep away the cobwebs of complacency. Dare to think the unthinkable. Dare to question the unquestionable. Dare to consider different concepts of life and death. And your Soul, your eternal "Self," will be all the richer for it.

SECTION ONE

The Mysterious Essenes

CHAPTER 1

How It All Began

It is possible to travel through time and space and visit long lost civilizations. It is possible to speak with those long dead and relive again with them their lives and their deaths. It is possible to travel backwards hundreds, even thousands of years to explore the past. I know, because I have done it - not once, but hundreds of times.

I have done it with regressive hypnosis. This is a technique or method that allows people to remember and often relive their past lives. The idea that we live not once but many times is called *reincarnation*. This should not be confused with "transmigration," which is the mistaken belief that man may be reborn as an animal. According to my research this does not happen. When the soul of man incarnates it will always inhabit a human body. He may, unfortunately, sink so low as to become animalistic in nature, but he will never take the form of an animal. This is an entirely different type of spirit.

I don't know why some people find the idea of reincarnation so hard to understand, when they can relate it to their own lives. Everyone is constantly changing. Not to change would mean you have stopped growing. At that point you become stagnant and start to die. We change so much that many times we may feel as though we have lived many different lives in this one. We go to school, marry, have children, sometimes marry again. We may change occupations, sometimes going in an entirely different direction. We may travel or live in a foreign country for a while. We may experience trauma and sorrow with the death or unhappiness of loved ones. We hopefully learn to love and attain our goals in life. Each of these are stages in our lives and they are totally different from the other. We make mistakes and hopefully learn from them. We hear people say, "I don't know how I could have done such dumb things when I was younger. It's almost as though it happened to someone else."

I know I could never return to the young teenager in high school that I once was. I would not even be able to relate to her, so naive and shy. We would not have anything in common now. And she would have never been able to understand the complex person I have become. Yet we are one and the same person.

This is the way I look upon past lives. We know we lived them, just as we know we lived our childhood. They could be called the *childhood of the soul.* Hopefully we have learned to apply the knowledge we have gained through hundreds of years of making mistakes, of being human. But just as there are people who take longer to grow up, there are also people who must live many lives before learning even one lesson.

We can look upon our own bodies as a form of reincarnation. We know our bodies are ever changing. Cells are constantly dying and being renewed in a never-ending cycle. We certainly don't have the same body we had ten, twenty, or thirty years ago. It has changed for better or worse.

We can see reincarnation as a school for the soul, a series of lessons and grades to be learned for our education and growth. Then we can stop cursing the bad times that often befall us and learn to think of them as tests and exams which we must pass or fail. We can't change what has happened to us in this life or in others. We can only learn from it and go forward, letting the past guide and teach us.

The doctrine of reincarnation is a philosophy, and as such it does not detract from any established form of religion. Rather it enhances, makes it fuller. Anyone who really studies the idea with an open mind will find that they are able to believe in both. The two really do not conflict at all. Reincarnation does not belong to the dark arts. It should not be lumped indiscriminately together with the occult. It is a tenet of love. and thus can be combined with any religion whose main basis is love. Many people groping blindly in the dark for answers may find what they are looking for here. It is like a bright light at the end of a tunnel.

You actually do live forever because the soul is eternal, it cannot die. Life is one continuous existence, merely going from one body to another. You change bodies as easily as you change a suit of clothes. A suit is discarded when it becomes too old and worn-out or too torn and damaged to be repaired. This is difficult for some people, they are reluctant to discard it no matter how ragged it has become. You do become attached to the thing, after all. But you *have* a body, you *are not* a body.

There will be those who think the idea of rebirth too complicated, too radical, too hard to understand. These are people who are perhaps not yet ready for the concept of reincarnation. These should endeavor to live the best life that they can through their own belief, one which they can relate to and feel comfortable with. No one should try to force these beliefs on anyone.

The concept of going back in time has a fascination for many people. Why? The search for truth, the allure of the unknown, or the desire to see how the ancients really lived? Perhaps a suspicion that somehow the past was better than the present? Is this why the stories of time machines are so popular? Maybe Man secretly wishes to unshackle himself from the chains that bind him to the present and to roam freely through time with no limitations or restrictions.

I am a regressionist. This is a modern term for a hypnotist who specializes in past-life regressions. I do not use hypnosis in the conventional manner, such as to help others lose weight, stop smoking or ease pain. I have been deeply interested in reincarnation for over twenty years. It all began when I watched my hypnotist husband conduct regressive experiments. He used conventional hypnosis methods and stumbled onto reincarnation quite by "chance" while working with a woman who wished to lose weight.

The story of our first adventure into the unknown and its tragic aftermath was told in my book, *Five Lives Remembered*. My husband was almost killed in a terrible car accident and spent a year in the hospital. After a long, difficult recuperation he no longer had any interest in hypnosis. His life has proceeded in an entirely different direction.

But my appetite had been whetted by the taste of the past-life experiences to which I had been exposed. The door had been opened on a whole new world of possibilities. I have always loved history and this was a fascinating way to explore it. It became more alive than the history books with their dry, musty facts and dates. This method was similar to going through a time tunnel and actually meeting people living in the past. It was possible to speak to those experiencing history as it was occurring. Yes, the door had been opened and I had glimpsed the unknown. I would not allow it to be closed forever to me. If my husband was no longer interested, then I would have to learn how to conduct my own research.

The conventional methods of induction did not appeal to me. I thought them too time-consuming and tiring - on both subject and operator. They contained many tests to determine the depth of the trance. I have often suspected most people subconsciously resent being tested. Conditioned by many years of schooling, they resent being placed in a position where they feel they must either pass or fail. It is difficult for them to relax if they are on the defensive. These tests are used to gauge the depth of the trance state under the mistaken belief that this has something to do with the ability to reach the subconscious. This has been proven incorrect. People are in a hypnotic state many times during the day and do not even realize it. They expect it to be different from what it really is, a purely natural condition.

At least twice during the day everyone passes through the deepest possible trance state. This occurs when they are falling asleep at night and just before becoming fully awake in the morning. It has been proven that every time we watch television and become absorbed in the story, we have entered an altered state of consciousness. It also happens many times as we drive down a monotonous stretch of highway or listen to a boring sermon or lecture. We all enter altered states very easily and the majority of people would be shocked if told they had been unknowingly in a hypnotized state.

I felt there must be a quicker, easier way of inducing trance for regression purposes that could utilize this natural state. I studied the modern techniques and found there were indeed many faster and simpler methods. These methods are currently being used by some doctors to control disease and pain. They mostly utilize the visualization areas of the brain, allowing the subject to participate in a game by using guided imagery. I improvised a satisfactory method and began experimenting in 1979. 1 found subjects easily because there seems to be an interest in this philosophical idea, even if the interest is only from the standpoint of curiosity.

Critics claim that the hypnotist tells the subject to go to a past life and the recalls are the results of the person wishing to please the hypnotist. In my technique I go to great lengths not to suggest. Under normal circumstances I never tell them to go anywhere. It all occurs spontaneously.

I planned to treat my method as a scientific experiment and see if it was repeatable. I wanted to use it on as many different types of people as possible. If the same results were obtained, I felt this would add to the validity of the theory of reincarnation. I tried to remain objective, but when ninety-five percent of those I hypnotized followed the same pattern - coming up with a past life and corroborating each other's stories - it was difficult to remain entirely neutral. People have said there could be other explanations besides reincarnation. This, of course, is possible. But my research leads me to believe the subjects are recalling actual memories from their past. As I regressed more and more people, I found the method repeatable on all types, even the uneducated and skeptical. Often the subjects did not believe in past lives or even understand what I was doing. Yet the results were the same.

Like others working in this field of reincarnation research, I hoped to add my data to the growing mass of material being gathered by others. Some researchers are only interested in statistics, how many people recall lives in certain time periods. But I love people, therefore I am interested in their stories. I prefer to work on a one-to-one basis with the individual rather than with group regressions. This way the whole story can be obtained. Also the operator (or guide) has better control over any trauma that may arise from the memories.

With this technique virtually everyone can remember their past lives even in the lightest hypnotic state. There are many different levels of hypnotic trance. These have been measured in the laboratory on scientific instruments. In regressions, the deeper the state, the more details it is possible to obtain. I have found the degree of trance can be gauged by the physical reactions of the subjects and the way they answer the questions. In the lighter states they will not even think anything unusual is going on. They will swear they are fully awake and cannot understand where the information comes from. Because the conscious mind is still very active they will think it is only their imagination. In the light states the subject will often watch the events of the past life as though watching a movie. As the hypnotic state deepens the subject will alternately watch the life and participate in it. When they are observing everything through the eyes of the other person and experiencing emotional reactions, they are dropping into a lower state. The conscious mind becomes less active and they become involved in what they are seeing and experiencing.

The best subjects are those who can reach the somnambulistic state. In this state they will completely become the personality and relive the life totally, even to possessing no memory of any other time period. They become, in all respects, the person living hundreds or thousands of years ago. They are in a position to relate their versions of history. But they can only tell what they know. If they were peasants they would not have knowledge of what is occurring in the king's palace and vice-versa. They are often ignorant of events which can be found in any history book but which had no personal bearing on their lives at that time.

They will remember almost nothing when awakened unless they are directed to do so. The subjects think they have just fallen asleep and any scenes that may remain in the conscious seem like the fading fragments of dreams. In the somnambulistic state they can release much information because they are, in all respects, that personality actually living in that bygone time period. To someone who has never seen this phenomenon the effects can be quite startling. It is a fascinating and sometimes unnerving experience to watch a subject change completely and take on the mannerisms and voice inflections of someone totally different.

The somnambulist is hard to find. Dick Sutphen, noted reincarnation expert, says they occur in one out of every ten subjects. He says that if there are thirty people present in a room, three of them will likely be capable of the somnambulistic state. My odds have not been that high. I have found it to be about one in twenty. Most people have a great curiosity about what is happening and they keep their walls and guards up, even in trance. This prevents them from dropping to the deepest state. I have found that an element of trust must be built before these walls will crumble. The subject must know they are perfectly safe. I believe the protective devices of the mind are still functioning because I have had people awaken immediately from a deep state if they see or experience something distasteful or frightening to them. This is much the same way we awaken ourselves from nightmares. My hypnotic technique is not control over another person's mind, but the ability to build trust and cooperation within that mind. The greater trust establishes a fuller release of information.

No, I have never yet found a Cleopatra or a Napoleon. To me it is a sign of validity that most people recall lives that were ordinary and routine. It is my opinion that if someone were to go to the trouble to make up a fantasy story to please the hypnotist (as has been suggested by "experts") he would create an exciting adventure. To me this would be a fantasy. They would see themselves as a hero performing wonderful and extraordinary deeds. Such is not the case. The occasional different, exciting life is unique. The dull, the boring, the mundane far outnumber these. This would be equivalent to real life. There are far more ordinary, common people going about their run-of-the-mill lives than the few who manage to make the headlines of the newspapers.

The regressions which I have performed are full of such cases. Soldiers who never went to war, native Americans who lived peaceful lives instead of fighting the white man. Farmers and early settlers who knew nothing but back-breaking work, sorrow and unhappiness. Some never did anything but tend their animals, raise their crops and eventually die, worn out before their time. The most exciting event in their lives was a wedding, the birth of a child, a trip to town or a funeral. Most of the people living today would fit into a similar category. No, the thing that is impressive about most of the regressions is not the person's deeds and adventures, but the very real, human emotions that they experienced. When a person is awakened from trance with tears still fresh on their cheeks after recalling an event that took place over two hundred years ago, no one can tell them it is fantasy.

It is similar to reliving a traumatic event from one's childhood, brought forth again with all the repressed feelings rising to the surface after many years. No one can tell you that such a childhood event did not happen because often you will remember it consciously or it can be verified by others. Thus the regression is similar to the dredging up of childhood memories. One can put it in its proper place, see how it has influenced the present life and try to learn from the unearthed memory.

One explanation for this phenomenon is cryptoamnesia or "hidden memory." This is the theory that you read it, saw it or heard it somewhere, sometime, and tucked it away in your mind. Then under hypnosis you conveniently bring it forward and weave a story out of it. To me this is not a sufficient explanation. If you retain hidden memory, you also retain the memories of everything that has happened to you in this life. This is a fact. But the somnambulist subject will forget anything that does not pertain to the time period being relived. There are numerous examples of this in this book. Many times the subjects will not know what objects I am talking about because they do not exist in their time frame. Or I will use a word or a phrase that they do not understand. It is often difficult trying to explain things we are well acquainted with in simple terms. Try it sometime. If the subject was using hidden memory, then why are these modern things forgotten? They are also part of the memory of the present personality.

Another theory is that the subject will "play it safe" and only discuss a time period or country of which they have some knowledge. I have disproved this many times. It is quite common for a subject to discuss a life in a culture totally unknown to them. Often they don't even know where they are, nothing is familiar. Their excellent recall of the country and the customs or beliefs can later be checked out through research. This has happened many times with the subject featured in this book. I would hardly call it "playing it safe" to discuss a lifetime that occurred two thousand years ago in a country halfway around the world. Yet her extreme accuracy can only be marveled at. Research has revealed her recall to be astounding. And this is only *one* of the lives that she brought forth during our work.

Since I am a writer with an insatiable curiosity, I became involved in this research project with a motive. I intended to regress as many volunteers as possible and compile their information in books describing different periods of history. I have had many people go to the same time periods and verify each other's stories by giving the same information about conditions existing at the time. This project may yet become reality.

But when I met Katherine Harris, (a pseudonym) I realized my work with her would supersede previous plans and become books by themselves. The information that came forth from her subconscious mind was unique and informative and I considered it to be highly important.

CHAPTER 2

The Subject

Who was Katherine Harris and how did our lives happen to cross? At the time of our meeting I had no idea what the fates had in store for us. I could not have guessed that we were about to embark on a journey that would last a year and take us backward to the time of Christ. I believe such meetings are never coincidental.

I was at a party given by a group of people interested in metaphysics and psychic phenomena. There were many there whom I had already worked with in hypnotic regressions, but there were also many strangers. Katherine, who had an interest in and a curiosity about the unusual, was there with a friend. During the evening talk got around to my work and as usual, many people volunteered and wanted appointments to be subjects. There is a greater interest in this field than most people realize. Often there is a genuine reason to want a regression, such as looking for karmic relationships or to get rid of a phobia, but for the most part there is just curiosity. Katherine wanted to volunteer, so we set up an appointment.

Katherine, or Katie as she was known to her friends, was only twenty-two years old when I met her that important day. She was short and rather buxom for her age, with close-cut blond hair and eyes that sparkled and seemed to see beneath the surface. Her personality seemed to radiate out of every pore of her skin. She seemed so happy and alive, so interested in people. I was to discover later through our association that often this was a facade to cover her basic shyness and insecurity. She was a Cancer, and people born under that astrological sign are usually not that gregarious. But she had a genuine sincerity about her. She really cared about people and would go out of her way for them. She possessed an innate sense of

12

wisdom that belied her true age. At the times when signs of immaturity would come through, it seemed out of place. I had to keep reminding myself that she was only twenty-two, the same age as my own son. Yet they seemed nothing alike. She seemed like a very old soul in a deceivingly young body. I wondered sometimes if anyone else got the same impression.

Katherine was born in Los Angeles in 1960 to parents whose job required much travel and frequent moves. They were members of the Assembly of God Church, so Katie's religious background was certainly not one that would encourage thoughts of reincarnation and hypnosis. She said she had always felt out-of-place at the church services. Much of the noise and gyrations that went on frightened her. As a young girl in church she often had the urge to cross herself in the manner of the Catholics. It seemed a perfectly natural thing to do. But after being sternly reprimanded by her mother, she thought it better not to do this in public. Her parents considered her the odd one in the family. They couldn't understand her reluctance to be like them. It was mostly out of concern for her parents' feelings that she requested to be anonymous in this book. She felt they would never understand, even though the idea of many lives was an easy concept for her to grasp. She didn't want to risk the possibility that her private life would be upset. I have agreed to respect her wishes and keep her identity a secret.

Her family's many moves through many states of the USA had finally brought them to Texas when Katie was sixteen. She had moved twice during her sophomore year in high school, and now again at the beginning of her junior year. She was tired of the constant adjusting to new schools, different teaching methods and temporary friends. Over the protest of her parents, she dropped out of school at the beginning of her junior year. This was the full extent of her formal education, two years of high school. This was to become an asset for our work. We could be positive the things she spoke of under hypnosis were not coming from her schooling. I know of no school that teaches such things anyway. They no longer even stress geography as strongly as they once did. She is an extremely intelligent girl but her knowledge did not come from books.

Once out of school and with apparent freedom, she found she

couldn't find work easily with such a lack of education or training. After a year of disappointing menial jobs, she decided at seventeen to take a GED test (high school equivalent test) and joined the Air Force to get job training. She spent two years there specializing in computers. Another important point for our work was that she never left the United States during her time with the Air Force, yet while in deep trance she has described many foreign places with minute detail.

When she left the service, she and her family moved once again to the middle-western city where I met her. She is now using her computer skills working in an office. She seems well-adjusted and has a normal social life. The extent of her spare time reading is romance and fantasy novels that are so popular now. The idea of researching in a library for the information that is so vital to these regressions would not appeal to her at all.

From the first session I knew this was no ordinary subject. She went deep quickly, showed sensory sensations such as taste and smell, experienced emotion and remembered nothing upon awakening. She had always thought she would have no difficulty going into trance, but she was also surprised at the ease with which it was accomplished. I knew I had found the perfect somnambulistic subject. Since this is the easiest type to work with, I wanted to have more sessions with her if she was willing. She was also curious and agreed to do it as long as her parents didn't find out. I hoped there would be no problems in this area, but legally she was an adult and could make decisions for herself. She then confessed she had been haunted by memories all her life that seemed out-of-place. She thought the answers might lie in reincarnation and she wanted to find out.

When it became apparent that I would be able to obtain much valuable information from this girl, we began to meet regularly once a week. Since I live in an isolated rural area, we agreed to meet at my friend Harriet's house. It was located in the city and was easily accessible to all parties concerned. Harriet is a fellow trained hypnotist. She had never worked with a somnambulist and was interested in my work with Katie. She was eager to see what would happen. After the information began to come forth I was glad to have Harriet as a witness. Later others were also present during the sessions. It was hard enough for us to believe what was happening. We could use all the witnesses we could get in order to rule out the possibility of an accusation of hoax.

After the first two sessions I conditioned her to go into a deep trance upon the mention of a keyword. This is much faster and saves time-consuming preliminary work. We had no idea where this experiment was going and thus our adventure began. A journey that was to take us to people and places we could not have imagined in our wildest dreams. It became a true journey through time and space.

In the beginning, she was never told to go to any certain place or time period. I let the information come forth spontaneously. A month passed and I decided to become more systematic and try to direct the regressions into some type of chronological order. I began going backward in hundred year jumps trying to discover how many lifetimes she had lived, but it is quite possible I missed some along the way. Many times obscure facts would come forth that could only be verified through diligent research. We even encountered the fascinating spirit realm where we obtained information about what happens after the soul leaves the body and enters the so-called "dead" state. Much of this will be covered in another book, *Between Death and Life*.

Each week I tried to go back at least one more life. I thought if any of them were particularly interesting we could return later and ask more questions. This was the method used in *Five Lives Remembered*, but the subject of that book only relived five lives. It had been much easier.

As I took Katie slowly back, we had uncovered twenty-six separate lives by the time we came to the beginning of the Christian era. The many lives seemed to be almost equally divided between male and female, rich and poor, intelligent and uneducated. Each one was filled with a wealth of detail about the religious dogma and cultural customs of the time period. I am positive even a scholar trained in history and anthropology could not come up with the incredible detail that she gave us. No, this knowledge was coming from somewhere else. I prefer to believe that she actually lived all these lives and the knowledge has remained hidden in the vast computer memory banks called the "subconscious mind". It only required pushing the right buttons and giving the mind the right signals to cause the knowledge to be brought forward and relived again. We have no idea how many more lives lie waiting to see the light of day once again. The stories of these other lives will be written in another book. It would do them an injustice to try to cram them into one book. There is far too much information.

When I found there was a possibility that the entity we had come upon could give information about the life of Christ, I thought it was important to stay with that time period and see what would emerge. I had no idea where the experiment was leading or if anything of value would come forth. But on the slightest chance that something could be found, I stopped taking her backward and kept returning to the life of Suddi, one of Jesus' Essene teachers, to get more information. We stayed with this for thirteen sessions, over three months.

If this life had been the first I had encountered while working with Katie, I would have immediately dismissed the whole thing as fantasy and stopped the sessions. Everyone automatically thinks if someone mentions having known Jesus that they must be on an ego trip. But this information did not come forth until I had been working with her for nine months. By that time I knew where she was coming from. I knew what tremendous capabilities she had in recalling past lives in great detail. We had built up a very strong bond of trust during that time. I believe this is the only way the story could have come out. It took much patience to continue working with one subject and to keep moving systematically backward. But if I had stopped too soon, this story would never have been written. Even knowing her as well as I did, I was still reluctant to tell anyone that I had discovered someone who was one of the Essene teachers of Jesus. I was sure I would get a smirk of disbelief and some snide remark, such as, "Oh, yeah? Now tell me another," as though I thought them gullible enough to swallow anything. I can understand that. I am sure I would have been skeptical if I had heard this from someone else. But I had to believe her.

There was no other way to explain what was happening. There was no possibility of lying; she was speaking from a hypnotic trance so deep that this was impossible. And the information that came forth demanded rigorous research and speaking with several experts on the subjects. Yet she never knew at any time where we would go next

16

The Subject

and what I would ask her. Her answers came spontaneously and naturally.

In the beginning days of our work, she wanted to hear the tape recordings after the session was over. Later she showed less interest, merely asking upon awakening, "Well, where did we go today?" She didn't care about listening to the session. She often expressed amazement because she said she knew very little about the time period or country covered.

After the Jesus material began to come forth, it started to bother her somewhat. Maybe it was her old religious background rearing its head. Especially when she began to say things that were controversial and contradictory to the Bible, it began to overwhelm her. She said it did not seem possible that all this was coming from her. It was mind-boggling. This one life bothered her more than any of the others we had gone through. Whatever the reason was, at this time she decided she did not want to have any more sessions. She was planning a move anyway. Her company wanted her to transfer to another branch office with a promotion and more pay. She also thought a year was long enough to work on regression experiments; it was time to call it to a halt. I agreed that she should pursue her life wherever it might lead her.

I would have liked to have had a few more sessions. I was doing research by that time and wanted some answers to things that were puzzling me. But I thought, "Would I ever have all my questions answered?" And even if they were, there would always be questions that someone else would come up with. We would probably never be able to answer all possible questions and confidently close the book on that life, to consider it totally wrapped up. As it is, I think I have covered a very wide range by asking about the living conditions and the customs and knowledge that were taught by the Essenes.

17

CHAPTER 3

Meeting Suddi

I was keeping fairly close track of the time-periods as we went slowly back. I had the different lives listed in a notebook. This was the only way I could keep them straight. She was never confused as to who and where she was, but many times I was at a loss, so the notebook was essential to me. I had to refer to it many times.

It is difficult to convey the appearance of this phenomenon through words on paper. The people she became were very real, with emotions, facial and body mannerisms that were characteristic of each one. I became so familiar with these different individuals that I was soon able to recognize each one before they gave their names.

In the last few weeks we had seen her as the doctor in Alexandria discussing the drugs and methods of surgery used in the 400 AD period. Then she was a yellow-robed monk in the mountains of Tibet talking about Buddhist philosophy in 300 AD. Then came the surprise of finding a girl around 200 AD, who could not hear or speak. Normally I would have directed Katie to go back another hundred years. This time my instruction had to be worded differently. Since she could not communicate very well we were not certain of the time period we were in.

The personalities would often have strong accents which made transcribing difficult. There is a strange pattern I have noticed about the manner in which the different entities speak English. It is as though they are mentally translating from one language to another. When this occurs the words are transposed out of their natural order. Often what sounds like bad grammar is another example of this strange phenomenon. It gives one the impression that the entity (the being with whom we come into contact) cannot speak English and is trying to find the correct words from somewhere in Katie's brain or computer banks. This often results in mistakes in grammar, sentence structure or word order that she would never have made in her natural waking state. I believe this is just another small point suggesting reincarnation. Her conscious mind would not do these things.

I came to know the entity called "Suddi" quite well and eventually could understand his strong accent. His voice also changed with age. He was young and vibrant as a child, then gradually more mature until he spoke with a very tired voice in his old age.

This matter of gender is going to present a problem in telling this story. She is a girl telling the story of a male. It would be confusing to constantly shift from "he" to "she" and back again. I think the solution would be to call the entity "he"' and only refer to "she" when referring to Katie's physical body and its movements. Similarly, in most cases, dialogue spoken by Suddi is preceded by the letter S:, while, in the later parts when we talk to Katie's "soul" after Suddi's death, the letter K: precedes the dialogue. I, Dolores, am D:.

I want the reader to meet him the same way we did.

Dolores: Let's go back further into time, to a time before this girl who couldn't hear and couldn't speak. I will count to three and we will be there. 1, 2, 3, we have gone back further into time.

Thus I had no idea of the time period we were in except that it had to be earlier than 200 AD. The personality that emerged was a man. He was walking, on his way to Nazareth to see his cousins. His voice came forth with such a strong accent that it was difficult to understand him. His pronunciation of the word "Nazareth" was so different that I did not recognize it until I later played the tape recording back and listened to it carefully. It sounded like *"Nathareth",* spoken quickly. He said it was located in Galilee. Here again he pronounced the word other than I was accustomed to hearing it. He said: *"Galilay".* These names did not become apparent until they were played back. So at the time I was not sure where Katie was. I proceeded, hoping that the tape recorder had picked it up.

There is really nothing unusual about finding a subject describing a past life in Israel. This has happened many times. I have regressed several who lived there during the Roman occupations but none of these ever mentioned or made any reference to Jesus. The mention of a location does not give any clue as to the circumstances of the individual's life. When I first encounter a new personality, I have certain routine questions I always ask until the location and culture are established. When I know where we are then I can ask more specific questions. I asked for his name.

Suddi: I am Benzahmare. (Phonetic)

It sounded something like "Benjamin" and I asked him if that was the name. But he again replied "Benzahmare" with the accent on the last syllable. He said the other name (first name) was not used unless you were important. I asked him what I should call him and he gave me permission to call him "Suddi", which was a "playname". (nickname?) The pronunciation sounded like Saudi or Saddi, with an accent on the last syllable. I will use Suddi throughout this book since it is easier than Benzahmare.

Many times in these ancient cultures the person does not know how old they are, or they have different terminology. But he said, "I have thirty years". He was not married.

S: *No. It is not part of my life. There are those who desire nothing more than a family. And there are those who have many things to accomplish in their lives, that to have a wife and possibly children would bring them sorrow. Therefore it is unnecessarily cruel to others to ask them to share.*
D: This is why you have no desire to marry?
S: *I did not say that I did not have the desire. I just stated that I probably would not.*

He said he usually lived in the hills. There was a community there that was maybe two days journey away. When I asked the name of the community, which is a normal question, the personality changed. Normally Katie would answer questions without hesitation. But Suddi suddenly showed suspicion and asked curtly, *"Why do you wish to know?"* This was unusual and I could not understand the reaction. I explained that I was just curious. After much hesitation he finally said it was called *Qumran,* which he pronounced as: Kum-a-ran. At the time this name meant nothing to me, and I resumed my questions. I asked about his occupation.

S: I study the books of the Torah and I study law, Hebrew law.

This also did not mean anything to me. As a Protestant I did not know what the Torah was and I thought he meant law such as legal law that is used in the courts. I was to receive much education within the next few months as I discovered the Torah was the Jewish religious book, and the law referred to the laws of Moses which the Jewish people pattern their lives after. I asked if he was what some people call a "rabbi". I assumed we had come across an educated Jewish man and I knew a rabbi had something to do with their religion and possibly education. We (the people involved in this experiment) have had little contact with Jewish people, knew almost nothing about the Jewish religion and had never been to a synagogue. He answered that he was not a teacher, only a student. So I at least found out that rabbi means: teacher.

When I am working with Katie I often feel very stupid because I do not know the basic things about the time period she is in. But then I never know where she will go and can not be prepared for all possibilities. So I must draw on what limited knowledge I may have or feel my way by questioning. I think the people who say I must be asking leading questions to get these lives to come forth, can see this is not true. I have no way of knowing what will happen next and often feel I am only going along for the ride.

D: What are you going to do when you finish your training?
S: Go abroad among the people and share with them what we have learned.
D: Does it take very long to become a teacher?
S: For some it is a lifetime. For others their path begins early. I cannot remember a time when I did not study.
D: Are the rabbis the ones that teach you?
S: You speak of rabbis. I believe you mean in the sense of the village rabbi? I have my masters who would teach me. But I am not taught by the rabbis in the village.

D: Who are your masters?

I meant by my question what religion or type of school they were affiliated with. But he thought I meant their names.

S: *There is Bendavid, who is the teacher of mathematics. There is Mechalava, who is the teacher of the mysteries. There is my teacher of the Torah, who is Zahmare, my father.*

He (through Katie's face) smiled at the mention of his father and I drew the conclusion that there must be affection there.

S: *And my teacher of righteousness is (a long name here that I could not transcribe). She teaches the things that have been handed down, all of the laws of truth, of things that are protected. There is Judith Beseziher. (Phonetic, difficult to understand.) What she has taught me are the prophecies of the stars, the knowledge of their pathways. It is said that when she speaks all listen. She has a great many years. She is perhaps seventy, maybe even older. I am not sure. She has great knowledge in other areas, this is just one.*

D: Do most boys have to study these things at some time in their life?

S: *There's a point in every Hebrew young man's life when he must study the law and the Torah, but it is usually when he has his Barmitzvah. But if you wish to become a master or a teacher to follow the pathway, you must always leave yourself open for more learning.*

D: Do you get teachings from any place else?

S. *You mean if the knowledge comes from afar, this does. But my teachers, they live with us. When my father was young, he traveled to many places that are known to us and studied many things which he tries to impart to me.*

D: Is this the custom that some will go to different lands to learn from others?

S: *So it is with us, yes. It is duty to pass on knowledge. For this is a great sin, to not share with those who have thirst.*

Suddi had not yet traveled to any other countries in the pursuit of knowledge, but he thought it was very possible that he would be fortunate enough to do so.

D: How is this decision made?

S: *There will be a sign for us that it is time and that he has come and that we must move. My father says that it will be told in the heavens and that we will know.*

I didn't understand what he meant so I asked who was coming. He answered in a very matter-of-fact manner, *"The Messiah. The time is known to a few."* I was not sure what to make of this statement.

D: Hasn't it been said that the Messiah has already come?

I was not sure what time period we were in, and I knew that the Jews have never acknowledged that the Messiah ever came. They are still looking for him to this day. I thought Suddi was probably a Jewish man living some time after the birth of Christ. There was always the possibility of getting some information about the man, Jesus. Surely a learned man would know the stories of his time.

S: *No, he has not come, for the heavens have not let it be known. It is said that from four corners that stars will rise together and when that they meet, it will be the time of His birth.*

D: But I have heard it is said that he has come already. Have you heard those stories?

S: *No, he has not come. For as long as there have been Jews there have been rumors of false prophets and false Messiahs. But he is not here.*

D: Have your people ever heard of the man called Jesus? Some people have said that he was the Messiah who came. They say he lived in Nazareth and Bethlehem.

S: *I have not even heard this name, it is unknown to me. There is no one in Nazareth that is of that name, otherwise I would know him.*

This time when he mentioned Nazareth it made me realize he might be in or near the Holy Land. I asked if Bethlehem was near and he acknowledged that it was.

D: I've also heard of the country Judaea. Is that near there?

S: *(Rather impatiently) It is here!*

She always knew where she was even if I was often confused. Now that I definitely had the country, the locale, I set about trying to establish the time period.

D: Who is the ruler at this time in your land?
S: *King Herod.*

I knew that according to the Bible there was more than one King Herod. One who reigned at the time of Jesus' birth and another at the time of His death. For all I knew there could have been more.

D: I have heard there have been many King Herods. Is that true?
S: *(He seemed confused.) This is ... Herod the first. There were no others. He is the father of Antipas and Philip, but this is Herod.*

I felt a shiver of excitement. Maybe Jesus had not been born yet.

D: What do you think of King Herod?
S: *He is very much under the thumb of the Romans. This is not good. (sigh) He is a blood-thirsty lecher.*

His emotion surprised me.

D: Oh? I've heard many stories, some good and some bad.
S: *Oh, no! You cannot know anything of Herod to ask these questions. I have never heard any good of Herod.*
D: Does Herod live in Jerusalem?
S: *At times. He has many residences throughout. Sometimes he would travel to other areas.*
D: Have you ever seen him?
S: *No! I have no wish to see that.*

It was very evident that he was not fond of Herod; he did not like discussing him. I was still wondering what time period we were in. It would be difficult to get a year since our years are reckoned from the time of Christ. These people must have used a different method of keeping track of the years, if he had not been born yet.

S: *There are twelve months for each of the twelve tribes. The year is.... (he seemed to be having difficulty finding an answer). The years are numbered by the years of the king. I'm not sure. I think*

Meeting Suddi

For some reason that even Harriet herself could not explain, she had an obsession with finding out something about the group known as the Essenes. She had said repeatedly, "I certainly wish you would hurry and get to that time period." She said later she somehow knew that something important was waiting there. When she said this I would answer, "But I don't even know when they lived." She said she thought it was during the time of Christ.

I would then state, "Well, we're heading that way," and I would continue my methodical plodding backward by fifty and one hundred year jumps, much to her frustration. Each separate lifetime held its own share of surprises and historical knowledge, so I was in no hurry to speed up the procedure that had proven so effective. Now that it was obvious we were in the correct time period, Harriet seized the opportunity and asked, "Have you ever heard of a group that is known as the Essenes?"

Suddi surprised us by answering, "Yes. Why do you ask of these?" Elated, Harriet answered, "I just wondered if you knew anything about them. If they followed your teachings." Suddi said: "They are my teachers."

This was a surprise and gave the promise of a monumental breakthrough to be able to learn something about such a secretive, unknown group. "Oh!" Harriet remarked, "We have been searching for them."

S: *They have no wish to be found. Unless they desire it, you will not find us.*

He had thus indicated that he was also a member of the group. I wondered if this secrecy would create trouble in finding answers about them.

D: I have heard the Essenes are like a secret organization. Would that be correct?

S: *They are greatly feared by those who are in power, because we have studied into the mysteries that others have only hinted at. And they fear that if we gain too much power and knowledge that they will lose their place.*

H: How do they differ from the regular Jewish community?

S: *There is more strict adherence to the laws. More adherence, to the average Jew means: upon the end of Sabbath he leaves the synagogue and he does not remember it again until the beginning of the next Sabbath. To us, the law and the Torah are all. We must not forget that this is why that we live. Much time is spent upon the defining of the prophecies given. And knowing that this is the time that they shall be culminated. And it is our duty to prepare others for this time, and to prepare the way.*

We were again surprised when he told us that women as well as men were members of their sect. They were teachers and students alike. This was surprising because women in the average Jewish community at that time were not allowed the distinction of equality with men. Suddi confirmed this, *"In most synagogues, women are not even allowed inside. They have the women's terrace."* I wondered why women were allotted this honor with the Essenes.

S: *It is said that one away from the other is not complete. So all knowledge must be shared, so that it can never be lost. I have known women who have more brains than the average rabbi.*

This statement amused and delighted us. But he became suspicious again when I asked for an idea of how large the community was. He asked cautiously, "Why *do you wish to know?"* I had to think of an answer that he would not consider threatening. "I'm just interested in the size of the community because of the living conditions. I would think if it were very large it would be difficult to house or feed." Suddi relaxed and said the number was not known for sure.

D: Is there any dissension between the Essene teachers and the Jewish teachers in the area?

S: *Yes, they call us crazy, because we believe that the time is at hand. They have given up hope for the coming of the Messiah. (He was frowning deeply and seemed uneasy.) I am curious to know why you wish this knowledge? I would prefer to not answer any more. There are many who would find out about our community and see it destroyed.*

I was unaware that the Essenes had enemies during that time.

D: You said you were going to your cousins. If your people have enemies, aren't you afraid that someone will find you while you're out like this?

S: *They do not know who I am. To them I am just a traveler. I do not have blue skin. (We laughed.) We may tell each other by certain ways, but others may not tell us.*

Since I had heard that the Essenes were a secret religious order living in seclusion like monks in a monastery, I asked if there was a name for their kind of religion.

S: *It has no name, we are known as the Essene. But this, as my father speaks, it is a school of thought, not a religion. (He had difficulty with that word.) We believe in God, the Father.*

D: Do you have a name for God in your language?

S: *Yahweh. It means. . . 'with no name, for God is the nameless one. He has no name that man has knowledge of. They are also known as the Elorhim and Elori. They are basically the same thing. They speak of God. There are many names by which you may call upon Him and He will know you speak of Him. These are just a few. When I speak to Him, I do not call Him Yahweh. I call Him Abba, which means Father.*

We had made the breakthrough into the time of Christ and had met one of the Essenes, the most mysterious and secretive group in history. When I realized the potential of what we might have, I decided to stay with this lifetime and explore it more fully. Who could tell? It might even reveal something about the life of Christ. And we might be able to find out some information about this little known group. Of course, Suddi was showing signs of suspicion and reluctance to answer certain questions, but I felt this could be dealt with. There are many ways of going around a topic to get the desired answers. Still, I never expected what would happen within the next three months. The incredible amount of knowledge and information that poured forth was like riding a whirlwind. It came so fast and furious it, at times, took our breath away. We did not expect what was to come and we got more than we bargained for.

In the next chapters, I have tried to compile the information according to content. It did not come through in this manner. It was like putting an incredibly complicated puzzle together, taking a piece from one session and a piece from another. But I think this way of presenting it makes for easier reading.

There is a two-fold purpose in this book. One is to present the accumulated knowledge about the customs and living conditions of the vague, shadowy group known as the Essenes. The other is to relate the life of Christ against this background as he was associated with this group, and as he was seen through the eyes of a loving teacher.

CHAPTER 4

Who Were the Essenes?

Before we began these sessions, if someone had asked me for information about the Essenes and Qumran, I would have told them I knew next to nothing. I wasn't even sure how to pronounce their name. The Essenes to me were a mysterious group shrouded in secrecy. I assumed, as others had, that they were a religious group similar to monks, living in isolation in a monastery-type environment. This was what I had heard.

There was also a rumor or legend that Jesus may have studied with them or at least visited them. But this idea sounded like all of the other legends about him. Legends that he had visited other parts of the world during the "lost years". When I have spoken with groups interested in metaphysics I have received the same reaction. The names are somehow vaguely familiar, but few can supply any information about them. I could not have even told you where Qumran was located. Harriet admitted she knew no more than I did about this group.

I remember the excitement in the early 1950s when the discovery of the Dead Sea Scrolls burst upon the scene. They were somehow connected with the Essenes and Qumran. I wondered sometimes what had happened to the unearthed manuscripts. After the first flurry of excitement, they seemed to disappear as surely as if they had been pushed back into the caves from which they had sprung. It seemed a pity, because they were said to be an early version of our Bible.

Brad Steiger, noted author and expert in reincarnation studies, suggests that regressionists working on verification should delay any research until they have finished their work with the subject or the time period. He says one theory is that through hypnosis the subject's awareness is greatly heightened. There is always the possibility, no matter how slim, that they could pick up the information from the minds of anyone participating, through telepathy or ESP. I believed this was sound advice and would better insure the validity of the material. So, except for looking at maps to locate Qumran, I bided my time. After three months of working on this, I thought we had enough information that it was at last safe to start my historical research.

I was to discover that even today, over thirty years after the excavations of the ruins of Qumran, the Essenes remain a mysterious, secretive group. I was disappointed to find the books were mostly repetitions of each other. All but one were written in the early fifties. They each described the discoveries of the scrolls and the later excavation of Qumran. Each discussed the translations of some of the scrolls that had been found intact. They all came to the same conclusions about who or what the community was. The authors all referred to each other as experts on the subject. I might as well have been reading one book. I wondered why, after all the glowing reports of the "greatest discovery in the history of mankind," there were no later books written about further translations of the scrolls. It was as if a door had been opened and then suddenly slammed shut.

The one exception was *The Essene Heritage* by Martin A. Larson, published in 1967. Here at last was a fresh approach. He dared to raise the possibility of a cover-up. That perhaps what had begun to emerge was too much for the conventional church to accept. There were possibly discrepancies between these much older versions and our modern day Bible. There were also indications that Christianity had not originated full-blown with Jesus but had its beginnings in the customs and beliefs of the Essenes. Larson suggests this would not be tolerated by the church. Modern clergy would think that the idea of Christianity before there was a Christ would be too much for the layman to accept.

John Marco Allegro also has like beliefs. He was originally a member of the international team of eight scholars who began the editing of the Dead Sea Scrolls. Of these men, four were Roman

Who Were the Essenes?

Catholics and he was the only member with no religious commitment. Ironically, Professor Allegro is now not even permitted to see the Scrolls! At least four hundred documents had been pieced together and prepared for publication by the end of the 1960s, but only four or five have been released to the public. He also asks searching questions as to why this information has been withheld.

The Scrolls were pushed quietly back into the woodwork and quite a few of them have disappeared again. One theologian was known to remark, "I wish they would just disappear and re-surface after about two more generations." He meant in this way he would not have to explain them to his flock. I think this is very likely what has happened. I also think they may have found some of the same things which I unearthed during our experiment - and they couldn't handle them.

The documents are supposedly now housed in the Shrine of the Book in Israel. This building was especially built for the study and translation of the scrolls, and to act as a depository to facilitate the piecing together of the countless fragments.

I know the information in this book could not have come from the minds of anyone involved in the experiment because the information was too obscure. But now I am convinced that it could not have come from the minds of anyone living today. I believe we have uncovered a more complete picture of this wonderful group of people than has ever been presented before.

If there were ever an attempt to wipe an entire group of people off the face of the map, that was what happened with the Essenes. There is no mention of them in the Bible. It has been inferred that all references of them have been deliberately deleted, because of the similarity between their doctrine and Christianity.

If it had not been for a few diligent writers and historians who lived at the beginning of the Christian era, we would have no knowledge of the Essenes at all. These ancient authors were: Philo, a Jewish-Alexandrian philosopher; Pliny, a Roman writer; and Josephus, a Jewish warrior and historian. I went to the source and read the translations of their works. I shall refer to them at times throughout this book.

31

Philo is said to have lived between 20 BC and 60 AD, so he would have been alive during the time period that our story covers. But his accounts are said to have been written from hearsay. He was not personally acquainted with the Essenes or their community. This might explain any discrepancies between his account and Josephus'. Pliny lived from about 23 AD to 79 AD, and wrote only a small amount concerning the Essenes. Josephus is considered to be the most reliable source and is the most quoted. He was born in Jerusalem about 37 AD, and actually lived within the community and had firsthand knowledge of them during their latter days. But it is said that he tended to color his report to make it harmonize with the systems of Greek philosophy popular at his time. He lived and wrote from a later time period than the life of Suddi. Yet these histories verify the incredible amount of accuracy we uncovered in our experiment. The descriptions of lifestyle and beliefs dovetail very well.

These are the only known written records about the mysterious Essenes. These authors only mentioned that the strange community was located in the Dead Sea area. Archaeologists never knew exactly where and had never tried to find Qumran. The terrible climate of the area is a scientist's nightmare and they had no desire to hunt for it without a specific reason.

After the destruction of Qumran by the campaigning Roman armies in 68 AD, the ruins sat atop the salt cliffs by the Dead Sea for almost two thousand years. Crumbling in desolate silence they went virtually unnoticed. The men who had devoted their lives to the accumulation and preservation of knowledge seemed to have completely disappeared beneath the relentless sun and the shifting sands of the desert. It was as if they had never existed. Although the ruins stood as a silent reminder of the great minds that once flourished there, they were not recognized for what they were. For ages people thought they were merely the remnants of one of the many Roman garrisons that sprang up after the invasion. Surely nothing of any importance could have flourished in such a God-forsaken spot.

The ruins were ignored completely until the discovery of the first Dead Sea Scrolls in 1947. The caves in the salt cliffs had held tightly to their secrets for two thousand years. Then fate took a hand and led the Bedouin shepherd boy, searching for his lost goat, to the discovery of the hidden scrolls in jars in a cave. The story of this exciting find has been told and retold. It is certain that much was probably lost or inadvertently destroyed before the enormity of the discovery was made known to the outside world and the scientists descended on the desert. With the help of the native Arabs more and more scrolls and tens of thousands of fragments were uncovered from neighboring caves. What was at first believed to be an isolated "lucky" find was soon being heralded as the "greatest discovery in the history of mankind".

As more caves yielded up their hidden treasure of knowledge, archaeologists began to wonder how such an accumulation came to be hidden in the desert. Only then did they begin to look questioningly at the nearby ruins. Maybe it was something more than just an army garrison, maybe there was some connection. The first excavations in the winter of 1951 turned up nothing to support the theory. But during 1952 it was proven conclusively that the scrolls had originally come from whoever had lived in the ruins.

Then the writings of Philo, Pliny and Josephus began to shed light on who the occupants might have been. Everything finally fell into place and Qumran was declared the home of the secretive, communistic Essenes. The word "communistic" has taken on a very different meaning in our world today, and some questions have arisen over my using this word to describe this ancient group. The Essenes were considered communistic in the purist sense of the word. They lived together in a community, sharing everything and needing no money.

All that is known today about these people has come from the ancient writings and what the archaeologists found in three years of digging. There are many gaps and questions. Maybe our experiment will help supply answers.

CHAPTER 5

Description of Qumran

The archaeologists believed the group living at Qumran was a religious order of men similar to monks, secluded from a world they could not identify with. They believed the Essenes lived by a strict code of discipline and rigid rules. I shall attempt to show that many of the scientists' ideas of these wonderful people are incorrect, according to the information received through Katie while she was in deep trance.

I have compiled all of the information gathered about the community of Qumran and will present it in one chapter, although it actually was scattered throughout the many sessions. Katie often repeated the same descriptions but she never contradicted herself. I believe the picture that emerged through the eyes of Suddi is much more human than the one revealed by the scientists' shovels.

I felt that in order to understand this person I had uncovered, I had to know more about the place where he lived and his way of life. Especially since this would also reflect the conditions under which Jesus lived during the most vulnerable part of his life. When I talked with Suddi as a child, he called the place a community. He never called it anything else. He did not understand the word "town" or "village" and did not know of any other place but Qumran. This is also what the archaeologists have called it, and they say it was not a city.

In his description, Suddi said, *"It is not very large but it is a place where there are many people. There are the libraries, the houses and the temple. We are in the hills and we overlook the sea. The buildings are of clay. They are made of bricks and they have flat*

34

roofs and everything is built together. " He said most of the walls joined each other.

I was confused when he said the community was enclosed by a wall that had six sides. It sounded strange, but the odd thing is that when you look at the drawing of the archaeologists' excavations, you can see it is definitely not square. It may be debated whether or not it is a six-sided shape, because it is not a geometrical six-sided figure. It is also apparent from the drawing that the rooms mostly all connect. Most are built with common walls.

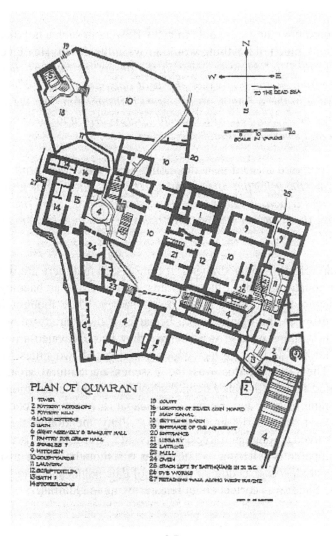

PLAN OF QUMRAN

1 TOWER
2 POTTERY WORKSHOPS
3 POTTERY KILNS
4 LARGE CISTERNS
5 BATH
6 GREAT ASSEMBLY & BANQUET HALL
7 PANTRY FOR GREAT HALL
8 STABLES ?
9 KITCHEN
10 COURTYARDS
11 LAUNDRY
12 SCRIPTORIUM
13 BATH ?
14 STOREROOMS

15 COURT
16 LOCATION OF SILVER COIN HOARD
17 MAIN CANAL
18 SETTLING BASIN
19 ENTRANCE OF THE AQUEDUCT
20 ENTRANCE
21 LIBRARY
22 LATRINE
23 MILL
24 OVEN
25 CRACK LEFT BY EARTHQUAKE IN 31 B.C.
26 DYE WORKS
27 RETAINING WALL ALONG WEST RAVINE

At times when I talked with Suddi as a child he was playing in a courtyard. When he was older, he also liked to sit and meditate in one of these. He said there were several courtyards within the community. I am accustomed to a courtyard being in the center of something, but these were scattered throughout. He said the study and library were in the very center, where everyone gathered for the classes. The papyri (or scrolls) were also stored there. In one of the courtyards there were fountains., In others there were gardens, not gardens as I would have assumed, but beautiful flower gardens. *"They are the colors of the rainbow. They are like many jewels that sparkle.*

I wondered how they were able to grow flowers in such a hot place. I didn't think much of anything would grow in the desert. He objected, *"Oh, but they do! Flowers grow in the desert, as long as there is rain. As long as there is water the heat does not matter. When the rains come in the spring, that the desert is all abloom. For the seeds that have been dropped will suddenly burst forth into flowers. The desert can be very beautiful. "*

In the courtyard located near the eating areas there were fruit trees. *"There are the trees that they grow up, the figs, dates, pomegranate, orange and lemon. It's almost as if they touch the sky. And there are pathways that you can walk among them, or you may sit among the flowers. "*

By again referring to the drawing, it can be seen that there are indeed several courtyards. In all the diagrams, however, the archaeologists have pictured the courtyards as being barren. They thought little would grow in the Qumran area because of the scarcity of water. They knew gains were grown because they had excavated around a spring known as 'Ain Feshka which was located two miles to the south. They thought this was the Essenes' agricultural area, and concluded that the isolated people subsisted on this cultivation and the keeping of bees, etc, eating only meager, monotonous food. But the ancient writers disagree with this. Pliny mentioned that the Essenes lived among palm trees. Solinus said, "Palm-berries are their food", apparently referring to dates. This was thought to be a mistake until the archaeologists dug up remains of date palms and date seeds. It seems Suddi was correct about trees growing in Qumran.

Description of Qumran

Suddi said that the majority of the Essenes did not live within the community walls. There was housing for the families farther up the hill to the north, outside the main complex. These houses apparently had the same building arrangement as the community, the joining together of buildings with common walls. The archaeologists believe the people lived in caves and tents, which seems strange to me. Why would they build such a beautifully efficient community and then go and live under primitive conditions?

As far as I have been able to find out, I do not believe many excavations have been performed in the area away from the walls. Their reports mention only digging in the main complex and exhuming some of the graves in the adjoining cemetery. Incidentally, the scientists still believed there was only a brotherhood of monks living in Qumran until they found the skeletons of women and children in the cemetery. They had to quickly revise their thinking, for it was apparent that families lived there.

Suddi's family lived farther up the hill than most. He could look out of the house and see across the Dead Sea for a long distance. The only people who lived within the community itself were the priests of Yahweh who took care of the temple, the scrolls and kept the fires lit.

Suddi lived with his mother, father and sister Sarah. I asked for a description of the living quarters. When the weather was hot they would sleep out on the flat roof. When it was cooler he shared a room with his sister. There was a room which was considered the family room, where the meals were cooked. His parents had their own bedroom, and there was another room where his father studied, which was full of many papyri. The quarters shared common walls with the other families.

The archaeologists have assumed from the ruins that everyone always ate together in the large dining hall within the community complex. But Suddi said the families mostly ate in their own quarters. If there were great occasions when someone would come to speak, then they would go to the main dining hall. The Essenes believed there would be less conflict if everyone had an area that was their own.

The library and the dining hall were both large rectangular rooms. Covered openings in the roofs allowed the light to enter. There were also openings in the walls which were covered to keep the sand out. He was not sure which was the largest building because he had not "stepped them off ".

The most common way of entering the community from the outside was through a gateway next to the high cliff. It was large enough to take a caravan through if need be. When I asked if there were any other ways of coming in, he acknowledged cautiously that there were, but would offer no further information. This was apparently one of the many subjects that I was to find he was not allowed to talk about. The Essenes were extremely secretive in many respects and I was to have difficulty breaking through this defensive barrier.

He said there were several buildings that had more than a single story. The library had a second floor. The assembly hall (dining hall) had the height for two floors but there was only the tall ceiling. He said the tower near the gate had three floors. The archaeologists mentioned there was evidence that some of the rooms had two floors. They said the tower had two storys, but they also mention a basement for storage, which would be the equivalent of three. The purpose of the tower was mostly for observation. From this vantage point the Essenes could see anyone approaching the community. Suddi mentioned it was also used for protection, but when I asked him to elaborate he refused to answer. This was another forbidden subject.

When he grew older, he no longer lived with his parents in the housing but had moved to a part reserved for unmarried young adults. Here the men and women lived in what he called "apartments", although he wasn't sure of that word. Where they had their meals was an individual preference. While living in these quarters, he often ate with the others for companionship and conversation. There were many tables in the dining room or "hall of meals," but the cooking was done in rooms off the hall or outside in clay ovens.

The scientists have said that the Essenes all ate together in the dining hall while solemnly observing ceremonies or rituals that went on while they were eating. Suddi disagreed: he said there was only the blessing, and that no teaching or anything else was done while the meal was in progress. It was also believed that they observed strict religious rituals during the day. Again Suddi disagreed, saying nothing was mandatory; it was left up to the individual. For the most part any religious observances were on the Sabbath.

If the people wished to eat in their own quarters they would go to one of the "keepers of the stores" and take what they would need. They would not go hungry, but there would be no "gluttony" allowed.

I was curious about the types of food that would be eaten. Millet was a main staple. This was a type of grain that was raised outside - probably at 'Ain Feshka. After it was harvested, the grains were winnowed and stored in great sacks. He described a dish made from millet. To prepare it you would *"take a handful and a pot of boiling water and throw it in with a little salt"*. Sometimes herbs were added. It sounded like a soup, but he said you could roll it and eat it with your hands, so it may have been some kind of bread.

Different types of meat were eaten: lamb and goat, occasionally an ox or a young bullock and different types of birds. I remembered the food laws in the Old Testament and asked about any restrictions. He said, *"You may not partake of swine or anything that the hoof has been uncloven. The swine, it eats anything. It would eat dung if this is what it is fed, it would not matter. Therefore it is considered unclean. You may eat only those with the cloven hoof that chew the cud. The camel chews the cud but we do not eat the camel."*

He personally did not like to eat meat although there was no strict rule forbidding those in the community to do so. It was his personal choice. *"It is not good to kill something for your own.. just .. for enjoyment. This is God's creature you are destroying. To eat meat is to tie one here, to tie one's soul to the earth."*

He did not understand the word "beverages," but they drank wine, water and sometimes the milk of different animals. As a trick I asked about coffee, but he said, *"I do not know this. This is not familiar to me. I have had teas that are made from mints and different types of leaves."* *"Vegetables"* was another word he did not understand even after much explanation. Other things were eaten besides the grain and fruit, but these were bought from passing caravans.

He described the furniture in the living quarters. *"There are the bed, frames that have ropes that are criss-crossed, in which to make a frame. And then the padding and all is put on top of this. And this is how you sleep, on this. There are chairs and tables. If you wish to sit or relax, take a cushion and sit on the floor. It is again preference. "* *The* frame of the bed was about a foot high. He did not understand what I meant when I asked about blankets or covers. When I explained, he answered, *"There is no reason to have these blankets. It would be too much. If you lived in the mountains, perhaps you would need them."*

He also didn't know what a pillow was, but since he had used the word "cushion" I knew he would recognize that word. He could not understand why we would want to put a cushion under the head while sleeping. *"The head is not elevated. The ideal way of sleeping is to have the feet higher than the head, to aid in circulation. To elevate the head, then you would have problems with your feet swelling. You do not? To elevate the head would be to bring about headaches and many other problems. To elevate the feet would aid in the circulation of the body and stop its settling down. "* They would either put a cushion beneath the feet or tilt the bed. The only other furnishings in the house were shelves that you could put things on, such as clothing and things of that nature.

I asked about decorations and he frowned, confused again. I was thinking about pictures or statues. The word "statues" disturbed him. *"We do not have statues! There are not statues made. We would occasionally have a painting. But there are no statues allowed in the community. It is to copy what God has made. It is not allowed in the Commandments to make of a graven image."* "Even if it wasn't meant to be a god? For instance, a statue of an animal?" *"Many false gods are worshiped as animals."*

I tried to explain that some people liked to have statues and paintings in their houses just because they were beautiful to look at. They did not intend them to be used in worship. But Suddi couldn't understand this concept. *"I would look at nature and find the beauty in this. Why look at a rough imitation when that the real thing is before you? I can understand the beauty and the need to create, but could you not*

40

create many things far greater? The paintings are very beautiful."

When I asked for an explanation of the paintings I was not expecting the type he was familiar with. They were painted on papyri or wood and hung about the house, but they were not pictures of objects or living things such as we would have. They sounded more like some type of abstract painting.

S: *Colors, and the way the lights and shapes and... I do not paint. I am not explaining this very well. They are things that speak to the soul. They are from within, rather than what the eyes would see. They are what the soul sees. They would have meaning only to the one that paints them.*

D: What about the Romans? They have many statues, don't they?

S: *Yes, but they are heathens. They worship them. They have them having qualities that are not there. They are just stone.*

D: Do they actually worship the statue itself, or do they worship an idea behind it?

S: *There are all differences. Some of them worship the statue as real, others say that it is just what it represents. Either covenant seems to be very dangerous ideas.*

He was very shocked when I asked if he had ever been inside a Roman temple. *"I have spoken with Romans about their beliefs. But in their temples they slay animals and defile the name of worship. It has become something of horror and unclean. There is one in Bethesda, this is the only one I know of. I have heard of the one in Jerusalem and different ones. Capernaum is said to have one. Of course, Tiberias has the temple. This was built by their emperor."* (*Tiberias* was pronounced fast and the syllables slurred together.)

I asked about Nazareth, but he said the village was too small, they would not bother to put one there. I thought he might have wanted to see one out of curiosity, but the idea was repulsive to him. *"Our temple starts from within. If there is a wholeness from within, it spreads without. You need no house or chamber to hold it."* I have always thought that the temple and the synagogue were the same place with different names. I remembered the story of Jesus in the Bible when he was found in the temple teaching the doctors.

S: *A temple is only for the worship of Elorhim, but the synagogue is*

41

also a place of teaching. The temple, it has the holy of holies,
where in the synagogue, perhaps, they only have the sanctum for
the Torah. The temple is to God; the synagogue is for the
worship in the manner of the Jewish faith.

D: So any person practicing another religion could come into the
temple, but not into the synagogue?

S: *Yes. In the synagogue there is a place for the Gentiles or also a*
women's court. And in the temple all are allowed who worship
God.

Although the Bible mentioned Jesus questioning the doctors, Suddi
did not know that word. What he considered a healer was called a
physician, and this type of person would only teach his specialty.
They would not teach in the temple. Apparently what is meant in the
Bible is someone like a teacher who is very learned, perhaps a
master.

S: *Those who would teach in the temple are the teachers of Law.*
There are priests, each has their own specialty. Like one would
have Law, and another would have the mysteries and others
would be speaking of the different knowledge that has been
passed on down. A rabbi would be different, he teaches Jewish
law and Jewish religion, as it were.

I asked for a description of the temple at Qumran and got more than
I bargained for.

S: *There is the area where the people would gather. They would*
kneel or sit on the floor. And then there is the altar. Behind the
altar is the curtain, the inner sanctum which has the veil across.
And inside there the Torah and the scrolls are kept, cabal.
During the studies or celebrations of holy days, whatever is
occurring, they would bring this forth and read of them and
share. There would be the sharing of souls, then discussion of
dealings of God and life and many things. In the synagogue the
women are not allowed except in the women's court. Here all are
allowed.

D: Are there any religious objects in the temple, for instance, on the
altar?

S: *There is the cup and usually an incense burner, this is truly all.*

D: What purpose does the cup have? What is the significance of it?

S: It is the passing between all and sharing in this manner. It bonds us together and makes us one.

There was an unexpected familiarity about this. Harriet excitedly asked, "Everyone drinks from the same cup? What do they drink, water?" *"There is usually wine."* This was a significant new development. What Suddi was describing sounded like Holy Communion or Lord's Supper. But this is supposed to be connected with Christ and he was not yet born. Suddi said no food was passed at this time (I was thinking about the bread or wafer in Communion) - only the cup was passed around among the people.

S: It is the cup of life blood. It is the sharing of life between all. The wine represents the blood of all and the sharing together.

D: This is the significance? It means that everyone is of one blood? Are only those members of the Essene community allowed to partake of the cup?

S: One must have accepted the precepts to be able to share of the oneness. Partly due to the fact that they would perhaps not understand what is the point that is trying to be brought with this. It is not that we do not believe that they are one with us, because we do. It's just that the sharing is brought about in their own time. If they are not ready for it, it is not stressed.

Thus a stranger passing through would not be allowed to participate in this. This ritual was performed at ceremonies where everyone would be together and able to attend. It was done on the Sabbath but was not restricted to that day. Suddi said that to his knowledge this ceremony was not performed by the Jewish community at large.

I felt this was an important discovery. Apparently when Jesus performed the Last Supper with his disciples in the Upper Room he was not instituting a new ritual. He was using one he had participated in many times with the Essenes. The symbolism of the bread is said to be a Jewish custom. I think he combined this with the custom of passing the cup and gave it a new meaning. To the Essenes this ceremony symbolized that they were all of one blood and the sharing of life between all. What could be more natural than Jesus wanting to perform this on the eve of his trials and eventual death? It was to be one last show of brotherhood between himself and his followers.

Sandalwood was burned in the incense burner, because *"It is said that it can help open some of the centers (chakras?) within ourself. Again, I am not familiar with the teachings of all of the mysteries and the ceremonies."* Whereas the passing of the cup was strictly a rite of the Essenes, other religions did use the incense, even the Romans.

It occurred to me that if they had one type of ritual that was familiar to the Christian church, they might have another one. I took a chance and asked about baptism. Suddi seemed confused, puzzled, because he was not familiar with that word.

D: It's a washing, a ceremonial cleansing with water.

S: *There is a ceremony of cleansing. After a person has had his Barmitzvah, they are taken out and they have to be considered to reach the age of consent. And they choose to follow the path of Yahweh or perhaps to fall off. If they choose to follow this, they are cleansed in the waters. And it is said that they are washing away their past and from this point they shall start anew. There are different ways of doing it. Some pour the water over and some make them lie down in, upon the water.*

D: Would you go down to the Dead Sea to do this?

S: *No, no one would go into the Sea of Death. It is usually done in one of the fountains here.*

D: Are there any special clothes that you would wear at that time?

S: *Either a robe made out of flax or none at all. It is part of the purification, the stripping bare of the soul.*

D: Does the priest perform the ceremony?

S: *Yes, or an elder. Usually this is only done once in a person's life.*

This would explain where John the Baptist got the idea for the ritual of baptism. When he was baptizing people in the Jordan River, it was nothing new. He was merely following an existing custom of the Essenes.

The translators of the Dead Sea Scrolls are aware of this coincidence. I found that there are numerous references to these two ceremonies in the scrolls. Many of these experts have come to the conclusion that this directly ties John the Baptist to the Essenes. It indicates that he was under their influence at some time in his life.

The Essenes dressed quite simply. Both men and women wore a plain robe made either *"of sheep's hair that was spun and woven (wool), or of flaxen that had been processed"* (linen). The robes were gathered at the waist and touched the floor. They were considered to be cool. Underneath the robes the men wore a breechcloth. Both sexes wore sandals. The robes were always white, although sometimes it was *"more of the color of the rich cream of the cows. 'Tis not quite white. "* It rarely got cool enough to wear anything else, but if it did, they had cloaks of various colors. The adult males wore a beard. *"It is a sign of belonging to the men community. "* Outside Qumran there were people who chose to be clean-shaven. *"There are communities that never cut their hair. The Romans wear theirs short. For us, it is permissible at any length, as long as this is well-groomed and clean. Most prefer it about to the shoulders. "*

If anyone left the community to go into the outside world, they were required to dress like the other people so they would not appear different. The outsiders did not wear white robes; they wore colored clothes with various head-dresses. So in this way the Essenes were unique and would have been quickly recognized as they would have stood out among the others. The ancient writings confirmed these facts about their dress.

It must be remembered that the Essenes were in danger when they were outside the walls. But as long as no one knew who they were they were safe. As Suddi said, *"We do not have blue skin."* Apparently they could not be easily recognized when they dressed like everyone else. But when in Qumran, everyone wore the same "uniform," so to speak. It would seem as though they were all absolutely identical, but they did have a method of identifying "rank". They wore a cloth band tied across their forehead. These bands were different colors according to the wearer's standing in the community. It was like a badge of office so they could quickly identify each other's status.

S: *Like the color grey, it is for the young students. The color green, they are a seeker. They are above the students' level. They have finished that which everyone must learn, but they are still seeking more. They are still recently admitted. Their soul still thirsts for knowledge. They are still a student, but they are not a*

45

master. And there are the blue, which is the master. And there is the white which is the elder. There is red, he is not really a member of any of these others. He is outside of this. He is learning, but perhaps for different purposes. This is for the outside students, as if he is only a visitor. The red shows us, though they are of a like mind, that they are perhaps not quite of us. It is really just the green, the blue and the white that are of ours, and then the grey for the young students.

D: Then if someone is wearing a red headband, they don't live there all the time?

S: *Well, it is not that they do not live here all the time. It is perhaps that they are from elsewhere to come to learn, to seek, to study.*

D: Then when they finish studying, they will go away again. Did they choose these colors for a reason?

S: *The blue shows much of the inner peace. It is almost up to the level of the white. The white is the ultimate in attainment. You are at total rest and have achieved all that must be achieved. The blue is just one step below this, if this is to be understood.*

These colored headbands were also worn by women since they were considered equal to the men and were also taught. He couldn't understand my surprise when I said, "In some communities girls aren't taught anything." *"But how could ... ? If a girl was not taught, how could she stay one with her husband or ... I do not understand."*

We were very pleased with his way of thinking, which must have been against the popular Jewish customs at the time. This would explain some of Jesus' attitudes towards women. They had not been treated any differently in Qumran during his time there. If a woman was not a student she could wear a scarf or a veil, according to her choosing. But mostly they wore nothing on their heads.

At the time, I was speaking to him he was wearing green. *"It means that I am a student. I am one step below master. I am not an unborn student, I am a searcher. The younger ones would wear grey."*

During the session when Suddi was describing the living conditions of Qumran, Katie was in deep trance but she suddenly and unexpectedly slapped her right cheek, surprising us. Normally, outside of hand motions and gestures to describe something, such swift motions do not occur. Later she began scratching the spot she had slapped. Suddi stated simply, "*Umm, the bugs are getting bad*" I found this very amusing because it was so unexpected. He said they were mainly gnats, *"little flying things"*, but there were many types of bugs there in Qumran, of which locusts and ants were a problem. When I asked about dangerous insects which might inflict a poisonous bite, he said he did not know of any, although he, himself was *"not into the study of lower life"*.

There were animals raised for food: sheep, goats and oxen. But I got the impression these were not kept at Qumran. They were probably outside the walls or near 'Ain Feshka where the agriculture was located. We got into an interesting and fruitless discussion when I asked if they had pets. He did not know the word. This is often the case when I am dealing with people from another culture; they do not understand or have an equivalent word. I am always taken off guard because quite often (as in this case) the word is a common one to us. I often have to come up with a suitable explanation quickly and this is difficult. Try it some time. I tried to think fast and find a definition for the word "pet".

D: Well, it would be an animal no one would eat. Someone takes an animal and makes it their own. They just keep it for their own pleasure, as a pet.

S: *This sounds selfish. How do we know that the animal has different pleasures from this?*

D: Well ... it would be like a friend.

S: *How can an animal be a friend? It has not intelligent conversation.*

He seemed totally confused. I said: "Some people like to have animals with them. They live in their quarters with them." *"This does not sound very sanitary."* We laughed. I didn't realize how difficult it would be to explain. No matter what I said, it did not seem to get any clearer. I asked if he knew what a cat or dog was. He knew the word cat, but not dog. Frowning, he said, *"I've seen ... jackals"* (pronounced: *yackals*). I suppose this was the best mental picture he could come up with for the word "dog". I explained that they were similar but not quite the same. *"I do not think that anyone could own a cat. This is curious. Why would someone want to have something as a pet that eats dead animals? I would not want one to live with me. They all have vermin. This is not good; vermin carry disease. We*

47

use sulphur to keep them away.

It was apparent I would not be able to define what we consider pets, so I went on. I wanted to know if there was any trouble with snakes in the community. He said there were many adders that varied in size. They ranged from quite small to quite large, several arm lengths long. They occasionally got inside the community and then they were killed because the bite of most was fatal. I was surprised by this admission that his people *did* kill sometimes. He had seemed so much against harming any of God's creatures and against any kind of violence. He said they would kill if there was a danger.

I was still trying to find out if they would ever use any kind of protection if they were threatened. He had indicated earlier that there was something, but it was one of the forbidden topics of discussion. This time when I asked if there was anything else they would consider a danger, he again went on the defensive and refused to answer. Any time this happened it was always best to change the subject.

During my questioning I often found that Qumran was far from primitive. I came across him once while he was bathing. He said this was something that was done daily, usually in the morning. The "room of bathing" was a large room where the bath comprised almost the entire room. There were steps leading down into the pool and there was an area to the side where there were benches for "disrobing". They would remove all their clothes to enter the water. Many people (both male and female) would bathe at the same time using pumice instead of any kind of soap. The water came into the pool from somewhere underground. It was a steady flow, always being refreshed and changed. He did not know where the water flowed to because he said he did not design nor build the system, but he believed the areas that the water ran through were covered. I suspect if someone were to ask your average modern city dweller about their water system, they would also have difficulty explaining it, unless they had some reason for being involved with its workings.

There were places in the community where the water came to the surface. The drinking water was obtained from two fountains. I thought maybe he meant a well, but he was quite emphatic in his definitions. He knew what a well was, and he said it was not that. *"It is where the water comes up from below and pushes up. It comes from the mountains, and comes up out of the ground. There is an area that is for storage of this water that holds quite a bit of water. It is square and perhaps as deep as a man's waist. And one and a half again as many lengths as your arms stretched. During the hottest months, many times they are kept covered so the water will not be wasted, and the dust will not get in to foul them."*

The water was removed with buckets; they had only to reach down and dip it out. This surprised me because the area around Qumran is so arid. I did not think there could be a steady flow of water. *"How not so? With this close to the Sea of Death, there is water here. It comes from many sources. As long as it is not in the sea it is all right for drinking and such."*

I wanted to find out if they had any sanitary systems that took care of urination or bowel movements. According to the Bible (Deut. *23:12-14)*, the people in Mosaic times were not allowed to do this within the city, as it was unclean. They had to go outside the walls, dig a hole and cover it up afterwards. Suddi was an expert on Jewish law so I wondered what he would say about this. I wasn't quite sure how to word it. I had no idea what other cultures would find offensive. "You know, whenever people have to urinate? For sanitary reasons, would you have to go outside the walls to do this?" *"No, there is a place that is used for this body function. It is a room that has several sections ... (looking for the right word) ... cubicles, in which you would urinate or have a bowel movement. I believe it is a pit system dug and they are freshened. I'm not very sure about the method that they would use in taking it away."* It was within the community walls and everyone went to the same place. There was water in these cubicles but he did not know if it was also flowing water such as in the baths.

S: *There are things that are put in with the water that is there, to keep it fresh.*
D: Isn't it in the Jewish law that they have to go outside the city?
S: *I know not. And what if a man had to wake up in the night? (He laughed) Would he then leave the city?*

So apparently all of the Jewish laws were not in effect among all of the people. It is doubtful that other cities in Israel had the wonders of sanitation and water supply that were present in Qumran. But the Essenes apparently had access to much information, possibly this type of engineering knowledge.

When the archaeologists excavated the ruins of Qumran, they were amazed at the wonderfully complex water system they found (see drawing). There were two baths with steps leading down into them, several cisterns (as the scientists called them) and water storage basins. There were also many small canals connecting the whole system which were probably covered over during the time the Essenes lived there. It is interesting to note that the scientists have assumed that the baths were open, while Suddi says they were enclosed within rooms and that the storage areas and the fountains were open.

They also assumed the Essenes trapped water coming down from the hills during the very infrequent rains and stored it in this system. But Pere de Vaux said that during the three years he and his party were at the excavation site, water only came down from the hills twice. It is hard to believe they could have stored enough water to last for long periods of time if they had to depend upon the unpredictable rainfall. Suddi said the water was flowing. I believe they had found a spring and routed the water to flow through the community. I believe that over the intervening period of two thousand years something happened to the spring, either through earthquakes or natural ground shifts. There are known springs in the area, the most notable one at 'Ain Feshka, a few miles to the south. Why would the Essenes put their agricultural area by a spring and then build their community in a barren area?

Also, when the Romans destroyed the community, it is known that they ruined the water system. Maybe they, through ignorance, closed off the source of the water.

The archaeologists found the remains of what they called a sanitary system, some kind of cesspool. They also discovered the ruins of a building with cubicles, which they have assumed was a stable. Was it?

As to Suddi's daily schedule: *"Usually I would awaken with the sun, go and bathe, and then I would break my fast. Study for a period of time and then begin lessons or go about the day's teaching. And break off again and eat midday meal. Then usually I would study. There is much I am in ignorance of. Then I have the evening meal and spend my evenings in contemplation."* "Do you have to rise with the sun?" This is one of the things the scientists have assumed. *"It is just a matter of custom. It depends upon what you do. There are those who would study the stars. They would, of course, stay up all night and sleep during the day. If you are studying the stars, you would not get up and spend all day awake and fall asleep when the stars are out. There are those who work late into the night, but most of us rise with the sun."* "Is there any set time you go to bed at night?" *"No, not generally, if there are things that you would have to do that would carry on late into the evening. It could be just studying. It could be speaking with one who hadn't been there for periods of time. Numerous things."*

If they stayed up after sundown, they obviously had means of producing light. I was aware that they used lamps containing olive oil in that part of the world. I had gained this information from other subjects. But I should have learned by now not to take anything for granted when using this method to delve into the past. While working with Katie, I never knew where an innocent question might lead. When asked about their lighting methods, his answer was unexpected and proved again that Qumran was not an ordinary place. Its walls held many hidden mysteries. *"We'd have either the lamps of oil or the lights that burned."*

When working with regression, you must stay alert and be ready to pick up and follow through on anything that sounds the least bit unusual. Since it is something common to their way of life, they will not elaborate unless you pursue it with questioning. You never know where it may lead. This is one of these examples. Why did he mention two types of lamps?

S: *Usually I use the one that has oil in it and then lit. But there are also the lights that have light with no flame.*
D: What is the power source?
S: *(He had difficulty explaining it.) I did not build it, I do not know. It runs off of a jar that it is placed on. The jar has some properties. It is placed upon a jar that has a ... (searched for the word) globe that comes off of it, that is lit. The jar is about... so*

... (he measured with his hands - it looked like about maybe five inches tall).

D: By a globe, do you mean a globe of glass?

S: *(Hesitated) What is ... glass?*

D: (How do you explain *that?*) Maybe you don't have it in your community. Glass is a material, but it's something you can see through. Like a pottery but it is clear. (This was difficult.)

S: *Sounds interesting. It is somewhat like this, yes. I do not know how it is made.*

Harriet suggested the idea of something similar to a crystal material and he answered with an emphatic, "Yes!" That would be similar to glass. At least it was a material that you could see through, so he had something for comparison. I asked if the round globe was like a sphere and he became excited that he had finally made me understand. But when I asked if the sphere was hollow, he became confused again.

S: *I know not about these things. I do not design them.*

D: But it sits on top of the jar, and the jar is pottery. Is that right?

S: *I know not. It looks of stone.*

D: Is there anything inside the jar?

S: *I have not taken it apart to find out.*

He was getting aggravated with my repeated questioning but I wanted to understand how this strange device operated, if possible, for such a thing should not have existed. I wondered if it remained on all the time and could not be turned off. *"No. It is turned off and on by placing it ... Either you have the type that you would place inside of another jar and this would cause it to light, or you would have one that would be given a twist and then it would cause it to light. But it is never on constantly* unless *it is something you wish. "* I asked if he liked it better than the lamp with the oil. He said the strange one was much brighter and there was not the danger of fire.

D: Are these made at the community?

S: *No, they are very old.*

D: They must have a great power source to have lasted such a long time. Are there very many of them in the community?

S: *There are enough. I have not taken count of them. They are everywhere. They are allowed to be where they are needed.*

Description of Qumran

In my research I found the description of objects that Pere de Vaux, the archaeologist, excavated from the ruins of Qumran. Among the many shards of pottery he found a few stone jars and a few fragments of glass. Could they have been the remains of the lamps and not recognized for what they were?

The thought of a jar working in this manner awakened a memory. I remembered reading something similar in one of Erich Von Daniken's books. His works contain many unexplained oddities.

The Community of Qumran

I found it on page 174, picture 252, *In Search of Ancient Gods*. It was a picture of a small jar about the size that Suddi had indicated, and it showed someone inserting an oblong black metal (?) object into the jar. The inscription said that it was a battery operating on the galvanic principle. It was very old, but even today 1.5 volts could still be coaxed from it. It is now in the Iraq Museum in Baghdad.

There was more information on this device in Charles Berlitz' book, *Atlantis, the Eighth Continent (pl39)*. The caption on a picture reads: "Dr. Wilhelm Konig, an Austrian archaeologist employed by the Iraq Museum, unearthed in 1936 a 2,000 year old vase, six inches high, which contained inside it a copper cylinder set in pitch, and inside that an iron rod secured with an asphalt plug. This object resembled others in the Berlin Museum, some larger with a repetition of the cylinder settings. There is no clue to their function except that they were "religious or cult objects". It occurred to some investigators, including Dr. Konig, that these might be dry cell batteries which, understandably, were no longer in working condition after several thousand years. However, when they were exactly reconstructed and provided with a new electrolyte, they worked! This ancient use of electricity may, of course, prove only that electric power was used for electroplating metals with gold and silver, as is still done in the bazaars of the Middle East. But it is also likely that it was used for the illumination of temples and palaces, although its use disappeared before the middle epoch of antiquity, that of the Greeks and Romans, who used oil for illumination. (Reference: Berlin and Iraq Museums)."

Mankind has become very smug, thinking he is the first to invent our modem conveniences. It appears that ancient man was not as primitive as we believe. They actually had many of these things, and since the blackout of the Dark Ages we have merely rediscovered them. An intriguing idea.

I wondered what other surprises might lie within the secretive and protected walls of Qumran.

CHAPTER 6

The Government of the Qumran Community

According to archaeologists, the community was governed by the rules and regulations set up by a group of priests. Based on their translations of the Dead Sea Scrolls, they think the Essenes had some very strict and seemingly cruel regulations. This was contrary to what I found. I did not think this sounded like the gentle and just Essenes that I had come to know, and Suddi's information proved that I was right in believing this way. Of course, many times the difficulty lies in the method and manner of translation.

According to Suddi, there was a council of elders that set the rules to govern the community, did the judging and ruled on any penalties, etc. It was said that at one time there was someone like a chief in charge of the council, but no longer, since it was decided that it gave one person too much power. The elders were chosen by those in their area or field of study. The qualifications depended on how long they had studied in the particular area and how much knowledge they had gained. The number of elders on the council varied from time to time but it was generally about nine or ten, depending on which area of study had an elder.

I wondered if everyone in the community had a vote as we do in our democratic countries. He said it was discussed among the families, but only the masters and students in the particular field of study had anything to say about it. It appeared that the choice of the elders rested with the intellectual part of the community, the ones who were studying in the various fields. The ordinary worker would have no say, but a woman would have a say if she was a student. When someone was chosen for the council it was a lifetime job, and there had to be a majority in agreement on any decision that was made. I wondered if there would ever be a case when they would want to remove somebody from the council. He said it had been done, but not within recent memory.

Suddi had mentioned penalties, and I was surprised that such compassionate people had to resort to punishments. I wondered what they could be.

S: There are a few minor ones. If an infraction is major, the person is put out of the community, but this is rarely used. It is only used in cases of violence, where another receives bodily harm. Any type of violence such as this. Violence is against what we believe. This is the only great punishment that there is, to be made to leave the community. And this would be for some very great wrong. Last time was when one of the students killed one of the others.

So violence *was* possible even in such an ideal environment. I asked if he knew what had happened in that incident.

S: No, we were not told the story. It was not ours to judge. It is his cross to bear, not mine.
D: I would not think that your people would ever get that angry.
S: He was just a student, he was not one of us.

He meant that the offender had not been born in Qumran. He would have been one who wore the red band.

D: What kind of punishment would be typical for a smaller offence?
S: There is punishment from one of our masters, yes. But this is between the two of them - the person who has done the wrong and the master he serves. As stated, the master would deal on a one-to-one basis and do what he saw fit. Sometimes fasts are required. Penance by studying certain things or the taking away of privileges.

The archaeological translators believe the Essenes were a religious order and the priests were the leaders, above everyone, the final voice of authority. Suddi said the priests would only have authority over the students they were teaching. They would not be higher than the council.

D: Do any people ever leave the community due to dissatisfaction?

S: *There are a few that leave for teaching purposes. But, why would someone wish to leave?*

D: I would agree with you, but I wondered-if you ever had any people who were dissatisfied.

S: *It would probably be possible. I have not heard that it is not. But why would they?*

D: If they were unhappy and thought they would be happier elsewhere. Is it allowed if they wish to leave?

S: *I suppose. (Indignantly) We are not slaves! We wear no chains!*

D: Then they stay because they want to. Is anyone ever turned away who wants to be a student here?

S: *Yes. Their purposes would be looked into by the masters, and they would know for what purpose this person wished to do this. And if they had any malice in their intent, they would be turned away.*

D: Has it ever happened that anyone gave them a problem, created any disturbance because they were not allowed in?

S: *Not upon recent knowledge. This is not to say that it has not happened.*

D: Do you know what would be done if this would happen?

S: *I do not know. I am not a master, it is not my decision.*

D: (I was still trying to find out about their defenses). Do you have any ways of protecting your community? I mean like weapons or anything like that?

S: *Yes. (He became cautious and hesitated). Different, methods.*

He said they did not use weapons in the conventional sense, but he would not volunteer more information. Then Harriet took a chance and asked, "Do you use the sound?" He hesitated a long time, then answered softly and cautiously, "Yes". I could tell we were on dangerous ground. He may have felt he had betrayed a confidence by revealing as little as he did. He seemed uneasy and I knew we should not pursue the question any further even though I would have liked to have found out more. I tried to reassure him by telling him how wonderful I thought it was that they had no need for weapons, and that in most communities that was the only way they could protect themselves. He thought I was too curious. I told him we wanted so badly to learn, but it was difficult to find teachers. Of course, he said there were many teachers there. Our problem was our inability to question these.

D: Does your community have any kind of rules that are different from the normal Jewish community?
S: *How can I say, when I'm not that greatly familiar with the outside and their laws?*

I knew from the Old Testament that the Jews believed in animal sacrifices. But when I asked about this practice he spoke emphatically against it.

S: *I do not sacrifice blood! Why would it be pleasing to Yahweh to kill something that He had created? This does not sound very logical.*
D: I thought you believed many of the same Jewish teachings, the Torah and the Laws.
S: *They are part of belief but they are not the whole.*
D: But the Jews follow this practice of sacrifice, don't they?
S: *Yes. From my understanding of this, these practices were borrowed from other 'religions, as you would call them. They were not something that were in the original teachings. But we do not sacrifice. We would place and burn incense on the altars, and such things as this, in a form of sacrifice. But this would be the only thing.*

He was so emphatically against this that I decided to change the subject and asked about any festivals or holidays that his people observed. He did not understand the word "holiday". "This is unfamiliar," he said.

D: A holiday is a special day that is different.
S: *You speak of holy days. Of course there is the Passover. Also the Days of Atonement and Rosh Shofar. It is the festival of the new year, new seasons.*

Because I am not Jewish, I had naturally never heard of any of these except the Passover which is mentioned in the Bible. I asked about the Days of Atonement.

S: It is the time each year that we lay aside the things that we have done and ask forgiveness for them. And we give reparation to those whom we have harmed in any way.

D: That sounds like a good idea. Kind of washes the slate clean, and then you start all over again. Are there any other holidays?

S: Just the festival for the harvests and different things like this, yes, also. There are many holidays and many things that are celebrated. We're not a morose people. We have a joy of life!

This would be in contradiction to what the translators think. They have assumed that the Essenes were a solemn people. I knew from the Bible about the custom of washing other people's feet, and asked if he had ever heard of this.

S: Yes. The time when this is mostly done is if a person comes over and he goes for a meal, the host will wash his feet. But this is a symbol of humility. It is also done on the Day of Atonement, to show Yahweh that one is humbling oneself in His eyes.

The Jewish New Year is now called *"Rosh Hashanah"*. The name Suddi gave was different, *"Rosh Shofar"*. Was this a mistake? I found that *"Rosh"* means "beginning". I was very surprised when my research disclosed that a special feature in the observance of Rosh Hashanah is the blowing of the *shofar,* or ram's horn, in the synagogue, as a summons to judgement or repentance. Could it be possible that it was called Rosh Shofar in those early days because of this custom?

I found the Day of Atonement is now known as Yom Kippur, the holiest day of the year for the Jewish religion. It is the culmination of the Ten Penitential Days that begin with Rosh Hashanah or New Year's Day. It is described as a day of judgement, an opportunity to seek forgiveness for sins committed against God. In the case of sins committed against one's fellow man, this is a time for asking their forgiveness also. The end of this day is also marked by the blowing of the *shofar* or ram's horn. Apparently Suddi was calling the whole ten day period the "Days of Atonement".

I wanted to find out more about the customs in the land of Israel. I asked about sanitation.

Jesus and the Essenes

S: I know that those who are clean are definitely less likely to catch illnesses. This has been known for a long time among the learned. This is why when that pestilence strikes, it always strikes the lowest of a town first. And then if it is a grave pestilence, it will continue on up into the highest. But this has a great deal to do with cleanliness. There are different tubs that are used for different types of washing. The man would not use the same one that his wife would wash in, for it would be considered unclean. The same with clothes, there are different things that are used for the washings.

He had already told me about the bath system at Qumran but wondered how the average person in Israel kept clean.

S: Water, if it is in plenty, you would bathe. Such as those who are near the sea, they would not have to worry about the water. But those who are in the desert, many times they use sand. If you're out in the middle of the desert, you would not use your last drop of water to bathe yourself with.

D: Is oil ever used on the skin?

S: No. Oil is not used because in this desert where that it is dry, hot and dusty, if you have used oil on your skin, all of the dust sticks.

When I asked for some more information about the laws of cleanliness, I did not realize it was such a complicated question.

S: (sigh) I shall explain further. I mean, do you speak of the cleanliness of animals or the cleanliness of the body or of the soul? There should be the bathing and keeping the body purified from all ills that might wish to enter in upon it. Fasting helps in keeping the body balanced.

D: Isn't fasting dangerous to your health?

S: If it is not done to extremes, or for the wrong reasons, it can be very helpful.

D: What about the cleansing of the soul?

S: There are many laws involving that. Many of them are laws of karma. (sigh) I am not the teacher of religion. You are confusing the Law with the worship that others have, of supremeness. This is not what the Law intended. There is much cloudiness in this area that should not be there.

He would not discuss karma at this time, but on other occasions he did. This will be found in another chapter. I returned to asking questions about their customs in Qumran.

D: Are the people in your community allowed to marry and have families?

S: *Yes. But for the most part the husband and wife are chosen for each other by the elders. It is said that a chart is cast when a person is born and they are matched in this. I do not know it.*

It sounded like the drawing up of a horoscope. I thought the Essenes were more democratic than to select the mates for the members. I have since found that this custom is very old in Asia and is still followed in some places. They rely very heavily on horoscopes even today.

D: Do the people have anything to say about it, or must they marry the one the elders pick?

S: *They can refuse to marry but then they would never have a mate. They are also allowed the choice to stay single.*

Women had much more freedom in Qumran than elsewhere in Israel. They could decide to remain single if they wished and could become teachers in the community. This surprised me because of the Mosaic laws in the Old Testament, and the Jewish customs which severely curtailed women's activities.

S: *Of course they can be a teacher, and why not?*

D: Well, women aren't allowed to do anything in some communities except marry and have children.

S: *If this is the case, then many times a great mind may be lost. This is very sad, for is not a child's first years formed with its mother? And therefore, if it is not a woman of intelligence, how can it be a child of intelligence?*

D: This makes sense to me, but there are many people who don't think that way.

S: *Then it is a shame for them. God created two forms, both male and female, to complement each other, not to be above or below one another.*

D: Are there any kind of regulations where someone like priests or religious leaders would not be allowed to marry?

I was thinking about the priests and such who might have to remain celibate. He frowned as though he didn't understand.

S: *Why? This sounds very silly to me. Anyone may marry if they wish to. It is said that two are born of a time to be destined to spend the rest of their lives together. If the other is not born then perhaps they would choose not to find another. But this would be perhaps the only reason.*

D: What about work in the community? Are there divisions? Is there some work that just women do and just men do?

S: *The women have the children.*

D: (We laughed) That's right! But what about cooking?

S: *Usually for the cooking, there are the servants.*

This surprised me. I assumed everyone would be considered equal in a society that was so socialistic, with no one in the servant status.

D: Wouldn't a servant be someone beneath you?

S: *They are humbling themselves, yes. It is someone who has chosen for some reason to serve others for a certain period of time. Sometimes it is a student who is doing this penance. There are different reasons for doing this, yes. A person sees something in himself that he perhaps does not like. And to cure it, he would serve another because he was too proud and had great pride. He would make himself lowly so that he would humble himself, to help overcome the sin of pride.*

D: Would it ever be someone from the outside that is brought in just to be a slave?

S: *We do not have slaves! We only have free men. Sometimes there are people that we have freed. My father says that he had seen in the market and bought a man who was made free. And this man decided to stay with us.*

In these cases, freed slaves were allowed to do any job they wished to, and they were also allowed to learn if they had the desire. The students often took turns serving and cooking and performing various other humbling tasks as a penance.

I asked if the community used money and he didn't understand what

I meant. I did a poor job of trying to explain about people owning things. In a communistic society such a concept would be alien. He could not understand the idea of buying anything either.

S: *We have some things that are ours; I have my flute. But if everything is everyone's, it is shared.*

D: Is there ever any argument or dispute that arises when people need to share a thing?

S: *Not that I know of, I do not say that it never has happened. But everyone has the same. Except ... you can own certain things by working at different things. Everyone is judged according to merit. If he is doing the best that he can do in whatever he is doing, then he is judged on the same basis as somebody who is, um.... if he is just good at tending gardens, but he's doing this to the best of his ability, he is considered equal to a man who is brilliant scholar, but is also doing the best in his field. They are the same, they are equal, because they are both doing their best at what they do. In this, you are judged on merit. If you are not working as well, perhaps you do not have as much.*

It sounded like a good system, but what could you give someone if they earned it, if the community used no money?

S: *Well, it depends on . . . like for someone who is being gardener, maybe new area to have space. If you were the scholar, you would maybe earn more papyri. It would depend upon yourself. No one goes without. If there is need, it is there. The things that are worth it are the things that are earned. The things that are needed are given.*

This made sense. Money would have no value because there would be nothing to buy.

He had mentioned the sin of pride, although I consider a sin doing something wrong to another person.

S: *To treat another as they would not wish to be treated, to speak down upon them would be a sin. For it is not your right to judge. You are not placed here to judge another, but to only judge yourself*

D: Some people think that the breaking of any of the

Commandments would be sins.

S: *It would be great wrongs.*

D: Do you have any way of atoning for any of these wrongs, these sins?

S: *One must ask for the other's, the person that this would be done against, one must ask for their forgiveness for having done a wrong against them. And after that has been granted, one would have to ask oneself to forgive oneself And this would be the hardest part to accept. Also, if it was perhaps to steal something, you would have to replace it.*

D: How would you do that if you have no money?

S: *No, we have none but we have things that are personally ours, that we would give up in exchange for something such as this.*

This would be a great deal more meaningful if you had to give the injured party something you really cared about. Apparently such wrongdoing was rare and far between, but it was a beautiful system.

S: *Why would someone wish to incur such great debts to do something to someone who had not harmed them?*

D: Well, I think if you go outside the walls, you'll find there are many people out there who do these things.

S: *(Interrupted) Then I do not think I want to go!*

It seemed rather a shame that someday the time would come when he would be disillusioned by the way others lived outside the community. I wonder if Jesus felt the same way when his time came.

D: Many people would like to have a community like yours.

S: *But it is possible for everyone! It is just based upon love. If you love others, then there are no problems.*

D: But everyone doesn't understand that.

S: *But this creates more problems if they do not realize this now. They would go on and, maybe forever, forgetting where they came from. This would not be good.*

D: That's part of the problem, they have forgotten. It's good that your people have been taught to remember, to carry these teachings. (Which are really no more than what Jesus was trying to show people.) Would we be allowed to come and live there?

S: *I do not know. We take people from other places, I do not see why not. You must go before the elders and it is their decision.*

Suddi was many different ages when I found him and asked questions of him. The foregoing information was obtained when he was young. The following questions were asked when he was an older man. I knew some of the laws in the Old Testament, but I wanted to hear his version. I asked what happened to widows at Qumran.

S: *They are taken care of. If they were from outside of the community, if they wish to return to their families, they are given enough property or what have you, for them to be accepted into their family's life, if they would wish. (Apparently they could not return to their home empty-handed.) If they are of us or just wish to remain, they are also allowed to do this. And we make sure that they are taken care of.*

D: You said that when one married, it had to be done with the making up of the birth chart. Would a widow ever be allowed to remarry?

S: *It is possible, yes. If she was young enough and it was ordained, yes. But here again, only if the charts are matched.*

D: I thought you said your people only married once. Would this be the only way someone would be allowed to marry another time?

S: *If the mate had died, yes.*

D: Doesn't the Hebrew Law say that if a man ... if one of his brothers dies, then the brother...

S: *(Interrupted) Then he would take her as wife. And the children, if there were any from that union, would belong to the eldest son. This is the Hebrew Law, yes. This is not of the Torah. It is, in a great many cases, not at all useful, due to the fact that ... just because a man and a woman would wish to marry and would perhaps be very happy, she would not necessarily be one with his brother, or the next surviving male, which ever the case may be, if she were to become a widow.*

D: That's true. They probably thought it would be a way that she would be taken care of.

S: *But there are greater ways of taking care of them that are much better.*

D: Is it ever allowed in your community for either a wife or a husband to set aside a mate? Do you understand what I mean?

I didn't think he would understand the word "divorce". His answer surprised me.

S: There are times when they would live separate lives. And I have heard of cases where, for some reasons that have been disclosed to the elders, they were made as if not having ever been married. The reasons are known only to the elders. It is not a usual occurrence.

It sounded like the equivalent of divorce or annulment. According to the Bible, it could be done, but under certain circumstances it might be considered adultery. At Qumran they would be allowed to marry again.

S: The marriage is made as if it was not. This is why that the reasons are only known to the elders that do this. It is not something that is commonly used. Therefore, you cannot, because you have problems, decide that you may make the marriage no more. It is very, very unusual.

This sounded very considerate. If only the elders knew the reasons for the divorce (or annulment), there would not be the gossip and public chastisement that sometimes accompanies this. Also if the elders were the only ones who knew what grounds would be acceptable, the couple would not be able to invent reasons to get out of an undesirable situation. This was much more private, strictly between the couple involved and the elders. I was confused, however, because it seemed to be against the Bible laws of accepted behavior.

S: In Hebrew law this is forbidden, yes. The man is allowed to set aside his wife, but if he re-marries, according to Hebrew law, he is an adulterer.

D: I thought if your people married, they married for life.

S: No. There are cases of mistakes, where the person or soul decided to change their mind. That another lesson had to be learned instead.

D: Then they are very lenient in this way, it can...

S: (Interrupted emphatically) They are not lenient, but it can be done. It is not easily obtained.

D: But if they can still only re-marry if the charts agree, that means there must be more than one possible mate. Is that correct?

S: *Not always. But if there was a good reason for the marriage to be made no more, there is very good reason to believe that there would be another mate.*

D: I thought they never made a mistake when they drew up the charts?

S: *No one mortal is infallible. We are not gods.*

This showed that the Essenes were more human than their neighbors if they could forgive mistakes and not make people remain together for life or brand them adulterers.

S: *It is said that in the early days of the world that man and woman were not married in the sense that we would know this. And that a woman had many mates, and also a man. In order to make as many different possibilities of mates for the children of the children, many mixtures were tried. And a woman would have many children by many different men.*

I suddenly thought of the many legends of half-man, half animal. He had said "different mixtures". I wondered if he meant they also bred with the animals in that long ago beginning world. This idea angered him, *"This would be wrong!"* So, apparently I hit a wrong chord. I at least found one thing that would be frowned upon.

D: But they would not frown upon the idea of having many mates to produce many children?

S: *No, it is only after the idea of shame and guilt were brought into the world that this was frowned upon.*

D: Doesn't it say in the Commandments that 'thou shalt not commit adultery'?

S: *But this was, again, delivered much later, after Adam and Eve. The Commandments were given to Moses.*

D: What would you consider adultery then?

S: *Adultery would be to lie with another and not openly with approval. If it were something that had been discussed between the two, and it was decided upon, then this would be acceptable. The whole idea of adultery was very strange. For did not Abraham have two wives? Therefore, if it was not accepted by Sarah that he have another wife, would he not also be an adulterer?*

D: But in what cases would it be wrong?

S: To hide this, to seek to make a fool out of the other party. Adultery is, in the case where everyone knows but the one who is being hurt the most. If it is discussed and openly agreed upon, this cannot be adultery. This is just a different type of sharing. It has been misrepresented for many, many years.

This seemed to be a radical departure from the concept the Bible presents of adultery. Apparently if all parties agreed and there was an openness about it, it was not considered adultery. It was only so branded if someone was hurt or if there was an intention to hurt.

D: This is something I think a lot of people don't agree upon.
S: This is something that many people will never agree upon.
D: (I laughed.) I agree!

I do not want anyone to think that I advocate adultery, and I do not necessarily think Suddi's viewpoint is right. But it is a different way of looking at something so complex. I can see how they could accept this even though it would be totally against the Hebrew laws and teachings. If Jesus was indeed taught by the Essenes, I think his exposure to these ideas would explain his defense of the woman who was about to be stoned. He would have understood that sex between consenting adults was not considered adultery by the people of the Qumran community. A great many of their beliefs and teachings can be seen in the life of Jesus.

I was interested in their death customs. I asked about the most infamous one of all, crucifixion.

S: The Romans use this. This is where a felon is nailed to a cross. First their arms and their feet are tied. And then spikes that are so long (he made a measurement of about six or eight inches with his fingers) are driven through here. (He pointed to the area below the wrist, between the ulna and radius forearm bones) And through the feet.
D: Why would they do such an awful thing?
S: If you see someone who has done a crime and has been hung out there for days dying and you know his torment, you would think more than once about performing the same crime yourself. It is not our right to judge them ... but to take a life!

She shuddered all over, as though the very thought of it was horrible to him. I decided to change the subject, and ask about burial customs. I asked how a body was disposed of in the community.

S: *A lot of times it is anointed with the oils and the incense, and then it is buried in cloths. But there are those of us who prefer to destroy the body completely and burn it. I prefer the idea of turning to ash.*

D: Do you think there is any harm in burning the body? In doing it the way you prefer?

S: *No, why would there be harm? To my knowledge, this custom is very old.*

I was curious about the burial customs because it says in the Bible that Jesus was buried in the sepulcher. I asked about putting bodies in caves, and whether he knew the word "sepulcher".

S: *This is done by the others, yes. A sepulcher means a tomb. It is a larger area that has perhaps been hollowed out and prepared. It is something that was brought over from the Egyptians. They believed that we must have many things to go with you on the journey.*

D: But the body will deteriorate. If it was put into a sepulcher, a tomb, a cave, it wouldn't be covered by the dirt or anything.

S: *Some type of door is set, either a stone or something. Therefore, it is closed.*

D: But you don't put them in caves?

I meant *his* people, but he interpreted my question in his own way.

S: *It is very rare for any of us to entomb the bodies of others. The body has no use after it no longer houses a soul. Therefore, why not completely start from nothing and turn it back to the dust from whence it came?*

D: What is the purpose of the oils?

S: *The largeness of this reason is due to the smell. In Judaea and Galilee and this area, many of the people, they will anoint the body with the oils. If it was an illness that caused the person to die, it is said that it will keep that illness away from the others. Then, if they are to be entombed or whatever, if a pyre is built, it is done the day that they die, before sundown.*

D: What are the names of some of these oils or herbs that are used?

S: *There is myrrh and frankincense and many others that I cannot begin to name. But these are the most commonly used.*

This was a surprise. I had only heard of myrrh and frankincense associated with the gifts of the Three Wise Men. I thought they were incenses and did not know they had anything to do with burials.

D: I have always heard that frankincense was only used to burn because of the nice smell.

S: *It is rubbed into the body. Other times it is then burned before the body is. The smell, the scent is very nice and therefore it protects the nose of the people who are preparing the body.*

My research disclosed that frankincense and myrrh were used chiefly for the reasons he stated, to overcome the smell of the decaying body. Frankincense was also used as a salve or ointment to heal boils and sores, so it may have had some preservative affects on the skin after death. It was also an excellent repellent used to drive away insects.

D: When you bury the body in the ground, do you put it in anything?

S: *Sometimes, very rarely though, for wood is precious and usually they are just wrapped in shrouds and laid in the tombs or in the grave that has been prepared.*

The cemetery of Qumran was found outside the walls and adjacent to the community. There were over a thousand graves. When de Vaux. was trying to establish the identity of the people who lived in Qumran, he considered many possibilities. The graves were at first thought to be ordinary Arab tombs. But the local guides said this was impossible because the bodies were buried with the head to the South and the feet to the North, the exact opposite of their custom. They knew they were the graves of unbelievers or non-Arabs.

It was a very unusual cemetery, unlike any ever found in that part of the world. A few coffins were found but no artifacts or objects buried with the dead, as was the custom in many areas. Pere de Vaux was surprised that there was no jewelry or ornamental objects in the graves. He said this meant the people were either poverty-stricken or had a rigid discipline that did not allow them to wear finery. They were also surprised when the graves yielded the skeletons of women and children. They had long assumed that only men lived there in a monastery-type community. So, again, the excavations seem to support our findings in great detail and accuracy.

D: What do the Romans do with their dead? Do they have different customs?

S: *They have as many customs as they have gods. They have more gods than man can count. I think perhaps that a nation has many gods because they are unsure of themselves, and therefore they create their gods in their images. Therefore, if the nation is defiled, therefore, so are the gods. The Romans, as soon as a new god has occurred on the scene, it almost immediately becomes as debased as the rest of them. In each nation there are good men, but Rome tends to destroy the ones who speak the truth. Therefore, this is not good.*

D: Do you have a Roman who is a leader over your area?

S: *There is a man who calls himself Emperor over us, yes. He considers himself Emperor of the world.*

D: Is there anyone who has control over your area?

S: *At present it is Herod Antipas who is our king. There is a Roman who is ... what do I wish to say ... ? um, governor of the area. Yes, Pontius Pilate. When he says to hop, Herod hops.*

D: Then he is more important?

S: *He is the man with the soldiers, therefore he is more important, yes.*

D: Have you heard any tales of him? Is he a good man?

S: *He is said to be just.*

D: What about King Herod?

S: *(sigh) That man is a fool! He cannot decide whether he wishes to be Greek or Jew. And therefore, he is not a very good one of either.*

D: Has he ever bothered your community?

S: *He knows better than to do that. To try would be his death.*

This again indicated that they must have had some secret way of defending the community, although they did not believe in weapons. In asking these questions, I was thinking about the Bible stories of Herod.

D: Does he have a queen or some female who rules with him?

S: Herodius. (He almost spit the word.) That is his whore!

I was surprised by his strong answer. I asked if he had heard any tales of her.

S: (sigh) She has been married three times. Her first husband she killed to marry Philip. And then she left Philip to marry Antipas.

He didn't want to discuss her; it was distasteful to him. I wondered how she could have had so many husbands. According to their law, didn't she have to put away one before she could take another?

S: There are many loopholes in the law, in which she managed to come around. It is said that when she first moved with Philip that her first husband was not dead, therefore she was able to set this aside. And now that her first husband is dead, she was able to bribe, kill, whatever, to be able to acquire Antipas as a husband.

It sounded complicated. It apparently was an illegal marriage, in other words.

S: The second one was not. Who knows about this one? She is to be the downfall of Antipas. It is her destiny. I do not know of which path that she will choose. I just know that she will cause his downfall.

D: When a person comes into a life, I wonder why they would choose to come in and do evil, or do things to make it difficult for others.

S: It is not really a choice. It is . . . some people would, through outside pressures, perhaps the people that they live with or the community that they live in, or people who are not good. They would pressure them into doing things that, inside, the person knows are wrong. No one chooses to be bad.

D: The choice is really up to the individual, depending on which type of influence comes along?

S: And they also have the choice to withstand.

CHAPTER 7

The Mysterious Library

During a session with Suddi as a young student, I received my first indication that Qumran was not an ordinary school. There were much deeper subjects taught there than anyone could imagine. I also learned that the library held many strange and wondrous mysteries. He was in the teaching area of the library, and I asked for a description.

S: *The buildings are together. They are not quite separate. They are all as one. The library is in the center building. It is very large. It has many windows and is very light. Light filters in from overhead, it comes from different openings. There are shelves on which the scrolls are placed. They are wrapped in skins and different things. Some are not even scrolls. Some are just things that have been printed on, many skins and placed together. There are many things here that we study. The most things that are here are the books that have all of the knowledge, that they say, as we know it. A man could spend all his years here and never finish all of the scrolls and books and things.*

D: You said before that the library has two floors. What is on the other floor?

S: *The scrolls. The center of the building is open so that you may look down from the second and see the floor of the first.*

It sounded as if an upper balcony encircled the room. This allowed the light to come down to the first floor. I wondered if there was any danger of falling.

S: *There are rails to protect you from this, if anyone was uncaring enough to try to walk off. The library, the central area is light,*

73

but back where there is storage of the scrolls and things, it is darker so that it does not damage them. There are windows in the ceiling. They are covered with skins that have been treated so that the light is allowed to pass. So that the dust and things are kept out but the light comes through.

In the area where they studied, there were specially made tables that were constructed to facilitate the studying of a scroll. From her motions and his descriptions, it seemed there were brackets mounted on the sides of the table, and the scroll would be placed parallel with the table and unrolled. I have always assumed a scroll was unrolled from side to side, not up and down. He indicated with his finger that he would read from right to left. I assumed this meant that he would start reading from the bottom of the scroll. He disagreed and said that it depended upon the writing. Some things began at the bottom and some at the top. He said the scrolls were written in every known language, *"One's Greek one's Vulgate, Aramaic, Arabic. There are the language of the Babylonians, Syria, the* (sounded like: 'ta') *of the Egyptians, the glyphs. "*

D: Where did all these come from? Were these all written here?

S: *Most of them were at least recopied here. But a lot of them were brought from other places and gathered. It is to be a continual hunt for new knowledge and it is never-ending. There are new things brought in every day. The room where they are copied, there is one of them off the library. It is even lighter than the library. There are large tables that are, again, upright, so that the scroll is in front of you. They are very similar to the reading tables. There is something behind this to keep the pressure even when you write across. A board is placed back here, it is at this angle, so that when you press downwards with the stylus, it is equal and it does not rock. These tables are made of wood. Part of the stools on some of them are made of stone, but for the most part they are made of wood. (They seemed to be very similar to drafting tables)*

D: What are you learning in your classes?

S: *(Big sigh) Everything! Oh, it is not too bad. The teach us about the stars and the mathematics. The law and the Torah and the different things like this.*

I wondered about the methods the ancients used in mathematics. As usual, I got more than I was expecting.

S: *It has been told to me by my teachers that an ass would know more about mathematics than I. (This remark caused laughter among the listeners.) To me the Law is alive. There is feeling and emotion and depth in this. Mathematics are cold and facts and figures, and what meaning has it to me? And therefore it is not important to myself. There is great importance given to mathematics. And there is hidden knowledge, it is said, in mathematics, which shall be later discovered and re-used. So we must learn the theorem and the ways of doing things, so that we can learn to do different things within the mathematics and hopefully use it through our lives. There are many different types of mathematics. They deal in absolutes and theorems. Saying that if this is so then this must also be true. Shapes and geometries is one form of mathematics, dealing with the shapes and depths and all of things.*

D: Let's see, you may not know the terms of some of the things we use. For instance, we have addition, subtraction and multiplication.

S: *Explain. These are unfamiliar to me.*

D: The ways you use numbers. Addition is taking two numbers and putting them together.

S: *To make them total? Yes, this is done. And also to increase them so many times of each other, this is done. Also to take away from. And different ways of figuring heights and solids and things. There are many formulae for these.*

D: Do you have any tools or instruments to help you make your calculations, if you know that word?

S: *Like for the... the term you used was... um, addition? The easiest one to do is the knots, the knot belts. It is a belt that has been knotted, and has the strings that are varying lengths. There is a knot that means so many in numerals. And there are people who are very good, that can sit there and calculate with these all day. These are tools you would use. You can have those that are very large, that are always hung. Or you can have one that is suspended from a belt, that is used for sitting there and doing figuring. Like if you were a merchant in the market or something. They would be able to use one of these to do this. It is used in adding and counting different things. The people who are educated or have to deal with numbers would have to know how to use this. (He laughed.) They say it is the easiest one to use.*

When I began to search through books for some verification of the things Suddi spoke of, I could find no mention of anything similar to this being used in that part of the world. But it sounds a great deal like the quipu that was used by the ancient Incas in Peru. The quipu was called a string computer and used for calculation in their society. It consisted of strings of various lengths, ranging from one inch up to around two feet and was suspended from a holder. The type of knot and its position on the cord represented numbers in a decimal system, from one to nine while a blank space on the string represented zero. Granted, the Incas lived half a world away from Qumran, but could it be possible that others also used this numerical method and its knowledge has been lost? The community at Qumran apparently contained an incredible amount of knowledge collected from everywhere. I was beginning to think anything was possible.

S: *Sometimes there are those who use the sticks which are different colors for different amounts. And there are many different ways of utilizing things to do this. They are just like so long. (He made finger measurements of about four inches long.) Like one color means one thing and another color... and you add them up and it comes together. I'm not very good at this. I'm not familiar with the meanings of them, but there are blues and reds and yellows and orange and a black and white. Different colors. I've also heard of another tool that is utilized that has a frame. It is beads on wires. I have seen one of these, but I do not know how to do this. They count these beads.*

This sounded like the Chinese abacus. It is very ancient and it is possible that they had knowledge of it. If they could have knowledge of that, I do not see how it is too far-fetched to know about the quipu, except that China was actually closer and they might have had easier contact through trade caravans.

S: *There are also mathematics used when that you study the stars. You would use the mathematics to plot the direction that one would come, from here at this point to over here. (He gestured.) And with the maps you would be able to do this. We have the charts that help us to remember where the stars are. There are stargazers that you would have. We do have a few that are very strong. (I asked for an explanation) From which you look through the smallest end of this tube. And you look at the heavens with this, and it is as if they are brought in front of your face. This is very, very old. It is said that our people, as they were, they did create this, but the art has been lost. It was not done here. It was many generations ago.*

A telescope! But they were not supposed to have been invented until many hundreds of years later. I don't know why this should really be so surprising. The art of glass making goes back to the time of the ancient Egyptians. Surely someone in all that time must have been curious enough to look through a piece of glass and noticed the distortion in size. Erich von Daniken gives two examples in his books of the discovery of crystal lens. One was found in a tomb in Helwan, Egypt and is now in the British Museum. The other is from Assyria and dates from the 7th Century BC. They were mechanically ground, and the knowledge to do this required a highly sophisticated mathematical formula. What were these lenses used for? Possibly stargazers?

There were three different stargazers located at Qumran that varied in size. They were not located in the library, but were in an observatory farther up on the hill above the community. Two of these were permanently mounted there and the third, a smaller one, was portable. There were certain masters who lived in the observatory and constantly studied and monitored the stars. The students were allowed to look through these stargazers, when they were engaged in this study.

I was still trying to absorb this new development when he threw another one at me. This whole session was full of the unexpected.

S: *They have models of the heavens that move constantly, as our system does. They have the model of the star system in which we live in.*

I thought, "Wait a minute, let's back it up here." Was I sure I was hearing him right? A model?

The concept of the model was so strange to me that I was determined to understand it. Thus I asked many questions trying to get a clear picture of what it looked like. The contents of this library took me off guard, although I soon learned that I should not be surprised at anything that might be in Qumran.

It was frustrating for him to try to describe and explain something that was so familiar to him. He became aggravated with my insistent questioning. He probably wondered why I couldn't see it also.

The model, or orrery, was located in the library as were many other of the mysteries. It stood in the center of the room. It was large, *"perhaps the span of two men with their arms outstretched. This is the width, and maybe twice as tall as a man"*. The entire apparatus was made out of bronze. At the center was a large round sphere that represented the sun. A staff ran through this and was driven into the floor. From the bottom or the floor level there were many other rods projecting outward. Each rod had a bronze sphere on the end of it. These represented the various planets in our solar system. Each was placed in the position it would be in orbit around the sun. There were no moons represented, only a sphere of equal size for each planet.

This whole model was in constant motion: The sun revolving, the rods moving their planets around the sun in the exact position and distance of their orbit and the smaller spheres spinning on the ends of the rods. The spheres moved in an oval, an elliptical circle around the sun. Suddi explained all of this with much motioning and gesturing. He described the orbit as: *"it is ellipt. It is kind of high here and narrows out at the ends. It is like a circle that has been stretched ... deep. "* It was amazing to me that the entire solar system could be recreated in this exacting manner. I could not understand what source of power would be used to keep it rotating.

S: *When the earth turns, it keeps this spinning also. The earth, it spins around and around, and-it is like, if you've taken something and turned around in a great circle. First it starts at the floor and once that you are going faster, it sails to the sky, you see. And it is like this. This is being kept moving by the same thing that keeps the thing that you would be drawing... up. The movement causes it to keep moving.*

I could picture this as if you have something on the end of a string and began turning in a circle. The object would leave the floor and rise upward as you revolved faster. It sounded to me as though the orrery might be a perpetual motion machine operated by centrifugal force. Maybe someone else has a better explanation for it.

The model was surrounded by a railing to keep anyone from approaching too close. It apparently was a very delicate mechanism, and its movement could be disturbed very easily.

S: The students are warned never to go near it. It is said that even to blow on it would cause it to stop and then it would take a great length of time to again start. Therefore we are not allowed near it.

Whether it was really that delicately balanced or not, the threat apparently worked and everyone kept a respectable distance away from it. Since the floor was stone, the motion of the people in the room did not bother it. He could not give me any information about how it was constructed or attached to the floor, since it was very old and had been there a long time.

I received another surprise when I asked how many planets were represented by the spheres. He answered in a matter-of fact manner that there were *ten*. This really shook me because even in our present day we are only aware of nine. The ninth planet, Pluto, was only discovered in *1930*. There has been discussion among astronomers that there might be a tenth one out there, because something seems to be influencing the orbits of the others. I tried to remain nonchalant as though nothing of importance had been revealed and asked if he could name the planets for me.

S: I will give them their Roman names which you probably are very familiar with. They are known by many names, but these are possibly the most familiar. (He spoke slowly as though thinking.) To the inside is Mercury and Venus or Mathusias (phonetic) and Terra and Mars and Jupiter and Saturn... Let's see, after Saturn comes Urana and Neptune and Pluto. And out past Pluto there is one called - let's see, I believe they gave it the name of Juna. Whose idea it was to name them after these, I have no idea. I think that is all of them. I know there are ten. Juna, the one out past the farthest, they say that it has a very erratic orbit. It is not elipt, but swings in and out, and does a kind of a loop around

Pluto. It takes a great deal of time to complete its orbit.

He gestured with his hands to show something that went in and out among the others.

D: Do any of the planets look different?

S: *On the model they are all the same, but they really are larger and smaller. They are each individual to each other. Nothing is the same in the universe. (His childish enthusiasm was bubbly in his desire to share his knowledge) Even two ants that you would look at and think, these are identical. There is something about the one that the other one does not have. There is nothing in the universe that is identical.*

D: Can you tell me, as we move out from the sun, approximately the relative size of each planet?

S: *(He may have been referring to a map or chart here) As the sun is here, and you have a small one, and you have like two that are fairly small, and you have one that is getting larger. And each one gets larger for a while. And then it is like it reaches midpoint, and then they begin again to decrease in size. The largest one is Jupiter and the smallest is Juna. And each one has moons, which are many in some of these. But they are not added to the model. We are just told that they are there. The larger a planet the more moons that it has. Saturn has rings that were made of... They say that possibly these was another planet that was there and it collected it and it is called... rings. As you look at it, you may see these. There are many hundreds and hundreds of them about it. These are also not on the model. We are told these things and we have seen these with the stargazers. Our planet is Terra. It has the one moon that has no air about it.*

I asked if he had ever heard of another planet that exploded many, many years ago. I was thinking about the theory of the creation of the asteroid belt. There was supposed to be something between Jupiter and Mars.

S: *Probably hit Jupiter. I know not of this. It is said that our universe is still new and still changing, so this is very possible.*

D: How do you know about all these planets? You surely can't see all of them, even with your stargazers?

S: *I have not seen them. It is said that much of the knowledge of our system, as we know it, has been handed down for many, many generations.*

D: Do you know who made this model?

S: It is said that the Kaloo did.

D: Who are the Kaloo?

S: How do I say this..? They are the people who left their country to share the knowledge that they had gained with others. And it is said that we are from these people. It is said that we are members of their dying race. We are taught to spread knowledge among the uninformed in hopes to bring about the age of enlightenment again. I do not know much about them. Some of the masters know in great depth the things that they teach and who they were. It is knowledge that is only allowed to the eyes of certain ones. And it is not permitted to speak among strangers.

I wondered if they might have had some connection with the lost continent of Atlantis, and asked if he knew the name of the place they had come from.

S: I do not know. It is said that this has been lost. They say that they came from the direction that the sun sets, from the West. That they settled in Egypt and then traveled this way. I do not know where they went. This was many, many fathers ago.

D: You said that you were to bring back the age of enlightenment. Was there a time when things were more enlightened than now?

S: I do not know much of it. It is said that it was when great things were done when all men were as one. And we have just some of the things, such as the model. Our things that were protected and kept to show that these things were possible. That they were not just legends. It is said that the Kaloo wander. That is part of their destiny. Some of them are said to have traveled in hopes of finding others of their people, and are still traveling. And it is said that some of these have forgotten even from whence that they started. Others are like us here, descendants of some and some others who were from here and are trying to protect some of the knowledge that was.

This would explain their care with the model. If anything happened to it, they wouldn't know how to make another one.

D: Is this why you remain isolated? Why you are away from other towns, other people?

S: *It is said that if we would go down to where that the others are, that a lot of the knowledge would be lost because the people would be drawn away. Because of the temptations and they would not care about keeping the old knowledge alive.*

D: Is there anything else that they have brought to your people?

S: *The knowledge that sometime in the near future there will be a Messiah. It is said that a lot of the places that they went they would speak of the story of his coming. And that they would know and they would tell the time that this would be. There is more knowledge, but it is things that are kept for those who study into those things. It has been decided that I shall study Law, and this shall be what I do the best. And therefore I have no need to know of these things, for it would just clutter my mind for other things. I have heard of them speaking upon the Messiah, but it is not something that they wish a child to know. I have not had my Barmitzvah. That makes me a man. Then I shall be part of the adult community. I have no need to know these things yet for my destiny. Therefore, why interfere with your destiny in this manner?*

D: If you are to be studying the Law, why is it necessary for you to know about the stars?

S: *It is necessary for certain reasons of day-to-day living, of perhaps knowing a little of our destiny but not too much. Also there are other reasons for studying the stars in the skies and those of our system. Because they are fixed in many ways. It is said that when that the planets are placed a certain way . . . when you are born they are this set pattern, and that this has great meaning with what you will do with your life. I do not know how to read this. Again, the masters are the ones who teach this. It is said that the stars will tell the people the truth of things, but we just study where they are and things about them like this. We study astron.*

He did not use the complete word "astronomy." In the dictionary, *astron* used as a prefix is Greek for star. He said the brightest star in their part of the world was called *Garata* (phonetic) and was located in the northern part of the sky. He said that some people thought the groups of stars looked like people or animals up there. To him it looked as if *"somebody just took a bucket of sand and just tossed."*

I wondered what else could possibly be in this fantastic library. He said there were skeletons of various animals that had been preserved for study. I should have been prepared for surprises by now, but the next answer took me off guard again.

S: There is much here. There is a great crystal that is... how do I say..? shaped with four sides that come to a point, and the fifth side on the bottom (a pyramid). It is an ... energy increaser, if I shall use the right terms. When the energy is placed into this, the output is far greater than what was placed there. It is used in different things. I'm not very sure what. It also is protected. There is a wall that has been built around it. The wall comes to about approximately here (about waist high). You can see it but you cannot come near it. The crystal sits on a pedestal behind the wall. It is shielded in an area where there are curtains that may be drawn around it. (With hand motions he showed it to be a large crystal, about two feet square. But the color was uncertain) It changes. It is never the same. You look at it once and you will see it is blue. You will look at it again and perhaps it is purple or green or...it is never the same.

He did not know where the crystal came from, it had been there *"for as long as I know."* The wall was for protection. The crystal was so potent it would burn if it were touched. Only one person had the ability to come close to it.

S: Mechalava, (phonetic: May-chal-ava) the master of mysteries. He is able to channel it and his students who are taught in these manners are. They focus their energy onto him and he transfers it to this crystal and it is used in many different ways that we do not understand nor are allowed to.

D: You mean the energy is stored from the students to the master and then into the crystal, rather than the other way around?

S: And then it goes out from the crystal for whatever use they would. They have the ability to channel it or direct it or focus it where they wish. It is said that Mechalava's will is the strongest. He is very old and he is waiting for one who is the same to be born, so that he may pass on the responsibilities. It will be started from the time it is just a little baby. Some of the knowledge has been passed, but not all. Mechalava would teach the things that are unknown to most of us. It is said that once all had this knowledge, and because of this, great damage was done.

Therefore, it was then only allowed to certain ones who had been deemed responsible enough to be allowed to have this knowledge. So that it might be carried down to a time when that again all would be able to have this knowledge and gain from it. Therefore, he (Mechalava) is involved in the continuance of the knowledge that is.

The archaeologists found two queerly placed bases of columns in one of the buildings. They were set close together in the ground, as if they had been stands for something. They had no explanation for them. Could I speculate that this could be the pedestal mentioned that the crystal sat upon?

I attempted to find out about some of the mysteries that Suddi may have been taught.

S: *I am not allowed to speak of it because this is part of the responsibility. Unless the student has been verified, we are not allowed to speak.*

I tried to get around his objections by asking in what areas the mysteries were, for instance, the law or the history. I thought we would be able to get information easily while talking to him at a young age, but even then the bond of secrecy was present.

S: *No, they are with ... other things. Part of it is the using of the mind. It is the source of great power.*

He steadfastly refused to reveal any more about the mysteries, so I decided to change the subject. Maybe later I would be able to uncover more through my roundabout methods.

D: You said that the crystal was the storehouse of energy? Can you tell me, are there any metals that you are aware of that also store energy?
S: *Several. Gold... to an extent, copper. It depends upon which vibration you would need. They would work for different things. Like the higher level would be the silver or the gold, and the lower level would be the copper and the brass. The stones have the greater storing capability.*
D: It seems that you have a lot of knowledge there that other people

don't have.

S: We must try to keep it alive and breathing, so that it will not be forgotten.

CHAPTER 8

The Twelve Commandments

During this session I was speaking to Suddi when he was twelve years old. I assumed he had not been studying long, but he disagreed, saying it seemed like forever.

S: I know not of others, but in where we live we start at about six or seven. There are those of us here who are of Hebrew descent. There are those of us who are Syrian. And there are those who are Egyptian. There are many here. We are all different people, but we are all of one thought and one belief. We are who believe in God Abba and are gathering here to bring forth light into the world where there is nothing but darkness.

Note the similarity between this statement and the sayings that Jesus was the light of the world.

D: I have heard people say that the Essenes are a religious group.
S: We are a religious group in that we believe in God. But to say our way is a religion is something different. Because that seems to be so inhibiting. It is not the same. There is so much more, because we are protecting and keeping knowledge alive and helping bring knowledge and light to the world.

While I spoke with him, he was copying down parts of the Torah. I thought the only reason they would have for copying a scroll would be if the scroll was in bad shape and deteriorating. But he said the original "skin" was still very good. His father thought it would help him to remember if he wrote it down.

S: He says it might help. My head is so thick, he will try anything. I

86

have no good memory. What can one say?

I was interested in their method of writing. He said when they were practicing they used clay tablets because they were not going to keep them. Only what was to be permanent was put on papyrus.

S: With the clay tablets it is easy for a student to see how he is forming a word. He sees it in the tablet and he gets the feel of what it is. And it is cheaper, it is easy to make more clay tablets or wax, which can be melted down and redone. But, papyrus, once it is used, that is it.

He used a stylus, which was a stick with a sharp point, to write on the tablets. On papyrus you could either use the stylus dipped in ink or a brush. He mostly wrote in Aramaic which was his native language. At that time I knew nothing about the languages in his part of the world, and I caused confusion when I asked about his alphabet. He had no idea what I was talking about, and it is always difficult to explain in simple terms something that we are so familiar with. It never occurred to me that people in other lands might not use letters as we do. These sessions proved to be very educational for both Katie and myself. He tried to explain that it was not letters but sounds that made up their language. I did not understand what he meant. Later when I began to do research I found that the languages in Suddi's part of the world are vastly different from ours. They use symbols that are similar to a form of shorthand. Each stands for a certain sound and the sounds make up the words. He was absolutely correct, and it was little wonder that I couldn't make him understand what I wanted. I asked him if he could read me what he was copying from. During his recitation he spoke several words that were definitely in a foreign language, then he spoke slowly in English as though he was translating what he was seeing.

S: It is part of the Commandments of Moses. It speaks of... it says... the Lord thy God... thou shall have no gods other than me. We are to not make images of stone... of other gods to worship. And we should... honor thy father and mother. And... thou shall not kill or steal or.... commit adultery. There are many of them. Moses was a great giver of law. These are just some of the first ones. He went on and on about them.

It was obvious he was reading from the Ten Commandments, but he startled me when he said there were twelve commandments. At the time I could not pursue it during that session.

Later when I was talking to Suddi as an older man, an excellent opportunity presented itself to ask him about the extra commandments. I had taken him to an important day when he was about forty years old. He was practicing his daily meditation. *"It makes me feel very good to do this. I feel grounded, like I have a basis to work from."* On this day he was meditating to calm himself because it was a very important day.

S: *Today I shall be tested and the decision shall be made. Whether or not I have merit of the blue band.*

When an Essene had earned the right to wear the blue band across his forehead, he had attained the rank of master. The test was the last requirement and the culmination of all his years of studying.

S: *A person goes through the lessons and he is tested by the elders to find out how much of the knowledge has been amassed. How much understanding is there. A man can have great knowledge and still not have understanding of it and therefore the knowledge is useless. To be a master, one must have the knowledge and have the understanding of it. Of whatever that they are studying, be it Law or be it the study of the stars or anything else. You must have understanding in order to be a master. Therefore you are tested by the elders. They shall all question me to find my understanding.*

D: Will it be a long test?

S: *(Quite seriously) Not if I fail right away. It could go on for quite a while. But I shall not fail. The answers they shall come.*

I thought this would be an excellent time to ask about the extra commandments, as this might be a question they would ask him during the test. He sighed and began reciting them for me while counting on his fingers.

S: *The first is: I am the Lord thy God and thou shalt have no other gods before me. Thou shalt not make graven images. (Big sigh.) Honor thy father and mother. Remember the Sabbath day and*

The Twelve Commandments

keep it holy. Thou shalt not steal. Thou shalt not commit adultery. Thou shalt not covet... ah, another's property. Ah... I remember slowly. This is seven? Thou shall not follow the ways of the path of Baal.

He broke down in frustration, and forgot how many he had named. But I had already heard one that I was not familiar with, the one about Baal. I told him this would be good preparation for facing the elders. He took a deep breath. *"I think I'm more nervous than what I ....* Then totally unexpected, he startled me with a question, *"Who are you?"* I was taken off guard and had to think fast. I have often wondered how the subject perceives me or if they do at all. Do they see me as an actual person or am I just a little voice buzzing in their head? On occasion their answers seem to suggest that they see me but I am a stranger to them. During one session a subject saw me dressed as the people in his culture, but he warned me I was asking too many questions and this was dangerous. For the most part, I think of myself as just a voice. I think in this instance Suddi picked up on me differently because he was meditating. This may have made him more open to my presence. In the past whenever this has happened and this question came up, I merely told them I was a friend and this answer has been sufficient. I don't understand why, maybe just the reassurance that I mean them no harm is enough. I asked him if it bothered him to speak with me.

S: *It makes me curious. You are here, yet you are not here. I think you are not from... now. It is... you are here in spirit, but not in body.*

I had the weirdest feeling that maybe, through some process we did not understand, I had been projected backward through time and was appearing to this poor confused man. It was a strange feeling, knowing somehow you were existing in two places at once. But essentially, wasn't that what Katie was also doing? I must be careful not to disturb or upset him, so I tried to calm any apprehension he might have so we could continue.

D: Does it disturb you?
S: *A little. Are you my master?*
D: Oh, I don't think I'm that high. No, I'm more like a guardian. I'm very interested in your life and what you are doing. Would that

be acceptable? I mean no harm at all.

S: *(Suspiciously) You mean no harm? I feel a... warmth about you, but some people who are very knowledgeable can project many things.*

D: I am interested in your welfare. That's why I ask many questions, because I'm interested in the time and the place in which you live. I thirst for knowledge.

S: *Yes, I feel very great curiosity in you. I can see an image, but it is... it is as if you are not here. (Was it like a dream image?) I feel no harm in speaking to those who do not inhabit the body, but not all of them are benevolent.*

I had to try to get his mind off me, so I directed him back to the twelve commandments. He sighed and went back over them again while counting on his fingers. This time he included another, *"Thou shalt do only unto others as they would do unto you."* This is the Golden Rule and is not normally included with Ten Commandments. I asked about that one.

S: *It has to do with having memory of if you treat others as you would wish to be treated. For this is what you shall carry forward with you. (Was he relating it to karma?)*

D: It makes sense, but we never placed it with the other ones.

S: *How not? I have heard that the one of the worshiping, not only the graven image, but the one of Baal, that it was tried to be struck at the time of Moses because of the calf. But I have not heard that anyone would try to take this "Do unto others." I have not heard of this. This would be very wrong.*

I agreed it was a good law and belonged with the others.

During another session I reminded him about the test and asked if he had passed. He was indignant.

S: *Do I not wear the blue band? Of course I got my master's. How could you no pass the test and not become a master?*

Thus he was at that time a master of the law, the Torah, but he considered himself at forty-six to be a very old man. I disagreed, but he insisted, *"But it is! It is of an age when that many men have died sooner. (Sigh) I am an old man."*

The Twelve Commandments

If a man in his forties was considered old in that time period, this made me suspect that Jesus was not a young man when he was crucified. In his thirties, he would have been at least middle-aged.

CHAPTER 9

Meditation and Chakras

Exercises for the use of meditation were given to us on two separate occasions, once when Suddi was a child and another time when he was older. I do not think it is too fantastic to assume that Jesus was also taught these procedures since they were in common use at Qumran.

As a boy, Suddi said there was meditation time set aside during each day.

S: *We just sit and we must be very still and must think about the way that we are breathing, and concentrate on it for a while. And when it is under control, you have learned enough that you do not have to think about it. Then you must focus on something. You take an object and put your point of focus somewhere in the middle of it and become one with it and study it and learn about it. Then you would release this. Once that you become one with it and understand this, you would then "unfocus" the focal point so that you are no longer in the center but around. So that it invokes everything that is around, surrounding you. I can not explain it very well. A student is taught to do this when they are nigh three, four years old.*

Thus the training of the mind began at a very young age in Qumran. Once during a session when Suddi was an older man, he mentioned that King Herod (apparently the first King Herod) would soon die. He seemed to have received this information through psychic means, and I wondered if others in the community had these gifts. Suddi was surprised by my question.

S: *Who is not? Everyone has this that I know. It is said that people in everyday life perhaps are not so ... let's see, what ... ? gifted? But we are taught from an early age to open ourselves up to that that is. But it is one ability that needs to be nurtured and developed. Anyone has the ability, but when you reach perhaps the age thirteen and you have never used this, and you have closed it off, you start to lose the ability to breach the gap. Because often you have been in the society of others who are head blind. Who cannot hear you, who cannot understand what that you are speaking. And therefore because of the high level of intensity, you have locked them out. And when you spend all of your life blocking out, it is very difficult to open up.*

D: Is thirteen a significant age?

S: *It is just a time where that the body is going through changes. It is said that there is a great link between the two. I'm not sure about this. I do not study into this. But this is what I have heard, that when the onset of manhood or womanhood is, it is also when everything opens up. In perhaps greater ways than it ever has before, if you let it. (It sounded as if it was connected with puberty)*

D: Then you should have this other ability developing before that age?

S: *Yes, You should at least be aware of it. So that its intensity does not frighten you and does not cause you to close it off. There are many different concentration exercises that may be used. The easiest one is to take something, anything that you are focusing on and use it as a focus. You would set it in front of you and gaze at it and become one with it. And so that as you are focusing, you narrow your attention down to this one point. And when it all becomes focused, you then just release it. (He made gestures as though letting something go, throwing it away.) And upon the releasing, you will begin to be aware of other sensations that are around you, and you would take note of these. And each time the awareness of these other sensations becomes louder, so that it is as if they have been spoken to you.*

D: Is there any danger linked with this exercise?

S: *I have never known of any. I would not do it where that there were of any interruptions or perhaps rude awakenings. There is no set time. Each time it would perhaps build up until the length was what became comfortable to you.*

I had talked to him many times while he was meditating. Often he would absent-mindedly rub the center of his forehead with the side of his right thumb, as though massaging. I wondered why that particular area, since this is where the brow chakra or third eye is located. This time when he did it I decided to ask about it. *"Tis a habit. It is a method of concentration. It is to focus the energy, your thoughts. It is an energy point."*

His descriptions will sound very familiar to those who have studied metaphysics. The term "energy point" would be a good definition for "chakra". The chakras are essentially energy points located in various places in the body. They can be mentally and psychically stimulated to help control the health of the body, and to promote psychic abilities and awareness. According to modern teachings, they are located in seven parts of the body:

1. Crown: on the top of the head where the energy of the body is supposed to enter;
2. Brow or Third eye: located in the middle of the forehead;
3. Throat: located in the front of the neck;
4. Heart: located in the middle of the chest;
5. Solar Plexus: located in the center of the abdomen;
6. Spleen or Sacral: located just below the navel;
7. Root: located near the sexual organs, between the legs.

The energy is supposed to enter through the crown chakra and energize each of the chakras in turn as it passes through the body. Finally the excess is released through the feet.

Since he called them energy points instead of chakras, I used his terminology. He said by rubbing that point during meditation it was helping to stimulate it. I was always taught that you should sit very still while meditating.

S: There are different forms of meditation. All meditation basically is concentration. Whether you are concentrating on a point that is here (pointed to his forehead) or whether you are concentrating on a point that is outside of you, yourself All meditation is, is a focusing of all of your thoughts and energies upon that one point.

I asked if there were any other energy points in the body. He pointed in turn to the different conventional chakra locations, except he had one more than the normal seven. He indicated that there are two in the upper chest area, one on each side. He also indicated one at each knee. I asked about the extra one in the chest area.

S: *One is at the heart and there is another energy point there. It is not open in all people. It is one that has been, for a good deal, lost. Sometimes it is to the side, it depends upon the person. This is how mine is. There is also one at the back of the head, at the base. (He pointed to the back of the head where it is connected with the spine) To a great extent it is dangerous to stimulate it. It can cause many problems. But it is there nonetheless. It is important to keep that one unstimulated. Most people would not be able to handle the stimulation. It is too powerful a force. I know of only one person with it open and stimulated, and he is a great mental builder. He is the master of the mysteries. (Could this be the same man who could channel the energy into the great crystal and direct it?) It is too overpowering for most people.*

I asked about the one at the top of the head, the crown chakra.

S: *It is not necessarily an energy point, but where the energy enters into the body. It is like, the feet are not really energy points, they are where it leaves also.*

I wondered if any of the energy points was more important than the others.

S: *They all have equal importance. It depends upon which you want to stimulate, what you decide to do with your life. If you wish for knowledge, the one here (the forehead) would be a good one to stimulate. The one in the throat would be for different health problems, also to do with energy levels and balances. The one over the heart is for the pure energy that radiates throughout the body. And the other one (in the chest area) has to do with your other self's energy and other knowing. How do I explain this? It has to do with the energies in which you control the being able to know things that are unknown to others, through just knowing. It is to do with mental communication. In most people it was*

95

closed forever.

It sounded as if it has a lot to do with psychic or intuitive ability since it was the one that the majority of people have lost the ability to use. Was this the one that was open at the time of the Kaloo? (See Chapter 15.)

S: *(He pointed to the solar plexus area.) This one has to do with the wholeness of self. It is important for balance again. It has to do with the connection between your higher self and your body. It has a great deal to do with this connection and the keeping it together and oneness. (He pointed to the two in the abdominal area, the spleen and the root chakras.) They are to do with the manhood or womanhood, depending upon the person. So one would be stronger in one. If in a woman you would have a stronger male center, you would have emotional problems. Likewise if you have a stronger female center in a man, you would have great problems with identifying yourself, as who you were and things of this matter.*

Could this be an allusion to homosexuality, if these chakras were not operating in the manner they operate in most people? I asked about the method of stimulation of the other chakras.

S: *There are different methods of stimulation that work upon different areas. Some of them you would just utilize the inner focus surrounded with light and feel the energy from outside drawing into you. This is probably the easiest way of doing this. There are more complicated methods, but they take years of study. You draw the energy through the top of the head directly to that part. When you begin to feel the tingling of it to know that the energy is there, you would direct it out. And then channel it for a while. And close it off on both ends, by releasing it through the feet.*

D: Is there any harm in keeping it going and not releasing it?

S: *Over-stimulation, yes. There could be great harm, if the person is not emotionally or physically capable of handling the energy. You can generate too much through lack of caution. You must channel it into other areas.*

D: Can you pass the energy on to another person?

S: *Oh, yes! This is often used for healing. You would just have to think it toward that person, and it would be up to them to accept it or not. It is not your duty to force anything upon them. It is offered, this is all one can do. If it is not accepted, it is channeled to someone else or released through the feet. It has to go somewhere.*

D: You said it was dangerous to keep generating it. How could this affect the body?

S: *If you were not releasing it, you could cause yourself to ... make your heart to stop, or many other things to cease to function. It is not a game, it is not a toy.*

D: Then is it dangerous when you teach children to do it?

S: *No, because a child is more open to the feelings. If it starts to feel like it is too much, the child is willing to pass it on. They are more receptive to this. The control is easier to learn as a child.*

D: I think now I can understand these energy points better. My teacher didn't explain it as well as you did -- In our community sometimes people take certain things, such as strong drink or certain plant substances into their bodies that make them act differently. Do you have such things happening where you live?

S: *You are speaking of, perhaps when a person drinks too much wine. Those of our community do not indulge in excess. It is not said that they do not drink, for it is very acceptable to drink wine. But anything in the excess is bad. It robs one of will to do this. You are replacing your own will with that of another thing or of someone else, because you are then easily controlled. It changes the flow of the blood, and the breathing also alters. So that more or less oxygen is allowed, depending on what is taken, and would cause differing results. This causes a lot of what you are calling 'personality change'. They would do things in these states that they would never do in their normal, in control, position.*

D: Does it enhance your ability to hear God if you get together in a group and go inside a building, like a temple or a synagogue?

S: *Some people need an outward added strength to say, "Yes, I have heard God". If you have faith and you believe, it is as easy to draw upon it alone, sometimes easier, than with a group in sharing. Though there are those who need that sharing, to be able to trust themselves enough to open up, to hear.*

D: Do you think people need a temple or synagogue?

S: *Not all. There are those who do, because their faith is not strong enough.*

97

D: Do buildings tend to build up vibrations from people?

S: *They would gain positive vibrations just in the same manner a building can hold negative. If it is a place where many, many bad things have happened, it would have the negativeness. If it is a place where there was much happiness and much joy, it would also have this. Buildings can have a strength that the person can draw upon. Sometimes it has to do with the place where the building is placed. If it is a point where there is great earth energy, it can help open oneself up. Though it can also be dangerous to those who are too sensitive, too open. Then you must block against this.*

D: How would one find a place like this?

S: *You must take someone who is open to find them, and they would be able to lead you to them.*

D: If you wanted to build a house, how would you know the right place to put it?

S: *You would decide on the area that you wanted it and you would walk and you would find a point. If there is one in the area, you would be led to it. If you are open, you would know. Inside you would feel it. You would feel the energy that would flow through you. It could also be a feeling of peace and contentment.*

D: Have you ever heard of the pyramids?

S: *They are in Egypt. It is a structure that has been built up to where it has a side that is like so. (She made motions with her hands, putting her fingers together like the top of a triangle.) And each one rises up like this and it has the four sides and it rises up to a point. It has to be of a certain height by certain width. Not so much as they have to be in equal measure, like one would be the same size as the other, but the space distance - if you understand what I am trying to say - it must be the same on all four sides. And the base must ... the equation must always be equal.*

D: What is their purpose?

S: *To focus power is part of their storehouse of knowledge. The equation, it also says, speaks of distances of the earth and of the planets and the suns. There is much knowledge that I don't understand. (He was very emphatic that they were not burial places for the kings) Someone lied! Perhaps this is some great lie to keep the knowledge from those who shouldn't know. They are storehouses of knowledge. The record is the pyramid themselves. There are other storehouses that have the scrolls that are elsewhere. But this knowledge is in the pyramid themselves. In the way they are constructed and the mathematics of it.*

Since he was well-aware of Moses and his teachings, I wondered whether the pyramids existed during the time of Moses.

S: *It is said that this was where their beginnings are. This I do not know. For myself, I believe that they have been here much longer than any small kingdom of Egypt. The knowledge is much greater than that of any Pharaoh I have ever heard spoken of.*

D: Do you know how they were built?

S: *I have heard many different ideas. I have heard that they used slave labor, which sounds impossible. You could not feed the people that it would take to build in this area. I have heard that they were built on the site. That the forms were placed and the dirt was put in and then it hardened and the forms were taken away. This is possible but time consuming. I have also heard that they used the music to raise them. I know it is possible to use music to raise things. But this is on a grander scale than I have known of being attempted. So I do not know. I think maybe a little of all three.*

Apparently it was a mystery even in their time. I had never heard of the idea of using music in this manner. Could there be a connection with their use of sound as a protection for Qumran? He had supplied a different type of insight about the pyramids, but no real answers. I assumed it would take special people to decipher the knowledge in the pyramids.

S: *It takes many years to be able to understand them at all. There are those who have this knowledge and are trying to pass it on.*

D: Do you know who put the knowledge there in the first place?

S: *It is said, again, that those who built the pyramids were those of Ur.*

Harriet had made a list of various terms and names she remembered from books she had read. They were really just jumbled bits and pieces. She asked if he had heard of the Sphinx, and he said it was the guardian of the knowledge. Harriet asked: "Have you ever heard of the Ark of Ammon?"

Suddi made some abrupt questioning remarks that were not English. He then corrected her pronunciation and answered, *"Yes, it is the symbol of life "* When she asked for an explanation, he became upset. *"You ask this as if you are unknowledgeable. Yet you have questions for me that show knowledge. Why? "*

"I'm curious as to how it is symbolized to your people. Do you have a symbol for it?" It sounded as if he said, *"The ark. "* I asked him to repeat it and it still sounded like that although I do not know what it means.

Harriet: Do you have in your writings anything about Horus?

S: *Yes. He is what among the Egyptians was the first of the gods to walk upon the face of the earth when it was new. It is said that he ... um, how do I put this? mated with the women of the land, and this was the beginning of Egypt.*

D: Was this before the time of the wandering of the Kaloo?

S: *This is something that comes out of the depths of endless time. There is no way of knowing when this was. 'Twas before the measuring of time.'*

CHAPTER IO

Suddi's First Trip to the Outside World

Suddi had been born and raised within the walls of Qumran, the isolated community atop the salt cliffs that surround the Dead Sea. I knew he had not lived his entire life cloistered there, because at our first meeting he had been on his way to visit his cousins in Nazareth. I wondered what he had experienced when he left the community. What his first impression of the outside world had been and what he had thought of the way other people lived. So I took him to that time to find out. He was seventeen years old and was making ready to go with a caravan to Nazareth. He had never been anywhere before this: Qumran was all he knew. I had hoped he might go to a larger city such as Jerusalem, which was actually closer to Qumran. But since I had no knowledge of Nazareth either, I thought it would be interesting to ask questions about the place where the Bible says Jesus spent most of his growing years. The caravan was one that frequently stopped alongside the sea to gather salt.

S: *It is all so different to anything I am used to. The caravan is very long, there are perhaps twenty camels, and they are all making lots of noise and squealing. And everything happens at once. I'm a little nervous and excited.*
D: Are you taking anything with you?
S: *A few things. I am to take a bag of some clothes and a little food and things like this.*

He had said before that whenever anyone went outside the community they had to dress differently so they would not be recognized. The other people in the land did not wear white robes.

S: I'm wearing the... (foreign word which sounded like 'Shardom') and the burnoose of the Arabs. (A burnoose is a long cloak with a hood.) It will keep the heat, the sun off, so it will not be so bad. A burnoose is much as a robe, but it is unusual having something about my head that is flowing. But it is not un-good, it is interesting. This is like a great adventure, it is something new and exciting.

The Camel Caravan to Jerusalem

He would be traveling alone. He was going to meet *"people from my family,"* his cousins, whom he had not met before. They had been living in Nazareth for many years. He planned to stay there for a few weeks, *"to learn what it is like to live outside".* They were to meet him at the square where the caravan would stop to sell the salt. I moved him ahead until the journey was over and he was in Nazareth. I wanted to know his first impressions of it. He sounded a little disappointed, *"It is very small."* "Did you enjoy the journey?" *"Except for the roughness of the ride, yes. It was an interesting experience. Camels are known for their want of tempers, but it was fun."*

The journey had taken a couple of days and they had only stopped at a few wells along the way, not at any other towns. I remembered some names of places from the Bible. I thought I would toss them in and see if he knew where they were. "Do you know where Capernaum is?" *"Ah, let me think here... On the northern shore of Sea of Galilee. I'm not real sure about where."* When I looked at the map in my Bible later, I was not really surprised to find that again Katie was completely accurate. Her knowledge was becoming commonplace now. Sometimes I wondered why I bothered to check anymore, except to satisfy my love of research.

D: Is the Sea of Galilee near Nazareth?

S: It is a journey away.

D: Do you know where the city of Jericho is?

S: To the North of the community.

D: Have you ever heard of the Jordan River?

S: Yes, it is the river that leads into the Sea of Death.

D: When you made your journey, did you go in that direction?

S: No. We went through the hills and mountains.

D: What about Masada? Have you ever heard of that city?

S: It is south. It is not a city, it is a fortress. At one time when Israel was stronger, it was a stronghold of protection. It has fallen into disuse, from my understanding.

D: Does the country around Nazareth look the same as the land around Qumran?

S. No, it is more green here. Away from the city, you can see out on the hills there are trees growing, farming being done. There are maybe a few more hills and mountains around Qumran. It is not very green along the Sea of Death. Only scrub brush grows there and not much more. Here there are orchards growing on the hills. But Nazareth is just a little town. (He again sounded disappointed.)

D: Is it as large as the community?

S: *Perhaps no. It is hard to judge. Let me think here. The area of land that is covered is perhaps the same, but there is not nearly the amount of people or the amount of buildings.*

This appears to be another indication that Qumran was larger than the area that was excavated by the archaeologists, because he may have been including the housing area and observatory in his estimate.

D: I thought that Nazareth was a large place.

S: *Who could have told you this? Nazareth is just a ... speck. It is nothing.*

D: What does Nazareth look like when you come in from a distance?

S: *Dusty. Very dusty.*

D: I mean, is there any kind of wall around the city or anything like that?

S: *No, it is an open village. It is not ... you could not call this a city. It is just worthless.*

His disappointment was very evident. He thought he was embarking on a great adventure, and Nazareth seemed to be a letdown. I suppose he expected something with more grandeur. Suddi had said that the buildings in Qumran were made of some type of brick. The buildings in Nazareth were not.

S: *They are square with maybe one, two stories in most, with the opening on the roof to sleep under the stars if you want to. They are much different from Qumran in the fact that there is an appearance of this way and that way. They are each different, there is not the sameness to everything. Here it is like some child had these things that would make houses and he just piled them, this way and that way. This is the appearance that you would get.*

This is what is different. They are square but they do not match. It is as if they do not fit together.

In Qumran the buildings were all connected and must have had a much more orderly appearance. I wondered if these had any individual courtyards with walls around them separating them from each other.

S: *Of course this depends upon the money situation of the individual. If there is more money, they would have a courtyard. If they are very poor, of course they would not. They could not afford the extra land that the courtyard would take. They would need to have this in the house or more room, whatever.*

D: Are there any large buildings in Nazareth?

S: *Nothing is large in Nazareth.*

D: Can you see where the water supply comes from?

S: *It is a fountain. It is actually a round opening coming out of a wall. A wall-type situation in which the water comes out. I'm not sure if it is a spring that runs or what. The water is constant, it seems. There is a... (hard to find the word) trough that is in front, in which they may put their jars there, to get the water. I'm not sure where the water goes. It must be piped elsewhere. There is no overflow from what I see. Either that, or they use it all. But it comes out at such speed that it must go elsewhere.*

My research revealed that Nazareth is still a little town today. The remains of Old Nazareth are farther up the hill from modern Nazareth. In The Bible As History, by Werner Keller, he compares the two areas, Qumran and Nazareth. "Nazareth, like Jerusalem, is surrounded by hills. But how different is the character of the two scenes, how unlike are they in appearance and atmosphere. There is an air of menace or gloom about the Judaean mountains (Qumran area). Peaceful and charming by contrast are the gentle contours of the environs of Nazareth. Gardens and fields surround the little village with its farmers and craftsmen. Groves of date palms, fig trees, and pomegranates clothe the encircling hills in friendly green. The fields are full of wheat and barley, vineyards yield their delicious fruit and everywhere on the highways and byways grows an abundance of richly colored flowers." Mr. Keller says there was a Roman military road that came down from the North and a caravan route not far South. There are also the remains of the caravan trails near Qumran.

Keller also writes of Ain Maryam, "Mary's Well," in Nazareth. It is a well at the foot of the hill where a little spring supplies it. Women still draw water in jars just as they did in the time of Jesus. He says this fountain has been called "Mary's Well" from time immemorial and it provides the only water supply for far and near. It is no longer outside but is enshrined within the 18th century Church of St. Gabriel.

Note the amazing similarities between these descriptions and the ones Suddi gave.

D: Can you see any marketplace?

S: *(Impatiently) We are in the marketplace. This is where the square, the fountain is all at. Can you not see? This is it!*

D: (I laughed) Well, I thought it was a larger city and that the market was somewhere else.

S: *I don't know who has been telling you about Nazareth, but I think you are pulling a leg?*

D: Okay, just have patience with me. Is the marketplace very busy?

S: *If you call a few goats and little boys running around and women standing in a corner talking, busy. Perhaps. But I do not think so. It is midday though and most have gone home to nap or to have their meals. 'Tis too hot to be out here doing much.*

I wondered if the people had any way to keep out of the sun when they sold their products in the market.

S: *If they are well enough, you would have like a fold of a tent. It would be brought over them and staked, so that it would cover their heads. But the very poor would not.*

D: Has your cousin come yet?

S: *No, he will be soon. I hope it is soon, I am very hungry. I still have some food left that I brought for the journey. I would prefer a good meal though.*

D: Do you have any money?

S: *I have a few shekels that my father gave me in a pouch around my belt.*

D: You told me you don't use money in Qumran.

S: *There is no need. What would you buy there? There is no one selling.*

D: What does the money look like?

S: *This that I have is round and made of silver. It has a hole through the top part of it, so that it may be looped upon a leatherer in the purse, so that it cannot be lost.*

All of the coins did not have a hole in them. He thought someone had put the holes in them. They were probably not made that way originally. I was hoping for something I could verify when I asked if they had any pictures on them.

S: *Some of them, yes. Some, it is hard to tell what they used to be. There is one that has the bird that is flying upon one side, and I think the face of a man upon the other. I'm not real sure, it is very worn. And most of the others, you cannot even tell. It is just a rough feel on the side of the coins, as if something used to be there and it was worn.*

D: Do you know where your father got the coins?

S: *I have no way of knowing. I did not ask, he did not tell me. He told me to use them wisely. And to guard them well, for people would kill for less.*

D: Yes, if some people saw them, they would think you are rich.

S: *They would not mistake me for someone who is rich.*

D: Well, what is your first impression of the outside world?

S: *I think I would be better happy home.*

D: Do the people seem to be different?

S: *People are the same. Maybe they're a little more narrow in their existence. They do not question anything about the day-to-day survival.*

D: What about soldiers? Are there any around?

S: *Why would there be soldiers here? There is not the garrison. If there was a garrison here, there would be soldiers. There is no place for them to live. We are not at war with the Romans. They know that they have captured the people of the nation. They are not worried. They have garrisons in other places, but why would they want one here? There is nothing here. They are stationed in the larger cities, and in places where there might be trouble. Who would ever come here and create problems?*

D: Have you ever seen any Roman soldiers?

S: We saw a few a day ago on the road, as they ran by us on their horses.

D: What did you think of them?

S: I did not have a chance to meet them, so therefore I cannot pass judgement. They had their helmets and their shiny swords. They were dressed in leather, it looked hot.

He was obviously growing impatient for the arrival of his cousins. He said they had a son who was about his age.

D: Maybe you will have a friend while you are there.

S: Perhaps. We shall see.

D: Will you have to work while you're there?

S: But of course! To eat you must work. This is accepted. How not?

I decided not to wait any longer, so I moved him ahead in time until he was at his cousin's house. His disappointment in Nazareth was erased when he was taken to his cousin's house in the hills a few miles from Nazareth. He seemed to be pleased with it. It was not a large house.

S: It is perhaps of medium size, several rooms, but it is a feeling of space, of openness. It is very nice. Up in the hills. It is a feeling of freedom. There are no others here always telling you that you should do things this way or that way. And the feeling of learning about oneself and depending upon oneself rather than others. This is very good. In Qumran there was always someone else around.

He had felt very much at home from the moment he saw his cousins. They knew each other instantly; it was as if they were old friends. The family consisted of Sahad, his wife Thresmant and their son Siv. His cousins made their living from a vineyard, trading or selling grapes and olives for fruits and various things. They kept what they needed and made enough wine for the family. A few sheep were raised for the wool. A man worked for them to help with the vineyards.

Mostly Suddi slept up on the roof because it was much cooler and quieter outside. He liked to fall asleep staring at the stars. His bed was a pad consisting of rushes and a few blankets lain over this. There was plenty to eat and he was introduced to some new kinds of food that he had never experienced before. One type of vegetable in particular, cabbage, was something he was not used to.

S: *They have figs. They have rice. This is something different than what I am acquainted with. I'm not sure I like it as well as millet or barley.*

D: Did they find any work for you to do?

S: *I just help out with whatever is going on during the day. Whether it be things around the house or out in the fields. We manage.*

D: Then you don't miss Qumran too much?

S: *I'm enjoying my time away. I'm studying here, only in different ways, not with scrolls.*

He was to stay there for two months altogether. This seemed to be a wise choice for a young man's first trip outside the walls. Nazareth was a small and quiet place. It might have been too much of a shock for him to go to a place like Jerusalem. For someone who had been raised in such a sheltered environment, that would have been a rude awakening.

D: How do you tell the months?

S: *The days are marked off on the calendars. It has the different points of what the moon is in, and as a day passes, it is marked off. This way we know when we enter from one month to the next, with the phases of the moon.*

The calendars were made on clay tablets. There were twelve months for the twelve tribes of Israel, and each month was composed of twenty-nine days because this was the cycle of the moon. I tried to get him to tell me some of the names of the months. He became confused and had difficulty. He said about six different words that were not English, but I can not transcribe them.

S: I know there are twelve. I do not know how that they count them (the months) off. This is part of the rabbi's day-to-day work. They let us know when the holidays are.

Research disclosed that Suddi was again correct. The Festivals were declared by the Sanhedrin in Jerusalem, and runners were then sent out to announce these to the rabbis. The month was based on the phases of the moon, which completes its cycle approximately every 29 1/2 days, with the new moon considered the twenty-ninth day. In those early days the months did not have names but instead had numbers: the first month, the second month, etc.

He understood the word "week," which was from one Sabbath to the next and was composed of seven days. Again he displayed confusion when I asked for the names of the days. He did not understand what I meant. They knew when it was time for the Sabbath because they marked it off from day to day.

I was surprised to find that even today the days do not have any names on the Hebrew calendar. They have numbers: Sunday is the Ist day, Monday is the 2nd day, etc. Only the Sabbath has its own name, although it is sometimes called the 7th day. As American Protestants this was something we would have never suspected. We are so accustomed to having names for the days and the months. This was another example of Katie's extreme accuracy. I took this line of questioning another step further, "Do you know what an hour is?"

S: It is from one knot to the next on a rope clock. There are rope clocks, which are lit and when it burns from one knot to the next, an hour has passed. (This sounded so strange, I wanted a better description.) It is a thing that is whole and it is made of very big rope. (With hand motions, she showed a thickness or diameter of about three or more inches across.) There are also candles that have the markings. When that it has burned so much an hour has passed.

Suddi's First Trip to the Outside World

D: Are these rope clocks in the houses?

S: *Some people can afford houses with clocks in them. Sometimes, there is just one per town, in which they would always know what time it is. Some towns do not have even that. Some just tell from where the sun is, what time of day it is.*

This was his first trip to his cousins in Nazareth, but he was to return many times throughout his life. At these times he would not travel with the caravan but would walk with an ass carrying his food, water and tent. The trip took at least two days, and he had to sleep out two nights. I once asked him if it wouldn't be easier to ride the ass. He replied, "Probably, but then we would have to have two to carry the load, so I walk. I tire, but it is good for the soul to continue on."

This became his favorite place to come when he wasn't teaching or studying. At his cousins', he would often go up into the hills to meditate, to commune. As he said, "I try to bring myself in touch with the universe. I meditate upon my look into myself and study upon what I am."

It was quiet there and he loved it. Later in his life when he became too old and sick to make the journey back and forth, he stayed permanently at the house nestled in the hills above Nazareth. And it was in this peaceful place that he eventually died.

CHAPTER 11

Suddi's Sister Sarah

For the most part, strangers were few and far between in Qumran.

D: What about people who were just wandering in the desert area? Would they be allowed to come in and stay for a while?
S: Not into the main part unless they had been verified by the elders. They would be given food and clothing and sent on their way.

This explained some of his reluctance to speak with me about things they considered secrets: to him I was a stranger. Even as long as we worked together, it was still very difficult to get past this natural built in defense.

Most of those from the outside came because they wanted to be students. They were the ones who wore the red band. It was not easy to become a student at Qumran. The elders would have to know the applicant's reasons, and they would have to pass an examination. *"Having not passed through this way,"* Suddi had no way of knowing what the examination consisted of. The majority of the students were born there, such as the case of Suddi and his sister Sarah.

Sarah was no longer at Qumran. She was living at Bethesda which was located in the area of Jerusalem. I was surprised that she was allowed to leave the community and live elsewhere.

S: Of course! This is no prison! 'Twas her desire. It was not her pathway to follow at this time. She has another life to lead. She met a student here who... they decided that they wished to be together, and were married and left.

D: Then there are people who don't live their whole lives in the community?

S: *There are many people in the world. Of course, not everyone who is born here wishes to stay here. And some who are not born here, wish to come. Therefore, it is a take and give situation. He was a student. One of those who was not one of us, but here instead to just learn of us and our beliefs, and have share of our knowledge. He was one of the students from elsewhere. He believed in some of our followings and teachings, but he was not of us. His father wished him to learn with us, and therefore they sent him to have the experience.*

He was one who wore the red band. He may have had to pay something for the experience, but Suddi did not know for certain. He stayed there for five years before he and Sarah married and left to live in Bethesda. A student could finish his course of study in five years, but it normally took a little longer than that. It depended on the student and his desire to learn and his ability to grasp the concepts. I asked what type *of* work Sarah's husband did in Bethesda. *"He does not* do *anything. He is rich. "*

I got the feeling he missed his sister and resented the fact that she left and went so far away. His tone of voice suggested he didn't like discussing it.

S: *His family is well-off and they are members of the Sanhedrin (phonetic: 'Sanhadrin'). It is the same thing as the Roman senate for Israel.*

D: You said your people were not allowed to have many material possessions. When someone comes, a student from the outside such as he was, and they are rich, are they allowed to keep their possessions?

S: *It depends on whether or not they wish to take this as their way of life. Some wish to come and just learn and leave. Others wish to come and to be accepted as a part, then they must give their possessions to the whole. But it is their choice. If they were to become a member, to remain here, yes, it would be then shared among all of the people, so that all would get what is deemed needful. Otherwise it is still theirs. Since he did not intend to stay, he was not required to give up what was his. He did not become a member. Everything is kept in a storehouse and if we*

*have any needs, you would let it be known, and if it was found
that you really needed this, you would be given that with which
to purchase it. The needs are filled with what belongs to all.*

This was apparently where the money came from that Suddi took
with him on his first trip to Nazareth.

D: Are the possessions or the money ever given back to the owner?

S: *I have never heard of this being done. The decision to stay takes a
long time to be made. And a lot of thought on both, whether or
not they are accepted as a member and their own choice.
Therefore I have never heard of anyone, after becoming a
member, wishing to leave. The decision to stay is not made
lightly or quickly. It is only done after much thought and asking
for guidance, meditation on the latter. All decisions that are
made, whether they be made- it does not always require time to
make good decisions, some people are just different. But we give
them a chance to make their own mind. It is not always a lot of
time, but a lot of at least soul-searching is done before the
decision is allowed to stand. It is different from person to person.
There are those who know immediately that this is what they
wish for the rest of their life. It is as if they had been born to us.
Others, it takes a while for acceptance.*

D: What about those who never become masters?

S: *There is much work to be done by those who are not masters. The
purpose (pronounced strangely) of things. Just the everyday
things that must be done. There is much work to do. To become a
master is not the path of all.*

D: If a man and a woman are married and live in the community and
have children, are the children expected to stay?

S: *They have the choice also, such as my sister made. It was her
decision that she would prefer to go with the man that she loved,
to share his life. This was her choice, and the men and women
are all given the same choice, whether they wish to remain or
not. The choice is usually not made before the Barmitzvah or
Botmitzvah, but sometimes they would know many years in
advance of this, that this is what they would not like to do. And
they would find something else. There are many pathways of the
same trail. They all eventually blend together.*

Because I knew nothing of Jewish customs, I did not immediately catch the significance of this passage. I was later told that Barmitzvah is the ceremony for boys coming into manhood, since "Bar" means "son." "Bot" means "daughter." The Botmitzvah is a fairly recent ritual for girls which was instituted mainly because of the Women's Liberation movement. I was told by a rabbi that this ritual should not be allowed because, "How can a girl come into manhood?" I feel that although the Botmitzvah has not been observed until recent times, this does not mean that the more liberal Essenes did not observe it during their time at Qumran. They believed in the equality of women. Women were allowed to teach and hold any office they were eligible for. It is significant that Suddi mentioned both rituals here. It may have been representative of either sex coming into *adulthood.*

I wondered why Suddi had never married. He had said before that the birth charts had to match in order for a couple to be allowed to marry. Was this perhaps the reason? There was no one whose chart was considered compatible with his?

S: *I did not wish... it is not that I did not wish. I did not marry because it was not my path this time. (Sigh) The person who I would have matched with was born as my sister.*

D: (This was a surprise.) There was no one else you could have married?

He became impatient with me; he did not want to discuss it.

S: *I could have married, but again I state it was not my path. When I decided what my pathway would be, it was discussed and it was chosen that I should be a teacher this time.*

I thought the research to locate Bethesda would be a simple matter because it is a name associated with the Bible. We have cities in the United States named after it, most notable: Bethesda, Maryland. But when we go on assumptions we often find them to be wrong when we search a little deeper. Bethesda is only mentioned once in the Bible, in John 5:2, and is described as a pool located near Jerusalem. Suddi spoke of it as though it were a place, a city. I am inclined to think it was, because I found that "Beth" in front of a name means "house of," such as Bethlehem (House of Bread), Bethany (House of Figs) and Bethesda translates as "House of Mercy."

Nowhere was that prefix associated with water except in this instance. Bible research shows that the pool was located outside the old walls of Jerusalem and within the present-day walls. It is an area known as Bezetha and Bethzatha in different books and maps, and appears to have been an area similar to a suburb of Jerusalem. I think from our story that they were probably all one and the same place, especially since his strange pronunciation often made it difficult to transcribe accurately. It had to be near Jerusalem because he said his sister, Sarah, had married into a family where the father was a member of the Sanhedrin and this court was located at Jerusalem. They were instrumental in the trial and ultimate crucifixion of Jesus.

CHAPTER 12

Going to Bethesda

During one of the sessions we came across Suddi as an older man. He was traveling to Bethesda to see his sister, Sarah. She now had two children, a boy, Amare, and a girl, Zarah. This time instead of walking he was riding the ass. Apparently he had become too old to walk the long distances he once did. He was grimly determined to make this journey although it was obviously a drain on him.

S: *(Sadly) She has a need of... to see me. It is to say goodbye. (He repeated solemnly)... It is to say goodbye, because soon she will... make the journey that we all must make.*

I was a little confused. Did he mean his sister would die? Was she sick? *"No. She just has wish to pass upon."* He was obviously talking about death rather than a real journey. He apparently had received this unwelcome news psychically and wanted to see her once more. He seemed very sad even though he had resigned himself to it.

D: Has she any fear?
S: *No. Why would there be fear? She just has wish to say goodbye. Simply, we know that we will follow. Death is not to be feared. This is foolishness. It is but a blink of an eye, if and then it is as if nothing had occurred. You are just without the corporeal body. It is like the projecting of oneself (Astral projection?) You find yourself the same as you were, but some way, how subtly different. But there is much of the sameness. It is but another step.*
D: Many people fear it because they are afraid of the unknown.
S: *Is it not more unknown what will happen to you in the next two*

days? Than it would be if you'd listened to what the prophets and the wise men had spoken of? You would know what there is to happen once you pass through that door.

D: Is there anything in your writings that indicate what we can expect when we leave the corporeal body?

S: *There are many things in our writings, yes. It speaks of the feeling of great peace that descends upon one. When you look down upon yourself and realize that you have passed over the threshold. That you are no longer one with the physical and are a being that is totally what you would call a soul again, or a spirit. There are people who are confused (after they die). They would be greeted by someone who would perhaps help smooth the pathways that they must walk. And all who are there to help, wish you well. There is no need to fear, for nothing can harm you.*

D: Is this found in the Torah?

S: *No, it is found in the writings of the wise ones, the Kaloo.*

D: In some of our books and scrolls they talk about places you can go after you cross over that are very bad, frightening places.

S: *Then this is something that this person has died expecting to see. For there is nothing there but what you create yourself. And in so believing, so it shall be. For thoughts and beliefs are very strong.*

D: What if someone was to die very suddenly in a bad way? Would their death be any different?

S: *No, but they might wake up confused about it, and therefore someone would be there to help them.*

D: What about a child who dies?

S: *A child is very close to what they were in the beginning, which is the soul. For they have not totally lost the memories of before. And therefore they are very accepting of this. More so than people who have perhaps lived for a great long period of time. Those want nothing more than to go back to the way that they were before they crossed. To a great extent it is easier for a child to understand. Children are more open to what is going on about them.*

D: When do they usually stop being open? Do their bodies physically have anything to do with it?

S: *A lot of times it is upon the reaching of maturity. But a lot of the closing off of children is done not by the children or by anything that their bodies are doing. But by others, and forces that are pressing and oppressing them. For in telling them that they have done something foolish, this is one of the worse things that you can do to a child. For they will then think that everything that they do is foolish, because a child takes things very literally. They must believe in themselves. And therefore we create the pressure that would close them off to a lot of this.*

D: Is there anything in your writings about evil spirits?

S: *There are no such things as evil spirits. There is nothing that is totally evil. There is always good in everything. It may be very small, but there is always some part of that that is good. The things that you are perhaps calling evil spirits are what others would call demons. The mischievous ones that wish to cause trouble because they get some type of enjoyment out of this. A lot of these are misshapen... how do I say this?... spirits who have been, through their experiences, changed. So that with love and guidance they may still follow the right pathways again. But with fear and intolerance, they are lost forever.*

D: There have been stories of evil spirits trying to enter the bodies of the living.

S: *There are instances when this is possible, but usually it is in the cases of either the person is very open to this or no longer wishes to inhabit that particular body. And would withdraw, leaving it open for others.*

D: Do you think people give them more power by fearing them?

S: *Yes. You surround yourself with good thoughts and energy. And request that only high-minded individuals surround you.*

D: Is it just your community that is aware of these things? What about the other people, such as the Jews and the Romans?

S: *The Romans are head-blind. They would not know truth if it came up and bit them in the ass. (We laughed and it was a relief from the seriousness of the discussion.) A lot of the people in the synagogues are so enmeshed in their own translations of the Law that they are caught up in this. They cannot see outside of it to experience the joys of living and dying.*

D: Then everyone doesn't believe the way you do. In your teachings do you have a belief in what we call reincarnation? The rebirth of the soul?

S: *Rebirth? It has been known for all, for surely it is true. Only those of the ignorant and uninformed can fear the thought of reincarnation, as you call it.*

Dr. Rocco Errico, an expert on the Aramaic language, says that in that part of the world the people tend to exaggerate and embroider their stories and statements. But when the statement was preceded by the words: "For sure, for surely, truly or verily," this lets the listener know the statement contains no amplification and should be taken seriously. This is especially true if the statement was spoken by a teacher. It means it is worthy of the listener's trust. This would explain the use of "verily" by Jesus so much in the Bible. A small, insignificant detail but one worth noting, because your average person would not know this was a pattern of speech in that part of the world, now as well as in Biblical times.

D: Many people say that you live once and die once, and that is all there is.

S: *There are those who say that once the body goes into the ground, that all that was that being has been lost and moulders with the worms. This is not true. If a person is dead or has become no longer inhabiting a body as we know, they must then go over what they have done. They must decide which lessons that they wish to deal with and proceed in erasing the debts that they have incurred. Then they go to school (on the other side). Then sometimes they decide to come back very soon. This is not always good because if you come back too soonSperhaps if it was not a very good lifeSyou have not had the time to understand what you have done wrong and to give yourself time to correct. Therefore it is not good to jump right back into existence as I know it and others know.*

D: Is it possible to remember past lives?

S: *Some of us, we know the lives previous, yes. Some of them that are important. It is easier not to remember it because if you remember, a lot of times you become overcome with great guilt. It is not perhaps necessary for that time. If it were necessary, you would remember. There are those in the community who are trained to remember. And there are those who would choose that path, but it is not for everyone. The elders would be able to tell you who you were, if it was asked. There are masters who have the ability, not only to remember theirs, but to help others remember. But for the most part, those who know who they were, remember. Usually Yahweh decides if He would grant this remembrance and then the pathway is started upon.*

Going to Bethesda

I had a book from the library that contained some color pictures of the area around Qumran. I thought it would be interesting to see if Suddi could recognize anything. I asked him if he would mind looking at them and he answered with a word that sounded like "sadat." I had Katie open her eyes and she studied the pictures with a glassy-eyed look. One of the photographs was of desolate mountains.

S: This is the valley to the south of here. There are hills that look of this. And the wadi runs... that way.

He traced his finger down what looked to me like a valley or space between the hills. A "wadi" is defined as a valley or ravine that is dry except during the rainy season. It also means the rush of water that flows through it. He was now looking at the picture at the top of the opposite page, It showed the ruins of a city from a long distance away.

S: Why are they so far away? You would not show anything about this. This has the look also of the same area, but this is not familiar to me. Here is a wadi that has water on. I know of very few wadis that stay wet when the hills are as barren as this.

The picture showed from a far distance what could have been a road or a stream. It was probably a road, but it looked to Suddi like a wadi. Maybe there were no roads as clearly defined as this in his day. I took the book away and had her close her eyes again. If that was in the area where he lived, it appeared to be very dry and barren. *"Yes, it is dry. There is very little rain."*

He said that when he went from Qumran to Nazareth he would follow the caravan trails through hills that were even greater than the ones in the pictures. It seemed to me it would be easier to just follow the wadi rather than climb the mountains, which looked very rough. But it was obvious I did not understand the culture. *"And if it rained up the hills, I'd be washed away. No."*

I wondered why he had never been to Jerusalem which was much closer than Nazareth and much larger. *"I have no need to go or wish to. I do not care that much for cities. They are noisy and full of undisciplined people. Why should I want to see confusion?"*

During my research I found many pictures in the books showing portions of the Dead Sea Scrolls. I thought it might be an interesting experiment to see if Suddi would be able to read any of this ancient writing. It might be possible since Katie was identifying so closely with the other personality. One sample was six lines of writing, each a little different from the other. It appeared to be examples of the script used in those times. I did not know at the time about the difficulty in reading their languages. This is explained in Chapter 14.

I had her open her eyes and she again stared at the page with a glazed expression.

D: Does any of that look familiar to you?
S: *(After a long pause as he studied it.) This was written by two different hands.*

There was a longer pause. Her eyes scanned from the bottom of the page to the top, and from the right to the left.

S: *It has the look of Hebrew. (He pointed to a line.) No, this is different. These two are different. (Pointed to other lines). And these two are the same but this is, again, different. I'm not sure, but I see simularness (phonetic) to this. It almost looks like somebody is just writing out the symbols. I do not make any sense out of this. It looks, like someone practicing form, but they are not the same people. It is different styles.*

I took the book away. At least I had found out that it appeared to be different people practicing writing. A friend of mine had given me an old newsletter put out by the Noohra Foundation. It consisted of two letter-sized folded pages. On the front page was a Bible verse written in Aramaic. It was a translation from John and spoke of Jesus. I handed it to him and told him I was not even sure if it was written in his language. He studied it for a few minutes, smiling all the time.

S: *I'm not sure I'm translating this very well. It... speaks of the Son of Man. (He seemed pleased to find this out.) It is the Vulgate, the language of the people. Some would call it Aramaic. It has a very strange dialect, but I'm making an attempt. (After a long pause)... It speaks of the Messiah.*

He suddenly pointed to a figure at the end of the inscription. It was different from the other writing., It puzzled him. He frowned as he studied the mark.

S: *What? That part on the bottom I believe is a different language. This is not Aramaic. This is out of the ancient writings. This is very strange to find this here.*

I pointed to another sign in the text that was similar to it. I asked if it was the same. He answered that it was close. There was no explanation in the newsletter for these marks, but they did appear to be different from the text.

S: *'Tis not of Aramaic, no. As I say, it speaks of the Messiah, but I'm not very sure of. . . (He stopped and began to finger and feel the paper.) This is odd. What is this? What is it made of?*
D: (I was taken by surprise and had to think fast.) Oh, it is made from the bark of trees. In some countries....
S: *(He interrupted me) How do they do this? Of trees?*

He kept feeling the paper and turned it over, studying its texture. I was a little worried he would get too curious and might notice that the writing inside was different. I did not know what effect it would have on him if he noticed too many strange things. Culture shock? I tried to get his mind off it.

D: Well, it's a complicated process. I don't really know myself how it is done.
S: *(He was still engrossed in the paper.) This is much better than papyri. It is very thick. It is more like the skins.*
D: Papyrus is thinner?
S: *Oh, much! It is very thin to write on. This would be very good for*

copying on, yes.

I took the paper away to get his mind off it, and got another book out. There was a photograph of a page from the Dead Sea Scrolls that had very clear writing. Across from this were pictures of the Qumran area that were photographed in black and white instead of color. But I was mostly concerned with the writing. I held the book so he could see it. I tried to keep it open to that page. I didn't want him to start wondering what the book was and how it was made. He announced, *"This is Hebrew, it is very old Hebrew. I am not a very good copier, but this is definitely Hebrew. See here, this letter and these ...* (he pointed to certain letters.) *It is something of the law. I'm not very good at this, I do not understand Hebrew well."* I told him I thought it was Aramaic. *"I do not know who told you it was Aramaic, but it is not! "* His attention was drawn to the picture on the facing page. It showed the Dead Sea and a portion of the rugged shore. *"What is this? It looks like the area around my home. There is the lake and the salt cliffs. Right? They have the look of them, yes."*

I knew he wouldn't understand the word "photograph," so I told him it was something like a painting. *"This is like no painting that I have ever seen."* I took it away. He was getting too curious and coming up with questions that were difficult to answer while spanning two thousand years. She closed her eyes again, and I thanked him for looking at the materials.

S: *It is hard to look at things close for very long. (She rubbed her eyes)*
D: Oh? Are your eyes bothering you now as you get older?
S: *Either that or my arms grow too short, I'm not sure which. I do not know who told you that that one was Aramaic, but it is not. The first one was Aramaic. It sounds like it might come from... ah, let me think.. Samaria. It has that dialect. It was Aramaic, but that one sign, it was not of the Aramaic. It doesn't belong there. It is very old.*

CHAPTER 13

Questioning

When I started conducting my research I was astounded by Katie's amazing accuracy. Suddi's description of the Qumran community has been verified by the excavation accounts of the archaeologists. The beliefs and certain rituals of the Essenes have been substantiated by the translations of the scrolls. But there were a few discrepancies, so I made a list of questions and asked them at our last session together. We had been working on this for so long and had covered so much material, I thought it was now safe to ask Suddi leading questions about things that I had read.

The scholars have given the name "People of the Covenant" or "the Covenanters" to the Essenes. Suddi frowned when I asked if the word "covenant" had any connection with his people. He said the terms were unfamiliar to him, and he could not understand why someone would give them a name like that. They were known only as the Essenes. He said, *"A covenant is an agreement between two parties to uphold a bargain."*

I asked if the name Zadok meant anything to him. One of the theories about the origin of the Essenes is that they descended from the Zealots who were led by this man. He corrected my pronunciation, putting the accent on the first syllable.

S: *(Sigh) He is a leader. Many follow him, saying that he teaches the Way of Life. He is a warmonger. He wishes to be rid of all oppressors now.*
D: Is there any relation between them and your community?
S: *They are not of us. The ones that we know of as Zadok are the Zealots that live in the hills. They are very wild. They say that*

most of them are touched by the moon. They also believe in the prophecies, but they believe that they prophesy war. And in order for the Messiah to come and be able to take his kingdom, that they must win it for him. And there is much bloodshed over this. If they would but look deeper into the prophecy, they would know that he shall not be king for an earthly kingdom. But you cannot tell them this, they would argue forever, to eternity.

D: Then people are wrong who think there is a connection between your people and them?

S: At least their information has come from strange places. Many tongues wrap themselves around tales and in the telling bend them.

The Jubilees are mentioned by the translators as a holy day, but it was unfamiliar to Suddi. He did say before that they were not morose people, they celebrated the joy of life. They may have called the holiday by another name.

A scroll called the *War of the Sons of Light with the Sons of Darkness* was one of the few that were recovered intact and much importance has been given to its translation. There has also been much controversy as to whether it should be taken literally or symbolically. It was supposed to be predicting a terrible war that had not yet occurred and instructions about what to do when it happened. This was very confusing to Suddi.

S: There are many such scrolls that speak of wars. But a war that had not happened? (He frowned.) Unless it was one that is someone's vision, I have no idea. In our scrolls it is the recording of events that have happened to the nations of the earth. We gather the information as much as we are able to. I know it not. Again, it sounds more like something that was a vision of someone than the meaning of an actual happening. If it is experienced with the senses, it is recorded and described at great length.

D: Who would they mean by the Sons of Light?

S: I would not know having not read the scroll. It could be anyone. To have not read it, to make a conclusion of this would be foolish.

A man called the Master of Righteousness has been mentioned in the

translations and has been confused with Jesus because their stories
bear some resemblance to each other. There are arguments over who
this man might have been.

*S: This name is familiar. There was at one time an elder of that
name, but he is not here with us. He lived long ago.*
D: Was he an important man?
*S: From the stories, yes. And he will be again from the tales that are
told. It is said that he shall return, I know not when. He shall be
born again unto this earth.*
D: Why was he such a special person that he was included in the
writings?
*S: It is very difficult to describe. He was as one step beyond others
around him. And had the ability to see to the heart of matters,
and to know what was right. This is part of why he was known as
the Master.*
D: Some people think he might be confused with the Messiah.
*S: No, the Messiah is our Prince, and the master was just a master.
He was not a prince.*

Part of the story deals with the Master of Righteousness and the
Wicked Priest. No one has ever been able to satisfactorily identify
either of these individuals.

*S: Wicked Priest? This is unfamiliar to me. This is not one that I
have read. I'm not saying that it does not exist. I have not read
all.*

The Master of Righteousness was supposed to have been crucified.
This is one of the reasons for the confusion between him and Jesus. I
asked if he knew whether the Master of Righteousness died in any
special way.

*S: I do not know the whole story. I've read very little on this matter.
It could take more than a lifetime to read all of the scrolls.*
D: Did he have anything to do with the beginnings of your
community?
*S: I do not know. From the tales that we have had handed down, this
does not sound to me correct.*

Another scroll that has been translated is called the Thanksgiving

Psalms.

S: (Frowning) Perhaps I do not know them by these terms. Explain. I am at a loss to understand. A psalm is like a message to God, in which you speak directly to God with your heart. It is very possible some were written down.

There was a man called Hillel who was supposed to be a wise teacher of the time. He had a following of people who called themselves Hillelites. It has been suggested that Jesus may have studied with him. Suddi recognized the name and corrected my pronunciation, with more of a roll on the I's. *"Who is reported to be a wise man, yes, if we speak of the same one. The Hillelites, they were his followers."*

D: What do you know of that man?

S: I do not know a great deal, other than he lived and he was a man of peace. Though I believe that some of his followers have since turned around to ways of war. I'm not very familiar with a lot of the people from the outside. He spoke a lot of words of truth. But his followers, they reasoned with their minds and not their hearts, and changed the teachings to what they wished to hear.

D: Is he still alive?

S: I do not think so. I think he no longer lives on this earth.

The Maccibees were people who were important in Jewish history. He again corrected my pronunciation: 'Mac-ki-bees'.

S: I do not know about them. I have just heard of them. They are a very powerful family. And many people will listen to what they have to say. The money has many friends.

D: Oh? I thought maybe they were wise people.

S: Some are. There are some wise men in each group, but then there again are fools.

D: Are they from the area?

S: I'm not truly sure. I believe they have a stronghold in Jerusalem (pronounced: Herusalem). *I'm not, again, too sure, but I believe this is what I heard it.*

The translators mention the Book of Enoch often in their reports on the Dead Sea Scrolls. It is not in the version of the Bible that we have at this time, but the scholars consider it important. It has created controversy among them. I asked if he was aware of this book.

S: *Yes, I have heard of this. It is taught.*
D: Is it looked upon favorably?
S: *It depends on who you speak to. It creates high feelings. As some may say, you either follow it wholeheartedly or you think that this is crazy. (So it also created controversy in his day.) I do not think much of it. There are those who believe it is everything of the truth and there are those of us who believe it is lunacy. But that is my opinion and others disagree. It is their right.*

It was looked upon favorably for the most part by the Essene community and some thought it was an important book. Suddi thought it was very possibly somebody's imagination.

D: Where did that book come from? Was that added later?
S: *The Book of Enoch is something that has been passed down from the Kaloo. What do you mean, added later? To what? I'm not understanding.*

I had made a mistake, a slip of the tongue. It was hard for me to remember that they didn't know anything about our Bible. So I referred to the Torah because that seemed to be the main book that he was familiar with, although I had no idea what it was composed of. He said the Book of Enoch was not in the Torah.

I read *The Secrets of Enoch* which is found in the apocryphal *Lost Books of the Bible*. Whether this is the version Suddi referred to or not, this one was confusing enough to read. It deals a lot with astronomy and symbolism and apparently contains hidden meanings. There may be other books that refer to Enoch.

I knew the names of different groups of people that are mentioned in the Bible. I thought I would throw them out and see what Suddi said about them.

D: Have you ever heard of the Pharisees? (He frowned.) The Saducees? (I again had trouble with the pronunciations.)
S: *The Pharisees, they are the well-to-do. They are the so called*

lawgivers. They are both members of the assembly, and they sit there and argue all day so nothing gets done. The Saducees have to do with the running of the temples and the laws that will be passed. And they also argue with Herod as far as what they wish to be done. They are always . . . one is getting at the other. They say that the one, the Pharisees have - because they have great wealth and they show this - that they are not as pious as these others. They say, "Walk around in ashes and sackcloth."

D: Have you ever heard of the Samaritans?

S: *From Samaria? Yes. (The word 'Samaria' was said so fast, it was hard to understand.) The Samaritans were people of the children of Jacob. And for some reason I cannot remember, there was a blood feud. And they are considered less than their brothers. They were as one at one point, but now they are looked down upon because they are perhaps not as good in the eyes of others.*

The questioning had been progressing smoothly and I did not know I had stepped on forbidden ground until I asked about Qumran. All I wanted to know was the meaning of the name. I was not prepared for his reaction. He excitedly spoke several words in a different language.

S: *What does it mean? I shall not speak of this. If you do not know the meaning, you have no need to know.*

D: I've heard it means 'light.'

S: *There are many essences to the term meaning 'light.' And if you do not know which pathway it belongs upon, there is no need for you to question. If it were important to you, you would have knowledge.*

This can be frustrating, but he made it very plain that he did not want to answer. Later my research revealed that when the Romans conquered the Essenes, the Essenes allowed themselves to be tortured to death rather than reveal the answers to questions of this nature. What seemed a simple topic to me apparently took on larger proportions to him. Of course, I did not know this at the time, and I was unaware which questions were the touchy ones.

D: Is there any significance about the fact that Qumran has been built near the salt cliffs?

S: *Not so much the salt cliff, as the* area. *It is a point of (sounded*

*like: 'ken' energy. This was not clear.) It is an opening. It is one
of the energy points.*

D: People have said it is an odd place to build a community. It is so
isolated.

S: That is one of the benefits.

D: They thought there would be no way anyone could live there.

S: (Sarcastically) And a man cannot live in the Sahara. But they do!

D: People have said it is so isolated and you cannot use the water of
the Dead Sea.

*S: There is water here that is drinkable and usable. We have what
we need.*

D: What is the meaning of the word 'Essenes'?

S: Holy one.

I wondered why he had no hesitation in telling me the meaning of
that word while he objected to telling me the meaning of Qumran.
This shows the inconsistency of the things he objected to.

Harriet was again referring to her list of questions. "Does the name
'Midrashim' or 'Mishna' mean anything to you?" The question
obviously upset him for he spoke several words excitedly in a
different language. There were many times like this that created
enough of an emotional outburst for him to slip into his native
tongue. *"Why do you ask?*

D: We just wondered if you had anything in any of your writings
about Midrashim.

S: (This again caused him to become upset.) I will speak not of this!

D: There's no way we will know the answers unless we ask
questions.

S: Why do you have questions that show only partial knowledge?

D: We have heard of these things and are asking if you can either
verify them or help us further in our knowledge. Sometimes we
have only bits and pieces of information.

S: (Interrupted) It can be dangerous to have just partial information.

D: (This was a surprise.) You think it's not good for us to know these
things?

*S: It is of concern, yes. In speaking of things that you know only
partial of and invoking words of power that you may know only
these scatterings of, you may be dealing with more than you will
be able to handle.*

This took us off-guard because we certainly didn't realize there was any danger involved in asking simple questions. We said we would abide by his judgement and asked what he suggested we do.

S: *Speak no more of it until you have the knowledge that may be gained. Because to speak of it to those who might trick you in some way into revealing what you have to better their cause, this could be very dangerous.*

D: How are we to get the other knowledge unless we ask questions? Is it allowed for us to seek?

S: *Seeking is allowed, but be very careful.*

D: It is not always easy to find the right people who can give us this information.

S: *It is true. But you must always protect yourself from those... and from saying too much to those who begin asking you questions in return.*

D: Then you think it is better *not* to seek this knowledge?

S: *I said that not! This* is your *meaning of that which I spoke. I state only to be careful. And to guard who you would share your knowledge with. And receive little or nothing in return.*

D: Well, the knowledge is enough.

S: *No! For knowledge can be very harmful. Because you would be tempted to use it. And not having full knowledge could cause danger to yourself and to others.*

I thanked him for warning us. This outburst was most unexpected and certainly out of character for the placid Suddi. He had refused to answer questions before but never came on so strongly. I still wonder what it was that we asked that triggered such an emotional reaction. I returned to my questions, a little more cautiously this time.

D: Have you ever heard of a book called the Cabal or the Kabbalah?

S: *Some of us have read it. There are scrolls that contain some of the writings, yes.*

D: Is it a complicated book?

S: *Everything is complicated if you would make it so. It explains many of the laws of nature and balance - how to use these for your own good. How to open oneself up to what worlds surround us in this world and others.*

He did not know who had written the Kabbalah but it was older than many of the other books they had.

Later, when I had a chance to do further research, I may have discovered the reason Harriet's question upset him so. I found that Hebrew theology is divided into three parts: the first was the Law which was taught to all the children of Israel; the second was the Mishna, or the soul of the Law, which was revealed to the Rabbis and teachers; the third part was the Kabbalah, the soul of the soul of the Law, which contains secret principles and was revealed only to the highest initiates among the Jews. The Midrashim referred to methods used to simplify or more fully explain the Laws. Apparently we had unknowingly crossed over into a secret area of teaching which Suddi and other Essenes were involved in. Maybe this explains his emotional outburst and his warnings about using words of power and speaking of things of which we had no knowledge.

The translators of the Dead Sea Scrolls speak of the *Damascus Document* and think there were probably other Essene communities, possibly one in the Damascus area. But I trespassed on forbidden ground when I asked about it. He answered in the now familiar, *"I shall not speak of this."* It was strange how it bothered him to answer certain questions yet he would answer similar ones with no difficulty.

D: Do you know anything about an Essene group in Alexandria?

S: *(Long pause) My father says that they have recently spoken of some teachers who have gone, not to Alexandria, but to Egypt. But I do not know. (Did he ask his father?) There are many others. There are one that I know of in Egypt. There are several in the area surrounding Israel, Judaea,(name of another country unclear but it sounded like 'Tode', phonetically.) There are many. We at Qumran are perhaps one of the larger but not the only.*

Strange how he only objected to speaking of the one at Damascus. He said that to his knowledge the other communities were also isolated but they all had the same principles as Qumran: the accumulation and preservation of knowledge. They were far from being a single isolated small group of people.

S: *If we were to preserve knowledge and we just stayed among ourselves, this very small group, how in that would the knowledge be preserved? If it was safeguarded by us and not shared? Therefore there should be others also.*

D: Some people have the idea that is what it is, a very isolated group that doesn't associate or pass the knowledge on.

S: *Some are fools.*

Scientists and Arabs scoured the caves in the Qumran area looking for more scrolls or fragments. In one cave, among the rubble of a caved-in wall, they came across a rare find, two copper scrolls. Scrolls had always been written on either papyri or leather. This was very unusual. Originally, they had been one continuous strip about eight feet long by a foot wide and had been cut apart for some unknown reason. The archaeologists could see symbols stamped into the metal, which was also unusual. But weather and time had taken its toll. The copper had become so oxidized that the scrolls were dangerously brittle to handle. They were so fragile it was impossible to unroll them. For four years they worked on the problem of how to open them safely. Finally, Professor H. Wright Baker of the University of Manchester, England, devised an ingenious method to cut the scrolls into strips. It worked so well that not even a single letter was lost.

After all the trouble, was it worth it? After translation the scrolls were found to contain a treasure hunter's dream. They were lists of buried treasure worth fabulous amounts. The inventory included gold, silver and other treasures possibly weighing more than a total of a hundred tons. Their estimated worth was over $12 million in the 1950s when the scrolls were translated. They would be worth much more now. The scrolls gave exact directions for sixty different burial or hiding places in and around Jerusalem and in the Judaean desert. The description of the scrolls and their translation is given in *The Treasure of the Copper Scroll,* by John M. Allegro.

He gives a detailed account. He was positive it was the inventory of an actual treasure and that the objects were buried in the places indicated. His only doubt was in the incredible amounts. He thought there must have been a mistake in translation, the amounts were too breath-taking. For instance: "a total of more than 3179 talents (a weight measure) of silver and *385* of gold; *165* gold bars, 14 silver pitchers and 619 vessels of precious metals." The directions were explicit: "In the cistern which is below the rampart on the east side, in a place hollowed out of rock: 600 bars of silver." All of the directions were this exact. Mr. Allegro says most of the places indicated would probably have been difficult or impossible to find after the Roman War devastated the area.

None of this treasure has ever been found. The last entry on the Copper Scroll gave directions to the location of another copy of the same inventory. Concealed "in a pit adjoining on the North the Great Drain of the Basin near the Temple". This duplicate copy was never found.

Some of the archaeologists have come to the conclusion that the copper scrolls are a hoax, that the treasure never existed. They said it had to be a hoax because where could the Essenes have gotten such fabulous amounts of wealth if they had been sworn to poverty? The scroll must have been more difficult to inscribe than the normal papyri. It would have been an awful lot of trouble to go to in order to perpetrate a trick.

Others say the scroll may not be speaking of an actual treasure but is using symbolism to convey another message that has not been figured out. I believe it was possible for the Essenes to have either accumulated that much wealth over the years of their existence, or that they were made guardians of wealth from another source.

The Bedouin of the area had been a tremendous help to the scientists because they knew every nook and cranny of the desert. It is possible that over two thousand years, they may have found some of the treasure. Also, because the duplicate scroll was never found, it is possible that someone found it years ago and followed the directions. I believe our modern generation was not the first people to find what the Essenes had hidden.

During this last session when I asked questions from my research, I decided to see if he might be able to shed any light on this puzzle. But how to do it without asking leading questions? Suddi was in the library on the upper level studying some scrolls, so it was the perfect environment. When I asked if he was studying any particular scroll, he answered with the now-familiar, "I shall not speak of this!" He would only say that it was not the Torah. When he went on the defensive about certain subjects it was no use trying to get the answers, unless I could do it by roundabout methods.

D: Do they ever make the scrolls out of any other material besides the skins and the papyri?

S: *There are other methods of making them. I am not a copier. I'm not familiar with them, but there are other ways, yes.*

D: Have you ever seen any scrolls that are made out of metal?

S: *Yes. (This apparently was another forbidden topic of discussion. He became suspicious again.) Why do you ask?*

D: I thought this would be an odd material to make them out of. It would be a lot more work. Wouldn't it be harder than using the stylus and papyri?

S: *(Coldly) Yes. (He asked suspiciously:) Why do you ask these questions?*

D: I just wondered why they would go to all the trouble of making one out of metal.

S: *They would contain more important information. There are some things that must be protected.*

He would not elaborate further. It seemed that if something were written on metal, it would be because it had special value. They were trying to use the most durable material to make sure it would survive. Thus I cannot believe the Copper Scroll was a hoax. The archaeologists were just two thousand years too late to uncover this fantastic treasure.

The archaeologists who excavated the ruins of Qumran have made no mention of finding any housing area. They have come to the conclusion that the people lived in the caves around the community or perhaps in tents or huts. They found pottery, lamps and tent poles in some of the same caves that the Dead Sea Scrolls were found in and thought this suggested that they lived there at one time. I could not understand why the Essenes would live in caves and tents when they were able to create this wonderful community with its marvelous water system. This did not make sense to me. I decided to pursue this.

D: You told me before that when you were a child you lived in houses that were away from the community, outside the walls?

Are there any caves in the vicinity of Qumran?

S: There are many caves.

D: Do your people ever live in the caves?

S: They said at one time they did, but there are not enough here now to have that as necessary. However, as children, we used to play in them.

D: You mean at one time there was more population, more people there? And during that time they lived in the caves?

S: Yes, 'twas in the beginning.

This was in the early times while the houses were being built. I thought that this would be the case. With such a wonderfully advanced community it would not be necessary for the people to be reduced to living in caves and tents.

During the excavations they found many coins, even bags of them. This helped the scientists to date the ruins. The coins belonged to the time periods from 136BC to 37BC, covering the period of Jewish independence and extending to Herod the Great. Then there was a gap, only a few coins found that were issued between this period and 4BC, the time of Herod Archelaus. There were a large number found dating after 4BC to 68AD, when Qumran was destroyed.

On this evidence the archaeologists have come to the conclusion that Qumran was abandoned for 30 years, since they found only a few coins from that time period. But this was the time when Suddi was living there and according to him the Essenes never left. Even the scientists could not come up with a satisfactory reason why they would leave. They could see evidence that the community had experienced an earthquake. (See the drawing of the community.) And they assumed this might have damaged the community to such an extent that the people left for these thirty years, but this is only an assumption. Even the ancient writers, who were so thorough in their histories of the time, do not mention that the Essenes were ever absent from the area. This was only the archaeologists' theory based on what facts they were able to come up with during the excavations. I conclude that if the entire treasure of the Copper Scroll could completely disappear, why not bags of coins? The ruins were known to have been occupied and ransacked by the Romans during the invasion. There were also other peoples that lived there afterward for a while before Qumran was abandoned entirely. I feel the archaeologists' findings do not contradict mine, but rather offer an alternate explanation.

I wondered how to ask him about this without putting ideas into his head. It would have to be worded carefully.

D: Can you tell me, Suddi, have the people lived there in the community all the time since it was built?

S: *Explain.*

D: Have your people always lived there in the community continuously, or was there a time when your people left?

S: *You speak of the time of the hiding. Yes, there was a time when they left for a period, yes. It has been spoken about.*

But this occurred before his lifetime. During his time there was never a time when the people abandoned the community.

In the drawing, it can be noted that the earthquake damaged one end of the community and left a large crack, part of which ran through one of the baths. The archaeologists also found evidence that some of the damage was repaired, especially around the tower. I wanted to ask about this, but 1 would not mention the word "earthquake."

D: Do you know anything about any natural catastrophes that have occurred since you have lived there?

S: *(Pause, as though thinking.) Ah! You mean when the... I remember when I was little my mother said that there was the shaking of the cliffs. At one time there was great fear that the whole place would fall off into the sea. I was two or three, maybe, I'm not sure. I have no memory of it.*

D: Did it do any damage to the community?

S: *There is a handspan gap where that part of it slipped and fell.*

Apparently he meant a crack. I asked where it was located. She used hand gestures in his explanation.

S: *Let me think here... it is along the wall. The wall runs like this, the cliff wall and it is on that way. On that corner, toward the bathhouse and the assembly hall and that area. It runs through in a diagonal. (I think this last word is correct. It was hard to understand.)*

138

D: Did the crack go through the bathhouse?

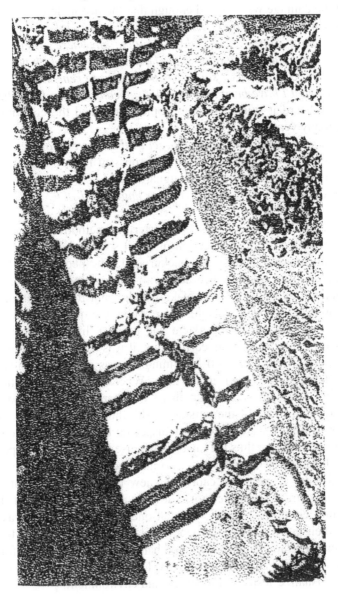

Ruins of Qumran showing the crack in the bath house steps

S: Yes, but the crack was not so that the water escaped. It was repaired. The people of the community took it in their stride. They knew it was about to happen, therefore there was no loss of *life. They had been told. (Did he mean psychically?)*

D: But the damage was not bad enough that the people left?

S: *For a while I think they probably stayed away while the repairs were being done. They could have gone anywhere. They could have gone and stayed only in the housing. They could have gone perhaps to caves. As I say I was too young to remember. I only know what I have been told. I do not remember never being here.*

D: I have heard it said that your people abandoned the community for many years.

S: *We made them think so. If they forget us they leave us alone.*

D: But surely people would come and rob you if they thought the community was deserted and unguarded?

S: *They knew better than that. It is never unguarded.*

This again seemed to refer to some mysterious method of protection. I have presented all of this section in detail so that the life of Jesus may be understood against this background. The people who lived there at Qumran were concerned with one main objective, the accumulation and preservation of knowledge and the passing-on of that knowledge through teaching those who were qualified to learn. The Essenes appeared to be placid and passive, living enclosed in their own little world. Secluded like this, it was a virtual paradise, a perfect place completely self-sustaining. It was amazingly modern by the standards of Israel at the time. Whenever anyone ventured outside the walls they saw that there was harsh contrast between their ways and those of the outside world, thus they preferred their isolation. But they were feared and suspected by the others who did not understand them, thus they had to disguise themselves. It appears that the location of Qumran was also guarded and known to only a few. I wonder if even the caravans knew the real purpose of the settlement. Strangers were not allowed in certain parts of the community either. Yet Suddi said that one of their purposes was to pass on their knowledge to the people at large. I suppose it had to be done subtly by the students of the red bands who studied and left the community to live in their own areas. I think this section makes it easier to visualize Jesus in this setting and environment.

This section displays Katie's great capacity for accuracy and detail about a culture she had no way of knowing anything about. Some will argue that she could have read about the Essenes and Qumran in the same books that I did and was thus prepared for my questions. I know she did no research; she had no interest in it. She never at any time knew what type of questions I would be asking. Throughout the section there is knowledge that is not found in any books. In this chapter there were some things dealing with the Dead Sea Scrolls' translations that even Suddi was unfamiliar with. This would be normal since he had not read all the scrolls in the library or they might have been called by other names during his lifetime. If Katie had been perpetrating an elaborate hoax she would have made sure she was accurate on all counts and would have been familiar with these translations. I believe the depth of the trance which Katie experienced made deception impossible. She slipped in and out of the personality of Suddi with great ease and literally became this ancient person in all respects during the three months we visited with him.

I wish to include here some quotes from Josephus that I believe have a bearing on our story. "There are also some among them (the Essenes) who undertake to foretell future events, having been brought up from their youth in the study of the sacred Scripture, in divers purification, and in the sayings of the prophets; and it is very seldom that they fail in their predictions."

"They despise suffering, and overcome pain by fortitude. Death, if connected with honor, they look upon as better than long life. Of the firmness of their minds in all cases the war with the Romans has given ample proof; in which, though they were tortured, racked, burned, squeezed and subjected to all the instruments of torment, that they might be forced to blaspheme the lawgiver (Moses) or eat what was forbidden, yet they could not be made to do either of them; nor would they even once flatter their tormentors or shed a tear, but, smiling through their torments and mocking their tormentors, they cheerfully yielded up their souls, as those who would soon receive them back again."

The Essenes had to swear "not to conceal anything from the brotherhood, not to disclose anything belonging to them to those without, even though it were at the hazard of his life. He was, moreover, to swear not to communicate to anyone their doctrines in any other way than he has received them."

This explains the difficulty I had obtaining answers at times, and why I had to turn to devious methods of gaining information. I am surprised that I was able to get it at all. I was trying to make him violate a strict, basic rule of his life, something that people under hypnosis will not do. They will never do anything that is against their morals. But these were not Katie's morals, they were Suddi's. This shows how closely Katie was identifying with the Essene and how completely she had become him. It also explains why it was easier to obtain information from Suddi as a child. He had not yet taken this oath and in his innocence he was unaware that he was revealing anything that was forbidden. We should be grateful that we were able to receive any information, even by hook or crook. This is another example of the great bond of trust that had been built between Katie and me. I do not believe this information would have been released under any other circumstances.

Ginsburg related in his book, *The Essenes and the Kabbalah,* published in 1864, that this secrecy was not uncommon, "since the Pharisees also would not indiscriminately propound the mysteries of the cosmogony and the theosophy, which, according to them, are contained in the history of the Creation and in the vision of Ezekiel, except to those who were regularly initiated in the order." The Essenes also knew of these teachings. (See Chapters 14 and 15.) Josephus said, "They take extraordinarily great pains in studying the writings of the ancients, and select that which is beneficial both for the soul and body."

Ginsburg: "They apparently studied the ancient books on magical cures and exorcisms that were the reputed works of Solomon, who composed treatises on miraculous cures and driving out evil spirits."

Philo: "They use therein a three-fold rule and definition: love of God, love of virtue and love of mankind." Note the similarity with the teachings of Jesus.

Writers in the 1800s said that Essenism arose out of the deeper religious meaning of the Old Testament. That the Essenes belonged to the Apocalyptical school, and that they must be regarded as the successors of the ancient prophets, and as constituting the prophetic school. They adopted some of the old Oriental, Persian and Chaldean ideas, and brought with them some practices and institutions which they mixed up with the Jewish views of religion. The Essenes aimed to reconcile religion with science.

CHAPTER 14

Scrolls and Biblical Stories

One of the activities of the community was the writing and copying of scrolls so that they could be passed on to other parts of the world. It was a publishing center, so to speak.

S: *We are put in charge of the saving of records, so that word shall not be lost. It is what they do at the library. Then they take the scrolls and they are sent to many countries and many places for protection, in hopes that at least some Of them will remain. There is so much here. There are all the stories, the communications of the different courts, the histories, and the day-to-day life existence. One would be of a great age before you could read all the scrolls.*

D: Do you know where else in your world the scrolls are kept? Are there other libraries?

S: *I suppose that there are. I have no way of knowing. (The old suspicion returned.) Why do you wish to know?*

I tried to fake my way through by saying I was curious and liked to read. If there was something they didn't have, I wanted to know where to look for it. My ruse did not convince him. He asked, *"Would you be able to read them?"* I had to think fast. I told him if I could not, I could always have someone translate them for me. This did not work either.

S: *Very few are even allowed to see the scrolls. They must have reasons.*

This surprised me because I thought anyone could look at them, just as in our libraries today.

S: *The openers would want to know why. If everyone had this knowledge, they could use it for harm.*

During the sessions there were many references given to languages spoken at the time. I thought the majority spoke Aramaic.

S: *No, they also speak Hebrew, Arabic, Egyptian. The language of the Romany. There are many, many different tongues.*

This reference to Romany surprised me because I knew this was what the gypsies call their language today.

S: *They are the wanderers. It is said that they are two of the lost tribes of Israel. How true this is, I do not know.*
D: What do the Romans speak?
S: *Latin Vulgate. Some of them Greek. There are also many dialects of Aramaic. From each little province you come, it is different. Each has its own way of expressing itself. My dialect is simply, I believe, Galilean. (Pronounced fast: Galilayan.)*

Suddi was able to understand the other dialects but at times it was difficult. These differences also affected the reading of Aramaic.

S: *There are so many ways of expressing and also the ways of writing are different. Unless you are very familiar, you can read something in there that is absolutely not there. You see, it is like this, one word would mean one thing to me and it could mean something totally different to you. It depends on the way it is in the structure of the letter. Also, if it is spoken, it is the way the voice sounds when it is spoken. It can mean a good many of things. There are several words that mean five, six, seven meanings. They are all different and diverse.*

This goes along with the other session where he said it was the sounds and not the letters that make up the words. I see it as a type of shorthand where the symbols represent the sounds. If there were many different dialects, the words would have different sounds according to who spoke them. The person who was doing the writing would make the symbols according to the way he spoke the language. I asked an Iranian about this and he said it was true in his language that the same word could have many completely different meanings. For instance, the same word means: lion, faucet and milk, each totally different. I asked him how they knew which was the correct word. He said it depended upon the sentence it was used in. When you consider this plus the fact that punctuation marks were not invented until the fifteenth century, it makes it clear what a nightmare the job of translating from these languages would have been.

D: Then if someone was to read one of your scrolls, could they get something different out of it?

S: *It is very possible, yes, to find something totally different than what was intended.*

Even though the symbols were essentially the same, the reader could get a different story if they didn't know what dialect the scroll was written in. I wondered how anyone could *ever* know what the writer truly meant to say.

S: *You would have to take it as a whole and find the way that the things fit together. If a word did not make any sense the way that it was in a part of it, then you would have to find another meaning for this.*

This would explain why some of our stories in the Bible could be different from the original. If someone inserted a different word during the many translations down through history, it would be very difficult to know which way the story was originally supposed to be read.

D: Are some of your scrolls in Hebrew?

S: *Yes, they are in all of the languages of the earth.*

D: Are mistakes also made in Hebrew?

S: *Yes, it is almost as easy in Hebrew as in Aramaic. The words have many meanings.*

Hebrew uses letters but they do not use vowels, only consonants, so many words are also possible.

All this would make it very difficult on the scribe. If they made one mistake they could change the whole story, even through simple ignorance.

S: Or fear, yes. I am not a scholar. I do not know of men's reasons for things.

With this information in mind, I will present Suddi's versions of the stories from the scrolls and the Torah. There are many differences from our modern Bible. It must be remembered these are what he was taught by his teachers, so it is the truth as *he* saw it. But he was closer in time to the originals, so who knows? Accept them as food for thought.

D: We have a book today that has some of your teachings in it, but it is supposed to have been written by many different people. They have names for the different parts of the books. One of them is called Isaiah.

S: Yes, there is the prophet Isaiah. You are saying 'book' ; it is not a book, it is part of the Torah. It speaks of the prophet Isaiah. And there is Ezekiel and Deborah and Benjamin and the story of Moses and Ruth, and many, many others. (Deborah was one Bible character I was not familiar with.) It is the part about the judges of Israel. She was one of these. She was one of the lawgivers. For the Israelis to have a woman over them was something of an unusual occurrence. And many of them could not stand the fact that they were being ruled by woman. She was a very wise person. Her story is not part of the Torah, it is in some of the scrolls.

In the Bible Deborah is barely mentioned in the 4th and 5th chapters of Judges.

I asked if he had ever heard of one part called Genesis, but he was not familiar with that name. When I explained that it told of how the world was formed, he said, *"You mean the foundation? It is just the Beginning."* He also did not recognize the name Exodus, but they had the story of Moses, it was very important to them. I am unfamiliar with the Torah that is used today in the Jewish religion but I asked him which parts were included in his.

S: The Torah, it consists of the laws and the prophecies. And then basically from the time of Abraham. There is very little of what went before. The stories are in the writings, but not in the Torah. It begins with the point of the creating about Abraham and that he is the leader of the people (of Israel) and it goes on from there.

D: Does it end with the stories of Moses?

S: *No, it ends with the prophets. Some of them are in the Torah, some of them are just in the other scrolls. But it is the work of putting them together. I'm trying to fit everything together of the promises.*

D: Who is the last prophet in the Torah?

S: *Let me think. I believe Zechariah. I thought it would be easier if all the stories were in one scroll.*

His answer caused laughter among the listening group.

S: *If they were all on one scroll, that would be a very large scroll. It would be too big to lift.*

We stumbled upon his ability to tell stories quite by accident. It had never occurred to me to ask Suddi for information of this type. The following stories were originally sprinkled throughout the transcripts and appeared over the three month period at random. I have combined them in this section for reading out of context. Since it is a known fact that our Bible has undergone many changes down through the years, there may be more of the truth here than we would like to admit. At least read them with an open mind.

SODOM AND GOMORRAH

I was asking him questions about the Dead Sea, or the "Sea of Death" as he called it. The Qumran community was located on the cliffs at the edge of this body of water. All I had ever heard about it was that it was very salty and would not sustain life. This peculiarity has never really been satisfactorily explained. With this in mind, I asked if the sea had any peculiarities about it. I was taken off guard by his answer.

S: *It has sometimes the smell of tar, or resin, or pitch, yes. They say that toward the South that there are pits of pitch and that this is part of it. Also nothing grows in the Sea of Death. There are a few plants along the edges.*

D: Is this why you call it the Sea of Death?

The Sea of Death

S: *It is called this because it is upon these shores that Gomorrah and Sodomon were brought to destruction. And it is to remind us of this.*

I glanced quickly at Harriet and saw she was as surprised as I was. This was certainly unexpected. We had heard the Bible story, but had no idea these two infamous cities were associated with the Dead Sea. Note the reversal of the names as we are accustomed to hearing them and the different pronunciation of Sodom. It was obvious none of this came telepathically from *our* minds.

D: Oh? We've always thought the name meant that nothing would grow there.
S: *(Interrupted) This* is why *nothing grows here.*
D: How were these cities destroyed?

Suddi answered nonchalantly, *"Radiation."* *Again* I was taken off-guard, and asked if he could tell us the story of what happened.

S: *It is said that they were displeasing in the eyes of Yahweh, for they had gone from the path of truth. And when that they were given the warning many, many times to become back to the path of righteousness, that they laughed. And it is said that Lot was in these cities and he was visited by two great beings, who told him to take his family and leave and they would be protected. And he was upset because, I mean, this was his city after all, and even though it was still bad, these were his people. But they told him they were not worth saving, that they must start over and start again from anew. So he took his two daughters and his wife and they left. It is said that his wife looked back on the city and in so doing that she died, from what she saw and looking upon the face of the destruction with her eyes.*

I remembered the familiar story of her turning into a pillar of salt, but Suddi said there was nothing unusual about her death other than she looked back and saw the destruction. I asked if he had an explanation for the destruction.

S: *Where these cities were located, there are pockets of the pitch and the tar and a great heat was caused. The lightning bolts, they struck from the heavens. And when they hit this, they caused destruction to reign (or could this word be 'rain'? An interesting difference in definition) And it caused to... explode. And the cities, they caved in about this, themselves, and sunk until that there was nothing left.*

D: Then you think that Yahweh caused all this to happen?

S: *It was his choice, yes.*

This was something I could not delay research on. He had sparked my curiosity. I did not see that it would jeopardize the story of the Essenes if I looked for information about Sodom and Gomorrah. Some of the best was readily available in my encyclopedia. The thing to remember is that we had no interest in looking it up before, we had never thought of a connection.

Archaeological and Biblical evidence supports the locating of the five Cities of the Plain (of which Sodom and Gomorrah were two) in the Valley of Siddim. This was a once-fertile plain located at the south end of the Jordan River-Dead Sea Valley. The early invaders of the area found that the valley was full of wells of asphalt - "Slime pits" in the older translations. Ancient and modern writers attest to the presence of asphalt (Greek) and bitumen (Latin) around the Dead Sea, especially around the southern part. In ancient times it was called the Salt Sea and Lake Asphaltitis. At the south-west corner rises a low mountain made up in part of pure compact crystalline salt, which the modern Arabs call Jebel Usdum, the Mount of Sodom.

Recent investigations by geologists have revealed the presence of petroleum as well as seepage of asphalt. They also suspect the presence of uranium but feel it would be too difficult to mine. Ancient writers wrote of the foul odors and soot arising from the Sea. It was so strong that it tarnished metals. Modern geologists say this is natural gas, which would have been unknown to the people of the past. They claim a possible explanation of the destruction of Sodom and Gomorrah is that oil and the gas fumes may have been ignited by lightning, or an earthquake overturned the hearth fires causing an explosion. In the Bible it says that Abraham saw smoke rising from the Plain, which went up "as smoke of a furnace," a fitting description of burning oil and gas. It also might fit an atomic explosion.

The surface of the Dead Sea, which is 1292 feet below sea level, is lower than any known place on earth. The sea then drops to a maximum depth of 1309 feet and is six times saltier than sea water, making it also the saltiest place on earth. This is a unique geological phenomenon. No other part of the globe, which is not under water, lies deeper than 300 feet below sea level. Absolutely nothing will live in the water.

According to Wemer Keller in *The Bible As History,* explorations in that area came up with something strange. Although the body of the sea is incredibly deep, the south end is shallow, no more than fifty or sixty feet deep. When the sun is shining in the right direction, the outlines of forests can be seen beneath the water. They have been preserved by the high salt content of the water. This is evidence that before the destruction of Sodom and Gomorrah the area was a lush and fertile plain. It is believed that the cities sank beneath the water in this area and this would explain why it is shallower there.

Salt is in the air, and everything in the area (including people) is quickly covered with a crust of salt. This could be an explanation for the story of Lot's wife turning into salt. When the explosion occurred, there must have been a tremendous amount of salt thrown into the air from the salt mountain located near the cities.

I would like to venture to draw my own conclusions as to what happened there. In order for the cities to sink and the area to be rendered lifeless and desolate for all time to come, I believe a natural atomic explosion occurred. Could this also account for the incredible depth of the sea? It is possible with the presence of uranium as well as the other highly volatile chemicals in the area. It is interesting to note that no Geiger counter readings for radioactivity have ever been carried out in the area, according to writer Erich von Daniken.

But this does not explain the presence of the two beings who came to warn Lot and his family. If it was a natural phenomenon, how did they know about it in advance? It has been suggested that instead of lightning triggering the explosion, it may have been ignited by laser beams from an outer-space craft. An open mind can see many possibilities other than the orthodox.

A new area of exploring this time period had opened up. Maybe Suddi could give us more stories and open up new avenues of thinking.

DANIEL

When I asked about the story of the fiery furnace, he said he was not familiar with it. So I asked him if he knew one about someone being thrown into a den of lions.

S: *You speak of Daniel. His story is in the scrolls. He was a wise man and a prophet. The people were afraid of his influence with this king. Because he was Jewish and did not believe as they did, they had him thrown to the lions. And so, when that he came out alive, they were fearful for they knew that his God was the true God. It is said that the angel came and shut the lions' mouths. I rather think that Daniel spoke to the lions. This is possible. Man can have shared conversation with animals. Are they not God's creatures also?*

DAVID

Suddi told me once that he was descended from the house of David, so I asked if he had heard of a story about David that involved a giant.

S: You speak of Goliath. It is said that Goliath was the head of the army of... I believe it was the Philistines. And the people of...- let me think, who was the king? I believe it was Saul who was king, and they were at war. And every day the Israeli army would go out and be defeated and many men would die, because of this leader Goliath. He would go out and he would challenge them all and would win.

D: Was he really a giant?

S: He was larger than most men would be considered. He was with the Philistines, but he was not a Philistine. In other words, he was of somewhere else. And it is said that David decided that he would take him on and would slay him, and he did. 'Tis said that he used his sling. That he was a shepherd and had much prowess with it killing wolves. It keeps the wolves and jackals away from the sheep if you are a good shot. So you do not lose many lambs. David was just from the threshold of manhood. I believe he was fourteen. It was something that he had been told that he would be able to do. It is not hard to defeat someone like that when you are in the right and they are in the wrong. In the case of that, it is better to slay one man to stop killing, than to let one man kill so many. So it is written.

JOSEPH

S: The story of Joseph is not of the Torah. It is said that he had many brothers by different mothers. But only one brother by the same, who was younger than him. Maybe he was the youngest, I do not remember. It has been a long time since I read this. It is said that he was sold into slavery by his brothers, because his brothers were jealous of the attention his father gave him. Because he was... let me think here. Yes, I remember, he was the youngest child of his mother and his mother died giving birth to him. And she was a much loved wife. And therefore this one was, how do you say...? probably spoiled. He received many things that the brothers did not think quite fair. And therefore, his father presented him with a coat with sleeves and he was....

Wait a minute! In our Bible story, his father gave him a coat of many colors. I interrupted, "A coat with *what?*"

S: A coat with sleeves. A robe that has sleeves. Usually the robe does not have sleeves, it is just an open robe. Anyway, it was nice and new and so they were jealous and they decided they wanted to take this from him and he said, "No! You know father gave this to me. " And they had an argument about it and so they threw him in a well, I believe it was, or lowered him down into it, I do not remember. And they said that, "Well, we cannot let him come back to father. He will tell what we have done." So they decided they were going to kill him. His brother of the same mother said, "No, no, we cannot do this. He is our brother. You know, we cannot do this. "And so, therefore, he decides that they would sell him to slavers that would go into Egypt and they would never see him again. So they sold him.

D: What did the brothers tell the father?

S: They brought the coat back and they had smeared lamb's blood, I believe, on the coat and said that he had been attacked by a lion and that he was no more. That this was all that they had found.

D: Then what happened after the slavers sold him?

S: His master finding out what an intelligent man he is put him to work for... let's see, bookkeeper, I believe, (I am assuming this is the word. It was pronounced strangely) and in charge of his estates. And his wife decides she wants Joseph and he says, "No, no, no. " So she gets him in trouble with that master, and that master throws him into prison. And, let me think now... There was an adviser to Pharaoh who had fallen out of favor who was also there, who had dreams. And Joseph being able to understand dreams, told him what they meant. And so when that the adviser to Pharaoh was released from prison, he told him to remember him. And in due time he did. And when Pharaoh had a dream, Joseph was remembered and brought to interpret and which he did. And in doing so he saved Egypt, because Egypt had seven years of plenty and seven years of famine. And Egypt was the only one that was prepared, and all the lands around were starving. So, it is said that when there were no more foods for his family to eat, he (Joseph's father) sent them (the brothers) to Egypt. And Joseph is said to have found out that they were there and accused them of stealing. And saying that they must leave the youngest son with him, who was the brother of the same mother. And they could not recognize Joseph because he had changed so much.

D: It had been many years?

S: *Yes, and... let me think. So they went home and they told their father and he was supposed to come back with them or something. I cannot remember. Anyway, they eventually met and everybody had to admit what had happened. But Joseph, being the great man that he was, forgave them and so did their father. And so they were great in Egypt. This is how that the family got to Egypt for they moved them there. It is a very long story and part of our history.*

ADAM AND EVE

Suddi had mentioned Adam and Eve earlier, so I asked him about that story.

S: *The story of the creation of man and woman, yes. Made from the clay of the earth when it was new, was Adam. And when God found that Adam was lonely and needed the other part of him, it is said that his rib was taken out. Though I cannot see this, man has as many as women. But, anyway, his rib was taken out and a woman was made, to be his soulmate, the other half of him.*

D: I wonder what the significance of a rib would be?

S: *The woman who is the ultimate mate is part of you and a part of a whole.*

D: Do you think this is just a story or did they actually...

S: *(Interrupted) I do not know. I was not there!*

He said the name of the place was Paradise. When I asked him about the Garden of Eden, he had not heard of that name.

D: Did Adam and Eve live in Paradise the rest of their lives?

S: *According to the legend they were cast out for trying to take from God what God wished to keep to Himself, which was the knowledge of shame. They ate from the tree of knowledge, which was very curious. Why would you wish for knowledge if you had the choice of life and you had the choice of knowledge? How many would not choose everlasting life? (I did not understand*

and asked him to explain) There were two trees. There was one of the tree of knowledge and one of the tree of life. Therefore, why did they say that they ate of the fruit of the tree of knowledge? Would not the most wish to live forever? This is very curious to me. I would rather be perhaps a little unwiser. If you live forever, you have much greater chance of gaining wisdom in that length of time.

His strange philosophy amused me, but it did make sense. I asked what the trees looked like.

S: *They were one of a type and they were giant in size. I have heard that they were made of pomegranates, but this is, again, a legend.*

D: Was there anything in your story about them being tempted to eat off the fruit of one tree?

S: *It is said that the serpent tempted woman. And in being tempted, when she succumbed to this, it was part of, according to legend, why women must suffer during childbirth. I do not believe this, for women do not have to suffer. This was something that men have added to this story, I think. Why should the bringing of life into the world bring suffering? Of course they do not have to suffer! There are many ways of bringing a child into this world without giving the mother pain. You would learn the cleansing and the calming breath, and using... drawing the focus away from too much what your body is doing as far as keeping the movements going. And you would focus instead upon what is very nice and calming to you. And the calmer the body is, the easier it is for the child to be delivered. (It sounds very similar to the modern Lamaze methods.)*

D: Are the women trained to do it themselves?

S: *There are women who are told the manner in which to do this. And of course there are other women and usually the mate is there with them. But I have not attended a childbearing.*

D: You mentioned the serpent. Do you mean it was a real snake?

S: *Some say that it was one of the beings of light who had fallen. He entered his spirit into the serpent. There are many legends about this but I do not believe in this. I believe that man created his own downfall through his acquisition of greed and lust. The more you have, the more you want. And man created his own fall from the Paradise that was. It is easier to say that the serpent*

156

*tempted, than to admit that that serpent is part of yourself that is
lower.*

D: What happened when they ate the fruit?

S: *It is said that they were cast out of Paradise. And they realized
that they had no clothes, and this was the bringing of shame into
the world. And since then they have been trying to cover
themselves up ever since. To have shame in the body when that
this is your temple, this is not a good thing. This is what God
gave you to spend your life in. You must treat it well, and treat it
so that it will last you a lifetime. And to be ashamed of what is a
God-given gift is a great sin.*

This reference to the body as a temple sounded like Jesus' comments
in the New Testament.

D: But you cover your bodies.

S: *But we do not hide. When we are children, there is a freedom of
going about as the day you were born. It is acceptable. It is not
shameful to have an openness about your body. You do not run
and hide for cover for someone to see you without your clothes.*

D: In some communities this is very frowned upon.

S: *And they are usually the ones that have the most trouble.*

This explains the daily mixed naked bathing in Qumran. It was an
accepted thing. He had mentioned a light being who had fallen and I
immediately thought of the stories of Lucifer as a fallen angel. But
he had never heard of any stories about him. He did however know
about the archangel Michael.

S: *I know of Michael. It is said that Michael is at the right hand of
God. He is one of the beings that never came here. He has
always been with God for he did not venture away. And
therefore he is as perfect now as on the day of Creation. And he
is like a messenger for God. If He wishes to speak to someone,
perhaps not quite so directly, God will sometimes send Michael
or Gabriel. (Pronounced very fast.)*

D: How does he speak to you?

S: *Thought to thought. How not?*

D: You don't actually see him?

S: *There are those who do. There are those who need to. But it is not
always a need to know in all who would hear him. He would*

appear to you or I differently. He would appear perhaps as something clothed in golden light, or perhaps just a sunbeam disclosed, or perhaps as a young man or even an old. It is all in how you view him, how you need to have this image of him. It could also be others. There are many who have not come yet. There are many who have not decided that this is what they wish to do. That they sit back and watch.

Returning to the story of Adam and Eve, I said I had heard a story that there were giants in the world in those days.

S: *So it has been told. According to the stories that have been handed down, Adam was just what God decided man should look like in the final choice. That there were many, many ones who came before who were not perfect, and therefore changed. And in the times before there were many things that are not now. So it is very possible.*
D: There are many legends about strange animals. Do you think that's where the legends came from?
S: *So I have heard. It is a great possibility.*

There is more about this in the story about the creation of the world in Chapter 15.

RUTH

During a session when I was talking to Suddi as a child, I asked him what his favorite story was. I was surprised when he said, *"I like of Ruth."* I thought this was a rather strange choice for a child to pick. I can think of lots of stories from our Bible that would seem more exciting to a youngster. I asked him if he could relate it and the following is a strange phenomenon in itself. Usually the hypnotist has to ask lots of questions to keep the subject talking. They become so relaxed there is always the possibility they might drift off into a natural sleep. I have never had that happen, but it is a possibility. Katie had always been talkative while "under" anyway. But this time, Suddi told this story and went seven and a half minutes without any interruptions. I did not ask any questions or do any prodding to keep the story flowing. I believe this is some kind of record, if there are any other cases of this happening. It is another example of how closely Katie was identifying with the personality from the past.

Suddi told the story eagerly with the bubbly enthusiasm of a child wanting to share his knowledge.

S: It is said that Naomi, her and her husband and her two sons went into the land of Moab (pronounced almost in one syllable) to earn a living. And that in doing so, these two sons grew up to an age and decided to take wives. Now it is said in the scrolls that we must not take wives of other than what we ourselves are. But they spoke with the priest about it and they were told, as long as they (the women) have accepted Yahweh as their God, they would be allowed to marry. So they picked the two wives that they would choose to marry, and they happened to be sisters. One was Ruth and I cannot remember her sister's name just now.

Anyway! So it came to pass that several years had passed and there was a great sickness among the people. And Naomi's husband sickened and died, and also her two sons. And she decided she would go back into her land, which was Israel, taking with her what few possessions she had, and going back to her people. Then she told her daughters that they were young and they should stay here and marry and be among their own people. And Ruth's sister agreed to go back to her parents' house. But Ruth told her that when she left the house of her parents, she was no longer their daughter, and that Naomi was her family.

Therefore, whither she would go, also Ruth would. And Naomi kept saying, "No, no, you cannot do this. It is strange. Our people are different." And Ruth says, "Do I not follow Yahweh as your people?" And she says, "Yes". "And do I not observe the laws?" And she says, "Yes". "Therefore, I am one of you." And so she decided that rather than go alone, for it would be a very hard journey, they would go together. And they went together. And they made it home. And when that they got there, of course everyone mourned for the fact that Naomi was without a husband and had no sons to carry on the name. She went back to her house. They were not really poor, but not having very much money for things to eat or anything. And such is how they lived for a while.

And Naomi had a cousin, whose name was Boaz, who was a leading man in his community. He was of the House of David and very important and a very righteous man and good. And he owned many fields and Naomi sent Ruth out to the fields for gleaning, which was allowed. And told her that this would be a good thing to do, knowing that this would catch the attention. For even though they were poor, it is to bring shame upon the house, to show them up. That they are living in the same town with cousins and they must go to the fields to glean. Therefore the attention would be brought upon them. She was hoping that something would happen of this. Or perhaps, many say that she knew of it and therefore caused it to happen.

But, anyway! So she went out into the fields and was gleaning and the overseers tried to discourage her and she said that according to the law she had the right to do this. Because they are the leaves that have been left. And this came to his attention of Boaz and he found that she was his cousin, being married to his cousin. Therefore they were of a family. And he, seeing their problem, sent many food things to their house so that they would not have to do this. Now, there was another closer cousin, who if Ruth wished to marry, would have to marry. Because it is the law that the nearest male relative to the man who dies childless must take his wife if he is unwed. And he could not stand the thought that she was a Moabite (pronounced Mobite) and different from his family. But also he could not stand that perhaps Boaz wanted Ruth for himself. Therefore he was in a quandary.

If he said that he would take her for his wife, he would have someone who was kin and not of his own. But if he let Boaz have her, he knew that this was what Boaz wanted. So he could not decide. And therefore the challenge was made. The challenge in front of the judge. That he must either accept her as his wife or to give him his sandal. Which is to say that the bargain has been struck and they have decided that this will pass. This is so that it will be legal, the sandal is passed. And therefore, he was shamed into doing this thing in front of the people.

Because he would not... there was no way, even to spite Boaz that he would take a wife that so much fuss had been made over.

And she was foreign and different, things like that. So, therefore, they lived and grew. It is from the meeting of Ruth and Boaz that the House of David was formed. They are very important. They are my people, their house. And, their son was... let me think. It was... David was their grandson, their son's son. And it goes on from there.

This was the entire seven and a half minutes spoken without interruption.

D: Why is that your favorite story?

S: *They are the story of my family. And this was the beginning of our house. (ancestor line, family tree)*

D: Was Ruth happy with the decision, or do the scrolls say?

S: *Yes, she was happy because it is said that, part of it, she went out and made herself known to Boaz, so that he would know that this was her choice. This is part of everything also. And together they broke bread and it was decided. And then they went through the public rescinding of rights.*

D: Well, if she hadn't come back with Naomi, she would never have met him.

S: *She would have. It would have been one way or the other.*

D: Are things like this pre-ordained, that people get together?

S: *If there are debts that must be paid, whether they be for good or bad, they must be paid. And therefore these things will happen. And we must learn from them. And learn not to challenge them, for this causes much heartache and much pain. If you would just make the best of the situations and learn from them, there is incredible good to be had.*

D: Just not fight it and go along with it.

S: *Yes.*

CHAPTER 15

Moses and Ezekiel

MOSES

The story of Moses was well-known and important to Suddi since he was a master and a teacher of the Torah, which contained the Laws of Moses. I obtained many pieces of this story during three different sessions. I have combined them together and they fit very well. They contain more strange differences than any other Bible story that I received from Suddi, different yet quite plausible.

Even from the beginning it was not like our Biblical version. We have been taught from Sunday School the story of the baby Moses being born of a Hebrew woman and hidden in the basket in the bulrushes until the daughter of Pharaoh found him and raised him as her own child in the palace. The following is the story as Suddi told it.

S: *His mother was princess in Egypt.*
D: We have heard the story that he was born to a Hebrew woman.
S: *No! He was born to a Hebrew* father. *(His voice showed aggravation) This was the story that was circulated around in later years, to protect her from a Hebrew child and a Hebrew father. Moses was the son of the daughter of Pharaoh.*
D: Why was this something they had to cover up?
S: *Because at that time the Hebrews were all slaves in Egypt. Though Moses was of noble descent, 'tis said that he was of the House of Joseph, (pronounced:* Yoseph) *he was again of a Hebrew slave in Egypt. I think the story was for her protection, that it was said that the child was found. It was said that he was*

162

found from the river in a boat of rushes. It is not the truth.

D: He was raised in the house of Pharaoh? Did anything happen later that made him leave?

According to the Bible story, after he was grown he accidentally became a murderer. When the Pharaoh discovered this, he wanted to slay Moses, but Moses fled into the wilderness to escape his wrath. Again Suddi's version disagreed.

S: *He was not made to leave. He discovered that his father was a slave. And his father being a slave, he also was slave. And said that he would live with his people. It was part of the training that was to stand him to good, so that he would be able to withstand what was to face him.*

D: Our stories seem to be a little different. We've heard that he went out into the wilderness.

S: *He was sent into the wilderness for daring to love princess Neferteri, who was to be the wife of Pharaoh. For this he was sent into the wilderness. This was after he decided to become a slave. If he was still Prince Moses, he would not have been sent into the wilderness. Rameses knew that Neferteri loved Moses and was jealous. Therefore he decided that to send one into the desert was to kill one. Therefore he believed he had done away with Moses. He did not know that the hand of Yahweh was on him.*

D: How did he learn of his destiny if he was in the wilderness? (I was thinking of our story of God speaking to him from the burning bush.)

S: *I do not know! I was not there! I have heard that he was visited by angels. I have heard that he just opened himself up to his inner being. There are many stories. I believe a lot of it had to do with... he just could not stand it. He was free and happy and his people were slaves in Egypt.*

D: Our story says something about a burning bush.

S: *I have heard of this one saying that God visited him as a burning bush. (Sigh) It sounds rather strange to me. Why would God burn one of his own bushes in order to gain attention of a mere mortal? Would he not just say, "I am Yahweh, you will listen to me?" I believe that He spoke to Moses' soul and Moses listened. Some people have it very difficult believing that someone can hear God inside. They must have some outward expression to say, "Yes, God has spoken to me. " To hear God one must just open the heart and He is there, in every breath and every moment. One must just listen.*

Of course this seems to be too easy for most people to accept. I asked if he had the story of the Red Sea and whether it was the same as the story we are accustomed to.

S: Who knows? Do you mean when that they crossed the Red Sea? 'Twas said in some tellings that the sea was parted, but this was not true. The truth of it was, they just crossed. They had the ability to... how do I say? That through the thoughts and efforts of all, that the energy just uplifted them. So that it is said that even their feet did not get wet.

D: Do you mean that they walked on top of the water or floated above the water?

S: Yes. Some could say that the waters parted, such that when they took a step, they did not touch the water. (He became frustrated at his inability to explain this satisfactorily.) To put the energy to walk upon the water, or however you want to say this, is with nature. It is not against nature. You are just enforcing, putting energy so that the surface is solid. You see? To part a sea is totally against nature. When you are doing anything with the laws of energy, you must always go with nature. To go against is to cause something else to fall out of place and to cause great harm and great damage. We are taught at the community to use energy in these ways. With faith, anything is possible. You must believe.

D: But there were many, many people crossing the sea. Do you think they all believed?

S: No. But enough did that they accomplished this and the others followed after. But the people of Pharaoh did not have the faith or the ability to do this, and therefore when that they took a step, they just went... whoosh to the bottom.

Even though I did not understand what was so obvious and simple to him, I proceeded to another mystery connected with Moses: The Ark of the Covenant.

S: It is the ark of Moses' covenant with God, yes. It is... how do I say this? A channel in which to communicate with Yahweh. It is part of the communication. It is also part of an energy exchange. It is said that it held all the secrets of the world and the universe.

D: It has been said that it contained the Ten Commandments.

S: *The books are there, yes, but it is, like I say, a* channel *to Yahweh. It is part of something that was once much greater in another time. And we were allowed to keep some of the secrets. In this manner you may learn the secrets of everything. The Levi keep the secrets of the Ark. They are the sons of Aaron.*

D: Where is the ark now? Does it still exist?

S: *It is protected. They (the Levi) have kept the secrets among them. It is said that in the time of Babylon and later, that several times it was captured by kings and emperors who wished to bend the power to their will. And in so doing their kingdoms fell. And the ark was again put in hiding many times. And it has again gone into hiding. This was a gift. The knowledge was given to Moses and Aaron to build this. And then Yahweh realized basically that man was not ready for this. And therefore man must be protected from this. The energy was too great.*

D: Can the ark be destroyed?

S: *No, never. It is only by an act or a will of God that it may be destroyed. It is protected by the Levi.*

D: I've always heard that the ark is dangerous.

S: *To those who have not pure hearts and right intentions, yes. It would kill you. The energy level of this is so great that it could cause your heart to stop or your mind to cease to function. To no longer inhabit the body.*

D: Is this why Yahweh thinks man is not ready for it?

S: *Because for many years man tried to bend it to his will, to do what he wished it to do. It is said that he who had this would rule the world. This is why it is in hiding.*

D: Will man ever be ready for something like that?

S: *Who am I to judge? It can only be hoped for. It is said that many people were killed by this. At one time it was in the inner sanctuary of the temple of Solomon. But the power of it almost destroyed the inner sanctuary and it was hidden from there also.*

D: Do you think the Ark of the Covenant had something to do with their ability to cross the Red Sea?

S: *The ark was not there. It was not made until... in the forty years of wandering. It was later made in which to store the tablets and the papyri of the Laws. Moses made the exterior, the Kaloo brought the energy source to put inside.*

D: People have changed the stories so much. Our stories are not the same as yours.

S: *It is said that every time a man tongue-tells a tale that it embroiders a little from this, yes.*

According to our Biblical versions, after they crossed the Red Sea the Hebrews were led by a cloud of smoke by day and a cloud of fire by night. Suddi had never heard this story.

S: *It is said that the staff of Moses, upon it had a great crystal that would glow. And this would tell the direction to go.*

This was another surprise. According to his story, if they were going in the correct direction the crystal would glow, and when they deviated from the path it would dim.

S: *It is said that during part of the journey, when they wandered about for so long, that the wandering was caused because Moses had lost faith and started to go in the direction that the people wished him to, instead of the way that he was being guided. It was that he had doubts. That he had lost the great faith that enabled him to do what had been done. And the dissenters were saying, "No, no, you are leading us wrong. You will do as we wish. We will go here." And this time is when they lost the way. Then it is said that he no longer could stand the fact that he knew they were lost, and his people were dying and suffering. And he prayed to Yahweh that he would again follow Him if He would just save the people. And it is said that He again would guide him.*

There is also the story of the people finding food and water by miraculous means to sustain them while they wandered in the wilderness.

S: *It is said that the manna grew on the trees. They said it was like bread which is manna, this is why it was called this. There are bushes in the wilderness that have the seeds. When they break open they have something that is... how do I explain this? It is very good to eat, it will sustain life. It is said that it was on these that they would live. I have never seen the bushes, so I do not know. And where these bushes were, they were able to strike the ground with the staff and water would come, so that they would have drink.*

D: Did Moses' staff have any special properties? It was used to perform many wonders.

S: *Moses found his staff. It is said that it was able to find water and things, but any staff will do that if properly used. It is said that the crystal was something that was handed down, many generations. That Abraham brought it with him and it was passed down and passed down. And Joseph took it with him into Egypt, to the land of Pharaoh. And there afterwards it was when that the captivity started. It was then passed down from father to son. It is said that his father, who was a Hebrew, gave the crystal to him when he became a man. It is said that for a time he wore it about his neck. It is something that was Yahweh's, therefore it was protected.*

D: Do you think Moses knew how powerful it was?

S: *I am not Moses, I cannot say. (We laughed) It is said that when that Joseph first came into Egypt, that the Hebrew were greatly honored. And then they became so many, that many of the Egyptians became jealous. And a lot of them were thrown into bondage. And it was from these that came the people who crossed the Sea, who followed Moses. It was these, their descendants, these descendants of the people of Joseph.*

D: How was Moses able to make the Pharaoh let the people go?

S: *Pharaoh was his brother. They were raised together. He was able to convince him through different methods and, some say, witchery. He cast the plagues upon them.*

I had heard of the plagues of Egypt since childhood and always thought them fascinating. They are found in Exodus *7-12.* Maybe this would be a chance to explore their meaning from Suddi's point of view. There are ten mentioned in the Bible:

1. The river water turns to blood;
2. Frogs;
3. Lice;
4. Flies;
5. Murrain, which is a plague or disease of animals;
6. Boils;
7. Hail mixed with fire,
8. Locusts;

9. Darkness;

10. Death of the first-born (resulting in the institution of the Passover).

D: Were the plagues real?

S: *Yes, but a lot of it was... Moses was a very intelligent man. The last plagues in which they said that the sky darkened and the waters ran red. It is said that, when the sky darkened he knew that upstream... he had been made aware of the knowledge that the volcano had exploded. (He had difficulty with that word.) And the fear of the waters running red? He knew that in a couple of days that this would happen, because upstream this is the color of the land. And if this would come into the river, the waters would run red. It was made known to him. There was supposedly the locusts and things. I do not know whether they all occurred. I do know that some of them were just being informed of the fact that certain things were happening.*

D: A very clever man. Then you think much of it was not really the wrath of Yahweh?

S: *Until the last, no. In which the starting of the Passover. It was, yes. This was done that Yahweh promised that an Angel of Death would be sent. This does not sound like the God that I know, to be vengeful. But, nor does it sound like the God that I know of, to slay all the men upon the face of the earth, as He did when He spoke to Noah and told him to build the great ark. This does not sound like my God, but these are what we have been told. It is said that there was the plague of the boils. It is said that this was part of the death that is brought with the rats. The painting of the doorways, I think that this has a lot more to do with the fact that the Israelites were kept healthy, rather than the Egyptians being struck down. I think that they thought themselves... immune.*

D: Yes, the story says that they painted the doorways and this made the Angel of Death pass over.

S: *This is what is said. I have also heard that they hung different herbs about the houses.*

D: Then you think it was a disease that was carried by rats, and boils were one of the symptoms?

S: *Yes, this is what I have been told. This is what our teachers think, that this is a very good possibility.*

D: It was only supposed to strike the first born.

S: *No, it was not just the first born. It struck the first born and half the people of Egypt. It is said that when that Moses told*

Pharaoh, he said that it would strike down his first born. It did not say that He would strike the first born of all. It just said that this was what he saw, and that this would happen. He did not curse it, he just foretold this.

D: Our story is that Yahweh did it to make the Pharaoh release the people.

S: *I think it had as much to do with Yahweh as it had to do with man. But Moses, with a little bit of foreknowledge a man can do much.*

D: You said he used witchery, too?

S: *This is what some people would call it, yes. The being able to see what will happen before it is occurred.*

D: You've already told us that there are masters in the community who have this ability. Could Moses have been a master trained in this?

S: *It is very possible. It is said that his father was a priest of the faith and of course his mother was the Princess of Egypt. He was taught by not only the Hebrew priests, but also the priests of Egypt. He was half Egyptian, why should he not be taught in this manner?*

It is amazing what can happen when you introduce an original idea to an open mind. I was suddenly able to look at things I had taken for granted all my life in a new light. The idea was radical, but could it be possible to explain the plagues of Egypt in this way? Suddi said the river ran red from the disturbance upstream. The Bible says the water stank and people could not drink from it. Could this have been caused by the volcano spewing sulphur into the river? Any country dweller can tell you this natural chemical will make well water undrinkable. And sulphur water can certainly stink.

The frogs left the river and overran the land. That could also have been caused by the changes taking place. Animals are very sensitive to nature. When all the frogs died, the Egyptians heaped them into stinking piles. Thus the plague of flies could have occurred naturally by their attraction to the dead frogs. He said the darkness was a result of the volcano, and this could also explain the hail mixed with fire. This phenomenon has been known to occur during volcanic eruptions.

Suddi said the plague that resulted in the death of the people and instituted the Passover was a disease caused by the rats. This would explain the plague of lice, because it is known that fleas carry the germs of the Black Plague. The disease of the animals and the boils as symptoms in humans could all be related. The plague of locusts could have been a natural occurrence or as a result of the volcano disturbing the atmosphere, It is strange how it all falls into place and must be considered as possible, yet it never even occurred to us until Suddi introduced the idea.

The Hebrews were slaves and their living compound was separate from the rest of the Egyptians. By staying inside their houses until the Angel of Death had passed over they were observing a self-imposed quarantine. They were kept away from the disease-carrying rats and the infected people. This is an interesting idea that could be open to all kinds of elaboration,

D: When did Moses first get the Commandments? Was it after the wandering in the wilderness?

S: *Yes, he had first heard the voice of Yahweh, and he was direct to Mount Sinai. And he went upon the mountain, and 'tis said that there he communicated with God and he received these Laws from God.*

D: Do you think he really did speak to God?

S: *Yes, it is said that he was someone different when he came from the mountain, than who went up. I think he was very much someone different. He was open to the knowledge and more.*

D: How did God give him the Commandments?

S: *I'm not sure. They were written out. Some say that they were written with the finger of God. I think it is more like some of our people who write the scrolls. It comes out through them. When they write on the scrolls, it just comes without thought. I think it was in this manner. They were carved out on clay tablets. (Such as were used in Qumran by the students for the practicing of writing.) He came from the mountain with the laws of God, and it is said that he was shining, that even the air about him shimmered. And when he came down, they had made the golden statue to Baal and Durue (phonetic), breaking most of the Commandments already. It is said that in his anger at them, that he shattered the tablets, and then had to go and have them again written. In being touched with God and the glory of that, he could not stand that the people were so base. He could not understand that, and felt that they did not deserve any word of*

God. Moses is said to have been known for his temper, so it was probably true.

D: Why did the people make the golden statue to Baal?

S: After forty years of wandering around in the wilderness and then suddenly having time to sit and do whatever they wanted to, they went a little crazy. The people had Aaron. But Aaron was not as strong as his brother in will, and was more bendable.

D: Was Moses on the mountain a long time?

S: I do not remember. I think a year, I'm not really sure.

The Bible says that Moses was so angered by the people's actions that in addition to shattering the tablets, he also caused the slaying of thousands of his own people in a burst of rage. Suddi does not agree. He says Moses' anger was spent when he destroyed the tablets.

S: He did not have authority over them. They were self-ruled. He again wrote the tablets. I do not know whether he went back to the mountain to get them. But this time the people were much more subdued. And they later found the land that they had been promised. It is said that Moses was not allowed to come into the land but died before. This was because of his doubts and following the wishes of the others. When that there was doubt and he stopped following the lead (the crystal) that Yahweh had given him. He showed himself that he was not yet prepared, that he needed more time. It was a new generation that went in. It was not those that wandered about the desert. I believe Aaron was the only one of the original who went in. There are many stories of Moses, he was very wise.

EZEKIEL

Much has been written about Ezekiel and his strange vision, so I thought this would be a good Bible story to ask Suddi about. However, I have the feeling he might have been confusing the stories of Ezekiel and Elijah, either because they are similar, or maybe the originals were more alike than our versions.

S: Ezekiel. It is the name of one of the prophets. His story is in some of the scrolls. Ezekiel was a prophet and a wise man and one of the teachers. He was odd, he lived by himself most of his life, having few students. And it is said that later in his life that he was told he would not die, because he would be taken directly to God. To me this sounds like vanity. Though it is said that he was visited by some of the others and taken away, I do not believe that these are people of God.

I did not understand what he meant by "others."

S: *There are others similar to us, but not the same. It was by these that he was visited. They are not of earth, they are from elsewhere, though we are not told where. We are just told that as far back as there is a remembrance, there have been visitors. And some people are more blessed, more chosen, whatever. I'm not sure what the qualifications are. But some are visited and some are, again, taken away. But some are left here to speak of the experience. It is said that his followers told of his leaving in a... I believe they used the term "chariot of fire." It may have looked to them like a chariot, but it was more like one of the flying machines of old than a chariot. It may have spit fire, I do not know. There were different types.*

Maybe the writers who have speculated that Ezekiel's vision was of a UFO may not have been very far from the truth after all!

S: *And he went. Whether he decided to go with them or they just decided they wanted him, I do not know. It is said that he has never been heard from again. I have no way of knowing. I'm not real familiar with this scroll, it is not one of the Laws. I have heard of it and read it when I was but a child.*

I was curious as to what he meant by the flying machines of old.

S: *Very long ago there were machines that had been built that went through the air like birds. The knowledge was learned and they used it. For the most part, it has been lost now, from what I understand. There are still some of the people, the masters, who have the knowledge but it is not used. The knowledge is in the library. It is part of the teachings of the mysteries. It is just better not to use this.*

D: Do you know how these machines were powered?

S: *No, I do not know. They used something for a central focus. Other than that I... again, this is not my study. I just know a little from what I have spoken to others about. It is said that the Babylonians had the knowledge in the early days. I do not know how true this was. The people who gave the knowledge to us were the Kaloo. It was before the speech to others was cut off that the Kaloo had the ability to do this. They had many great things, but the ability to use them was lost. Or if not lost, decided that it was better not to be utilized, because it had brought about so much harm and destruction.*

D: If your people have the knowledge, could they make these flying machines if they had to?

S: *If it was necessary, probably yes. I'm not an engineer. I do not know.*

He gave a description of them: *"They were made out of different things. Some were made out of wood, others made out of metals, bronzes, gold, strange blends of metals. Some were very small and some were quite large."*

I assumed they were used for travel, but I was surprised again when I asked him their purpose. He answered nonchalantly.

S: *They used them in war. They were utilized for travel also. But the greatest ability that they considered of them was the ability to overcome an enemy from great distances, utilizing these. They had weapons that were placed upon these machines.*

D: Did the enemies have the same kind of machines?

S: *Not all of them. Most of them did not.*

D: Does your story say what happened to take the knowledge away?

S: *(Very calmly) The world was destroyed. A cataclysm. I do not know of exactly what type. It was as if the forces of nature just rebelled and the earth exploded.*

He never ceased to shock and amaze me with these unexpected statements.

D: Do you think it was caused by the war that was going on with these machines?

S: *I do not know. I was not there.*

He said the Kaloo were some of the people involved in this war but he could not remember who some of the others were. I wondered if their fighting was confined to just one part of the world.

S: No, they were fighting in several areas. There was great unrest.

This gave me a very uncomfortable feeling. This sounded too much like what is going on in the world today. Could history be repeating itself? After this destruction occurred, he said the Kaloo began to wander, thus not everyone was destroyed.

S: No, but those who were left were hopefully very much wiser. Because they had gained knowledge they were allowed to keep the learning, and the ability to do this. Provided that they would not utilize it again to destroy themselves and others along with them. It was forbidden. The knowledge is preserved in hopes that someday it will be able to be used safely.

D: How did these people escape?

S: I do not know. The story is unclear. There was knowledge that it would happen. They were sent out before the destruction began. Away from where the destruction began.

D: Do you think anyone will ever find any of these flying machines?

S. It is possible. Metal lasts for a long time. There are bound to be some of them somewhere.

D: Do you think anyone will ever find any of their cities?

S: I do not know. There is no specific place that we are told of this is where that they are from.

So asking about the Bible story of Ezekiel produced a bonus I had not been prepared for.

CHAPTER 16

Creation, Catastrophe and the Kaloo

THE CREATION

When he was telling me the story of Adam and Eve, he mentioned the story of the Creation of the world. I decided to pursue it.

S: The Formation, yes. It is not from the Torah, 'tis from before. It is said that in the beginning there was just dark. All was dark and there was a void. And God seeing this, He decided that there must be something done to fill this void. There was nothing *there, it was empty. And God said that there must be something there, for this is empty and I am empty. Therefore it was out of Himself that all of this came, for when it was decided... there was instantly something there, the masses. It was as great clouds that were forming and coming together so that they were brought into essence. And this went on for a while. The forming of these things, what would later be, yes, the stars and the planets. It was part of God. There were definite bodies being formed, of planets and stars and different things. And this was found to be good. But again there was an emptiness, a feeling of not being whole. So then He decided to place beings upon this. And there were much decisions to be made about what they would look like. Many tries and changes and finally He settled upon the animals that He wished to be there.*

D: Did anyone help Him make any decisions, or did He do it all by Himself?

S: There were the others. The Elori, the whole, everyone. I'm not putting this across very well. (Sigh) It is not Elori, it is Elorhim, they are all. In essence, everything, everyone together.

175

D: I've always thought of Yahweh as being an individual....

S: *(Interrupted) Yahweh is... He is ours, He is to us as the others are to others. He is the individual that is interested and concerned with us. There are other... gods, as you would call them. Other beings that helped and worked with Yahweh. They are total, they are together. They are part of a whole. As one, but separate. They each have their concerns, but when it comes to things they must do together, they do it as one. When they are together there is a wholeness, a completeness that is there. Upon occasion they are allowed to work together. But once the decisions were made as far as which divides which area, they kept more to themselves than they did before.*

The concept of One God over all dies hard. Suddi said that Yahweh was part of the Elorhim but was not *over* them. They did not need anyone over them, *"They* are." Each one had their own area, so to speak, but they also worked collectively together if need be.

D: Is Yahweh concerned primarily with our planet or our solar system, or just our people?

S: *All. Our galaxy.*

This difficult concept he was trying to convey was still confusing to me, so I switched and asked about the decisions that were made concerning what to put on the planets.

S: *There were many things that have been changed. Many things were placed there and decided that it was not whole. It was not complete, and changes were made. Therefore they were no more. They had to see which would fit and be the whole and be complete there.*

It sounded like experimenting. They tried different ways and if they did not work out they were destroyed.

S: *Or they were changed, yes. Some of them were of the right ideas, but not perfect. Therefore, they were changed and made different. And when once that He found that these were good, there was much desire of His children to find out what experience would be here.*

D: What do you mean, His children?

S: (He had difficulty finding the words to explain) The... angels.
(pronounced 'an-gels'.*) The spirits that were formed at the*
moment when... See, at the moment when there was nothing and
then there was, there were parts *of them that had been formed*
and were smaller beings of light and essences. This was formed
at that moment.

As though when everything was created out of the void, there was
such a tremendous burst of energy that little sparks flew off, and
these little sparks became the individual souls or, as he called them,
"angels." In that respect we were all created at the same time.

S: And these were some that were curious and decided they would
see what it was like to live in this existence. The earth was not
barren, there was life and things. The trees had been created and
the water and the lands had settled and... we could go on forever
with what had been done in this time of before they ever stepped.
Everything was in an age of 'Let's see what we can create and
how beautiful we can make it'. And it just continued on for a
long time.

Apparently this occurred after the earth had been developed and life
was established. The animal kingdom was already well-formed and
primitive humans were existent when the spirits became curious to
try this new experience.

S: There were beings on earth. These were what the souls once
entered their existence into. To bodies similar to these when it
was done, when it was finally set, that this was how it would be.
First a few at a time came, the venturous and the curious. Then
there were more. Soon the earth was greatly crowded and these
were some of the times when great evil was here. For the
existence in these bodies had warped them, so that they were not
perfect any longer, and had problems and vices and things.
D: Well, when the Elorhim were putting these spirits on earth, did
they allow them...
S: (He interrupted emphatically) The spirits were not put. *They were*
allowed to experience this. It was their choice. It was never a
force. Things were very beautiful for a while, as long as they
were not earthbound. For a great long time they were able at
will to leave the body, so they kept it from being warped. When

they were allowed to leave the body, the body was left to breathe and to continue on existence usually with a shape-like form. And when they communed with the other spirits who had not had these experiences of earthly existence, they saw what they were and how beautiful that was and became once more this, the beauty and the things. It was when they lost this communication and this ability to communicate with the others, to know what they really were, that they became changed. It was when they lost this ability that they started changing and growing misshapen.

D: If the body is misshapen, is this a negative force that this body has to deal with?

S: *No, no. It does not have to do with this. Some people who are misshapen are very beautiful. Perhaps they wish to better themselves because they are handicapped. Perhaps they cannot use an arm and they must compensate and be greater for it. And the people who are greater for it are so much more beautiful and more toward the perfect than those who just sit and say, "Oh! I have this arm! Oh, help me, help me!" Do you understand?*

D: Yes, they are having to work harder but they are growing because of it.

S: *Growing so much more, yes, if they accomplish this.*

We understood now, he did not mean a misshapen physical body, but a misshapen or warped spirit.

D: Did people live longer in those days?

S: *How not? Because every time that you left your body it recharged and more energy was able to be entered into it, therefore they only left the body when it was their choice. (Died?)*

D: This leaving the body, does this resemble our periods of sleep?

S: *Somewhat. These are people, when they sleep they are able to do these things. There are some who still do it at will. This is a great, great ability. It is not exactly the same. It is different. There must be more control.*

This sounded similar to out-of-the-body experiences. In those early days this rejuvenated the body and thus the body lived much longer than ours today.

D: Whenever Yahweh and the Elorhim were creating, did they put life on just one planet, ours?

S: *(He interrupted indignantly) No! There are many in his area, it is said. They put life in different ways, yes. It is said that at one time the moon had atmosphere and was alive, and it is now destroyed and dead. I know not much of this, I have just heard of this.*

D: If there is life, do any ever visit from one planet to the other?

S: *If the knowledge is beneficial for them to do this, they are allowed to do this. For the most part if they are dangerous to others, they are not allowed to ... what do I say?.... yes, communicate.*

D: What people would be considered dangerous?

S: *The people who would destroy themselves would be dangerous to others. Mankind has done this! Man has destroyed himself many times, through different methods. God has almost obliterated everything that was, because of man's horrors that he has done. Men kill. Animals do not kill animals except for certain reasons. It is man who will kill another man for* no *reason.*

D: We have always heard the stories that Yahweh destroyed mankind. Do you think it was man's doing?

S: *Is God so judgmental that He would destroy even the innocent? No. This is something that occurred because of man. Is it not easier to lay the blame about Yahweh, than to shoulder it yourself?*

D: Can you give us an example of one time that mankind destroyed his world?

S: *It is said that this is why the Kaloo wander, because the world was uplifted and changed. There are many methods of using power and forces which I do not understand, but are no less real because of this. They wanted to use the power for their own selfish ends and means. They were people who quest for the self and what was not necessarily good for them, pleasures, different things like this. They destroyed themselves and caused themselves to be destroyed.*

By using more energy than was wise, by using it in matters that were not good and disturbing the natural balance of nature. I know that there was a void created and where there is action there must also be something that follows. Therefore when they took and took and took, there must be a pulling back. When the earth pulled back its power, there must be some great damage done. And it was this force that caused the destruction.

179

D: Then you think it was a natural thing rather than something they caused to happen?

S: *Yes, but it was something that they had created. They* did *do it, because they had been warned. They had been told that this would go on and therefore they brought it upon themselves.*

This makes one wonder if this might have something to do with ecology and environmental problems.

NOAH

The biblical account of Noah and his ark has always been a favorite of mine, and I was curious to see what he would say about it.

S: *Yes, about the flood that came? It is strong of hope, this may be why it is a favorite. It is one to show that it* shall *continue, no matter how dark it looks. It is said that Noah was a great individual, a very good man. And God saw this and was pleased, for He knew that he had kept what was good and right, and all of his sons followed the ways of Yahweh.*

D: Why would Yahweh cause a great flood?

S: *Again I believe that it were more a case of continually fighting against the earth. Also, I have heard that this possibly occurred in the time before everything was settled. Or, approximately the same time that there was the explosion of power. This could cause this to happen. If the seas changed, therefore would not the water just tend to go everywhere in many ways, rain, or different things like that?*

I do not think that all of this was of a rain of forty days and forty nights. This could not happen. It may have rained for this period of time, but I believe it had something to do with the changing of what land was there so that the seas would rise in one place and fall in another. I think that during this time that there were other changes as well as the rain that caused the floods. And it is said that Noah took, let me think here, seven of clean and... two of unclean. The animals that were taken were seven of clean and two of unclean. If an animal was not... if you were not able to eat this, then there were only the pair taken, so that there might be others later.

180

Creation, Catastrophe and the Kaloo
I asked for an explanation of the clean and unclean animals.

S: Let me think. It is said that the clean are those of cloven hoof and of the cud. For if they have but one and not the other, they are not clean. Such as the swine has the cloven hoof but chews not upon the cud, therefore this is unclean. The oxen, having of both, the bullock may be slain and eaten. The sheep, also having both, may be eaten. But the camel, though it chews cud, does not have the hooves. It has more of pads rather. They are cloven but it is totally different, and therefore they are not eaten. The horse has no hoof that is cloven and therefore is unclean, and the ass. Noah was told to take seven of the clean, so that there might be food and the animals that would be eaten could continue on (they would reproduce), so that they would not starve. He had prepared a large... (He had difficulty finding the word) ark that he had been given the dimensions. I do not remember these. The animals had been called, and they came and the choices were made, and they were brought aboard. And everyone laughed, of course, because, I mean, he was building this great boat in the middle of desert. And they say, "You're crazy." But he tells them, he says they should be warned because Yahweh has spoken and He shall make His wrath known. And this, of course, they laughed at him for saying fairy tales and things.

You see, they could not understand that they were doing this. That this would be occurring because of them. And they did not even want to understand that this would happen if God had decreed it. They chose to ignore this, though they had been warned. Noah took his sons and his wife and the sons' wives and their children. He took all that he could fit that were there, Provisions had been made. Grain had been stored and different things like this. It is said that he was out there for approximately two turns of the moon. Sixty days ... no, fifty-eight. (Here again showing the use of a lunar calendar.) There were signs. First the dove was sent out and it returned home. Then the second time a crow was sent out and it did not return, and by this they figured that it had found something. And then again the dove was sent and it returned bearing part of a bush, I'm not sure what, and it returned to its mate with this. Therefore they knew that it had found land. And they were able to find this point, 'twas a very high mound, and to come to land. Then they began building of civilization. The first thing they did was offer thanks to Yahweh that they had been spared, because there was destruction all around.

I was wondering why the significant rainbow had not yet been included in the story.

D: Was there anything else that happened at that time that was important?

S: *The children of Ham were cast out because of something. I do not remember, he did something and displeased Noah.*

Where's my rainbow? I hinted around about Yahweh giving them a sign as a promise that He would never do this again, but Suddi did not have anything like that in his version of the story. Finally I just came right out with it.

D: I see our stories are a little different. We have the story of the rainbow. When the ark landed Yahweh put the rainbow in the sky and said, "This is my promise. I will never do it again."

S: *This sounds very lovely, but I know not of this.*

D: You have no story then of where the rainbow came from?

S: *(He laughed.) 'Twas here! I don't know, I've never questioned. Some say that it is a sign that God is pleased, that Yahweh is smiling. It is very beautiful.*

I remember about why the flood came about, though. This was part of the time when that man was struck, so that he no longer was able to speak one-to-one to everyone. This knowledge was lost and it was closed up. And therefore there was great confusion upon the world. They spoke to one as one, to think was for the other to know. And this was lost, this ability, because of their doing. They thought, they told each other, "If we do this great thing, we can become as great as Yahweh and find the way to be even greater, to have more power." And because of this, it had been lost and the confusion was brought. Yahweh took away this ability and man was struck dumb because he had never had to communicate with others in any other way, and it was a great loss. Then he learned to speak with the mouth with words. Before this, there was no need.

Creation, Catastrophe and the Kaloo

This story sounded familiar. Maybe this was where the story of the Tower of Babel came from and what it is supposed to signify. The loss of telepathic powers through misuse.

D: Before this ability was lost, could they communicate with people over long distances?

S: *Yes, it was as if they were with you. It was taken away because man was proud and doing many things that he was not... he was subverting the law of nature. And therefore he caused great destruction. And this was lost because of this. It is said that the very earth exploded, as if to spew man off its surface.*

I wondered if this catastrophe was the same one Suddi had mentioned before that was connected with the wandering of the Kaloo.

S: *I do not know. You see, our knowledge comes down to us in bits and tatters and pieces and we must piece this together here and say, "Well, what is this?" And so not all threads are whole. And this is what we are trying to do. We are trying to make everything whole and put it together.*

D: Put all the pieces together and see if you get the whole story. That's why I'm interested. You know when books are changed from one language to another, many things are added and taken away.

S: *Sometimes it is intention.*

D: That's why we're curious, because our books are written differently.

S: *What do you mean? These books... what are these? Why would it be much different if it is supposed to be as the Torah, which is the work of God? Why would it be different?*

D: (I had to think fast again.) Well, you see, in the times that I live in, different languages are spoken. And whenever they change something from one language to another, the words are changed and the meaning is changed. In our ... what would you say ...? translation? That is taking something from one language and...

S: *(He interrupted me) And putting it in another, yes, yes. Perhaps something has to do with the person who is also writing it?*

D: Could be. You understand because you have other languages in your time, too.

S: *Yes, the people no longer speak of one tongue. This is because of the great harm that man did.*

D: Some people where I come from have mistaken ideas.

S: It is said with each telling of tales, the tale grows longer.

D: And many mistakes are made with the retelling. There is much to learn, isn't there?

S: To stop learning is to die.

THE WATCHERS AND THE KALOO

Suddi had already said that much of their knowledge had been passed down from the mysterious Kaloo. But I wondered if it could have also come from *other* sources. This was a subject Harriet was greatly interested in. With the protectiveness Suddi had about certain aspects of the community, there was a likelihood we would not get any information, but I thought it worth a try.

We were speaking to him as an older man.

Harriet: Have you and your community ever had contact with beings from another world or another planet?

S: Yes.

This was a surprise, because the question was just a stab in the dark. When the same question had been asked of the child, Suddi, he didn't see how it was possible to come from points of light.

S: It is those of the Watchers who guard what we do. They are pleased in our efforts to keep the knowledge, to bring about the peace.

His answers were evasive. He said they were contacted in different ways. Sometimes it would be in person. His caution came back strongly when I asked if they ever came to the community. *"I will speak of this no more! It is not a subject of discussion!"*

Any time this would happen it was useless to pursue the line of questioning. His need to protect would always override Katie's answering my questions. Sometimes the answers could be obtained by using different wording or by going all around the question. But he would never discuss this subject again. At least, not while he was *alive.*

When a subject is in the spirit state, the so-called "dead" state between lives, I have been able to obtain much information. Most of this will be presented in another book. I will present only what is relevant here. While Katie was in this state after the death of Suddi, I thought it would be a good time to find out more about the Watchers. He was never quite as secretive in that state. I said I wanted to try to find the answers to things that he had not been allowed to discuss because it had not been permitted in his culture.

K: *There are still many things that cannot be known now.*
D: That can never be known?
K: *No, just at present. There is much knowledge being gained, but there are things that must also be protected.*
D: Yes, I can understand that. But I think there are some things that are important enough to pass on to other people.
K: *(Emphatic) But it is not for you to decide what is important. But if it is permissible I shall answer.*

I could understand him being protective while he was alive because there were things he had sworn to protect. But I did not think I would also encounter a protective attitude on that side.

K: *There is more danger in the knowledge that all share on this side in the hands of the warped on yours.*
D: Have you ever heard the term 'the Watchers'?
K: *Yes, the Watchers are those from outside, from other worlds, who have been for as long as there is memory here on this earth. They have been studying mankind as a whole and hopefully... They wish us to succeed. They wish us to find the right path. But they are there, perhaps, just in case it is not found.*
D: Then there is life on other worlds?
K: *And why not? Have you the conceit of all the universe at saying that this is God's only point of life? That He created all of the heavens and all that is, and decided that on this one minute, insignificant planet, that this was the only place that He wished to make life? This is the greatest conceit that there could be.*

After he calmed down, I asked him to continue about the Watchers. He spoke very deliberately.

185

K: *The Watchers mean the highest intentions. They wish to hurt no one. I'm not saying that there are not those who are of the same high-mindedness. There are others. But the Watchers are our own protection, and more or less, safety valve. If we were to completely destroy ourselves, they would try to avert this, by whatever means that they could. Because, for us to destroy this earth, would it not have repercussions upon the whole universe? You cannot destroy one body and not have echoes ... forever.*

D: Do any of the Watchers ever incarnate on any of the planets?

K: *They have assumed forms that would be considered human, yes. They have done it on our world many times. But it takes a very special individual to be aware of them. One who is very open to influence, of emanations from them. Because the replicas, as it were, are very good. The beings, the forms that they assume are replicas. They are not exactly human. But then there are also those who would take the forms that humans would consider more normal. They would have bodies, yes. They are not to the point that they are just beings of energy. There are those that are, but they are not of the Watchers.*

D: Then they are not born into a body as a baby, as humans are?

K: *There have been* spirits *of Watchers who were born into bodies, but then they are as human as you, with a more high-minded soul perhaps.*

D: You mentioned beings of energy, are they different?

K: *Yes, they have passed the need for a physical body.*

I have read the term "light beings" in many books. He said this could be another term for them.

K: *Some of them are souls that never left the side of God at the Formation. Some of them are those who have again attained that perfection. Some are from other worlds that are beyond the capability of human understanding. They are so far advanced that they look on us as a human looks on an amoeba.*

D: Do you think we will ever attain that type of development?

K: *(Sigh) Not with the present pathways.*

D: Do these others also revere Yahweh?

K: *All revere Yahweh! God is* all *and* all *are God!*

D: Is there any special way that the Watchers help?

K: *If they influence one person he could possibly influence... even a country. Then they have done good. They have done their purpose. In this manner they are helping to keep the peace. Helping to ... how do I say that?... keep the balance, as it were, intact.*

D: Do they have spirits such as you and I?

K: All spirits are the same.

D: Do you know which other worlds they come from?

K: They come from several groups, but that is not knowledge that I am to be allowed to pass on.

He was apparently being censored from that side also. He did however admit that they were from within our galaxy, but not from our own solar system. They have been watching the earth since there were men placed upon it. I asked about any possible life forms in our solar system.

K: Yes, there is life here other than ours, but perhaps not always in life forms as you would consider them. Some are spirits. But there are places here that there are the beginnings *of life.*

I tried to take him to around the year 70 AD so he could possibly observe and tell me what happened to Qumran. It was supposedly destroyed in 68 AD and I thought I could find out about its fate. But when I took him there, he was in the resting place trying to forget everything.

When people have crossed over, they often go to the schools that are there. But if they have had a series of especially difficult lives and they do not desire to go to school at that time, they will go to the resting place for a while. When a person is there, they sound very sleepy and will not communicate. This place was also mentioned in my book, *"Between Death and Life."* The spirit just wants to rest and sleep and not be bothered about anything. I have had people stay there for a few years or a few hundred. It depends on how hectic their last life was or what they are trying to forget. Time does not matter there any more than time matters while they are at the school. But when they are in the resting place, it is useless to ask questions.

Thus I tried a different tactic this time because I was curious to find out what happened to Qumran. I took Katie to just before she went to rest. Sometimes when a person has crossed over they have the ability to see future events if they wish to. Maybe she could look ahead for me.

D: From your viewpoint you can see many things that are going to happen. You were so closely tied with the community for such a long time. I wonder if you can see what is going to happen to Qumran?

K: *Many shall be slain, and it shall be overrun by the Romans and ransacked. For its need is past.*

D: Do the Essenes know this is coming?

K: *Yes, and it is their choice to stay. The secreting of knowledge was begun many generations ago. Much of the knowledge has gone into hiding. The knowledge that shall not fall into the hands of others, until it is time to be unearthed at a later date. Then it shall be uncovered when it is time for that knowledge.*

This happened when the Scrolls were found in the many caves. Literally "unearthed," as he said they would be. But what about the other important things that have not been found? The mysterious objects in the library: the model, the star gazers and the crystal? He said it was very possible that the model would be taken away and hidden, but he was not certain.

I thought if anyone ever found it, they would not know the purpose of it anyway. It would only appear to be rods and bronze balls. It must have been a soul-searching decision to take the model apart, because they knew in so doing no one would know how to start it again. But it was probably better to hide it than to have it fall into the hands of the Romans. This was one of the things they had been sworn to protect since the Kaloo gave it to them aeons ago. All of these decisions must have been very difficult, for they knew they were coming to the end of an era, the closing of a door. The only solution they could think of was to hide the valuables in the hope that maybe somewhere, sometime, someone would find them and be able to understand what had been so precious to them. They must have known they were taking the chance that time, the elements and marauders would take their toll.

When I asked about the crystal, Katie's body suddenly jerked uncontrollably. I did not understand this physical reaction but he said, *"It is gone! It has been moved. It is not in the area. It was placed on another source of light"* I did not think at the time to ask him what he meant by that, but now I wonder if it was possibly taken to another planet? I asked why the question had bothered him. He paused as though he was listening to someone.

K: *They say it is not time for that.*

D: Well, I would like to make a guess. Do you think the Watchers might come and help take some things away?

K: *It is possible.*

D: Yes, that would be one way these things would not be found again. If all these things are gone, people in the future will never know how advanced the community really was.

K: *They will be hence, at the time when the world is ready to hear it.*

D: After the destruction of Qumran, will any of these people be left?

K: *Yes, they will go elsewhere. Some will survive with knowledge. Others will survive with only memories, to be reawakened at the time of need.*

I wonder if he meant the kind of memories we were now awakening with our experiment?

I changed my questioning to see if I could find out anything about the mysterious Kaloo.

K: *They are those who you think of. They are from that that you would call in your time 'Atlantis'. Part of this name difference is, when people speak of what is called Atlantis, they do not realize that instead of just being one, that there were many governments, many countries on that continent. The Kaloo were not made up of all of the people. This was but part of that.*

D: Do you know what happened to them?

K: *There are still some alive on earth. They are the guardians of some of the secrets that are being protected. They guard many things. Knowledge of them shall resurface.*

D: What happened to their country?

K: *Great destruction occurred because they did not follow the laws of nature. But those who are wise in the ways knew that it would come about, and sought to save knowledge so that the spark that was mankind would not be snuffed out.*

D: Was the catastrophe a natural phenomenon?

K: *It was a combination of nature crying out against what mankind had done to it.*

D: While he was alive Suddi talked as though there was a great explosion.

K: *There was partly an explosion, that was some of it. They misused the balance of nature. When you draw too much off of nature and do not replenish, you cause imbalance, therefore this is what occurred. Many were warned very early that this would happen and left the area. Some left on airships, some left by the seas in hopes that at least some of them would survive.*

D: Was a crystal involved in any way with the final destruction? (Other writers have suggested this and I wanted to check it out.)

K: *Yes, one of them. There were several. Some of it is to do with overload, misuse, mis-channeling of power. So much, it ultimately has to come back to where it began. For every action there is a reaction. This is what they did not take into consideration.*

D: Suddi told me there was a war and they used the airships.

K: *There was, this was part of the ending. But the war that he spoke of has not been.*

This was a shock we were not expecting. It made the hair stand up on the back of my neck. When I was transcribing the tape about the war, it made me uneasy. The world conditions that Suddi was describing were too similar to our own. It sounded so much like history repeating itself that it made me uncomfortable. This statement only reinforced that feeling.

D: Why did Suddi think it had already happened?

K: *Confusion of information.*

D: He did say it comes down to them in bits and pieces. But he spoke of airships of old.

K: *There were airships of old, yes. But the war that he spoke of had not occurred. He was speaking on one hand of the warships of old, which did exist, and on the other hand of a prophecy that was made of one that would exist. This is what you have when you have pieces of information. Those who think they are in a place to be able to know and make judgement upon, they would fit them askew. They fit their ideas, and therefore they must be correct.*

D: I don't know if you are allowed to give us this information, but can you tell us when the war will occur?

K: *The war that he spoke of, the prophecy, what many do not understand is it does not have to occur. This is a prophecy, and prophecies can be changed. If enough entities put the right energy into it, that this does not have to happen. Nothing is set until it has occurred.*

D: He said the Watchers were some that might try to help.

K: *They are trying to help, but they cannot do the job of thousands of men with only a handful. It must come from the desire among the people to avert this catastrophe. They must be made aware of what could happen. They must know what would happen if the prophecies were allowed to be fulfilled. If it is presented correctly, they will at least nurture the seeds.*

D: Why is it so difficult to get information from Suddi? If this is so important, he should cooperate more.

K: *Each entity has the personality at that time. Therefore the habits, what has been ingrained in each of them is there. If someone told you, as you are, to do something that was against everything that you had been taught, you could not do this. Therefore, do not ask it of him. For you would hurt if you would take the feeling of trust and misuse it.*

SECTION TWO

THE LIFE OF JESUS

CHAPTER 17

The Prophecies

There were many ways this regression material could have been presented. The incidents in the life of Christ were actually dispersed throughout the entire three months that we worked on this. I could have left them in context and written the life of Suddi in chronological order. But I felt the story of Jesus would have been diluted, lost among the tremendous wealth of material. I feel the life of Christ is too important for that. I believe it should stand alone, so I decided to combine all of that material into one section.

It could have been a book by itself, but then it would have lacked the basis I have tried to present. I wanted to show what life was like in that desolate community and let the reader come to know the personality and wisdom of one of the Essenes. Thus, with the life of Jesus presented against this background, we can have a better idea of the environment in which he lived and studied. And to see some of the beliefs and knowledge he was exposed to during his most vulnerable years. Only in this way can the missing parts of his life take on new emphasis. Only then can he be seen in a new light and hopefully be understood as the great human being that he was.

It has already been shown in the earlier chapters that some of the Christian beliefs and rituals have come directly from the Essenes, notably the rite of baptism and the passing of the cup. When the Dead Sea Scrolls were translated, these two rituals were mentioned as being part of the Essenic daily life. Many writers have commented on this after studying the translations. The similarity between these facts and what Katie recalled surprised me and was something I would have never suspected. I was amazed again by the accuracy she had shown in the reliving of Suddi's life.

In his book, Ginsburg says as the Essene advanced through the different stages of development within the community, he or she came to the highest level he could attain. "At that point he became the temple of the Holy Spirit and could prophesy. Above all things the gift of prophecy was regarded as the highest fruit of wisdom and piety. Then he advanced again to that stage in which he was enabled to perform miraculous cures, and raise the dead."

I think this passage leaves little doubt where Jesus learned these abilities. It sounds to me as if these studies would come under the teachings of the Master of Mysteries. Suddi, being taught foremost in the Torah, the Law, had only minimal training in other fields. But Jesus had to learn everything from all of the different masters.

The Scrolls are still being studied today, but reports ceased immediately after the translations began. Why? What did they discover in the ancient writings that they did not want the world to know? Did they find the same things I have? Were they afraid the Christian world would be shocked by the findings that Christianity was not created with the ministry of Jesus, but was born out of the teachings of these apparently self-denying men and women who devoted their lives to loving all mankind and preserving knowledge for future generations? I am not the first to bring forth this idea. I was surprised that many other writers have come to the same conclusion after examining the evidence.

One of the first was Dean Prideaux, who wrote *The Old and New Testaments Connected* in the 1600s. He said that people in his day were inferring from the agreement between Christian religion and the documents of the Essenes, that Christ and his followers were none other than a sect branched out from that of the Essenes.

In 1863, Graetz wrote in his second edition of the third volume of his *History of the Jews,* that Jesus simply appropriated to himself the essential features of Essenism, and that primitive Christianity was nothing but an offshoot from Essenism.

Again from Ginsburg's 1864 book I quote: "Those who style themselves the true evangelical Christians are very anxious to destroy every appearance of affinity between Essenism and Christianity, lest it should be said that the one gave rise to the other."

This idea has been brought out more and more by the writers of the books on the Dead Sea Scrolls, that the connection is very evident and very real. One author stated that most of the theologians know this and only the layman is ignorant.

In the December 1958 issue of National Geographic, there was an in-depth article about the discovery and translations of the Dead Sea Scrolls. I quote: "Certain striking parallels exist between the beliefs and practices of the Essenes and those of the early Christians... Scholars of all faiths recognize these parallels. They are facts."

Still, everything that is known about this wonderful group has been obtained from the ancient writers and the excavations of Qumran. I hope that what I have found will open another door and allow a glimpse for the first time of their lifestyle and beliefs. A glimpse that is impossible to attain from the sifting and dating of remains and artefacts found in a silent ruin. I hope the scientists will use this book as a valuable tool to understand these mysterious people and Jesus' association with them. Maybe at last the whole story has been revealed and Jesus emerges even more wonderful and glorious than before. We can appreciate him as a living, breathing human being as seen through the eyes of one of his loving teachers.

D: You said that you spend time with the defining of the prophecies. Can you explain what you mean?

S: *Throughout the Torah there are many prophecies given. More than half of them upon his birth. They say the Messiah is coming. For us, we must know the time, and show that we may know him. It is for us to keep this knowledge so that in the future it may be shared with others who have gained understanding. We are studying how that ... it is said that out of whose House that he shall come. He shall be of my house. He shall be of the House of David. And he shall be born in the city of David, which is Bethlehem. It is said that he shallbe spurned by others because he comes from Nazareth. And nothing good comes out of Nazareth.*

D: Why? What is wrong with ' Nazareth?

S: *At one time it was fit for nothing but cutthroats and no accounts.*

And it is said that nothing good comes from there.

D: Then why do you think he will come from there?

S: Because the prophecies say.

D: Do your prophecies say when this will happen?

S: It is said that the time is soon, very soon.

D: Will he be born or will he just appear?

S: He shall be born of woman.

D: Is anything known about the parents?

S: It is said that they will know her when they see her.

D: What about the father?

S: Only that he shall be of the tribe of David.

D: Is there anything else you can share with us?

S: It is said that Elias shall have to come before to pave the way.

D: What do you mean?

S: He shall be reborn. He is to pave the way. To let those know who are listening that the Messiah comes.

D: Do you know who he will be reborn as?

S: I do not know.

D: What about the Messiah, is he going to be the rebirth of someone else?

S: He is Moses or Adam, it is the same.

D: Can you tell me how long the Essene sect has been here? How long it has been formed?

S: It is said that the first ones were not even Jews, but were known as the men of Ur. It was far in the past. They brought the knowledge of some of the prophecies and the symbol of the cross.

D: Is that one of the symbols that the Essenes use?

S: Yes.

D: What type of cross is it? I've seen many kinds and they're all shaped differently.

S: It has two short arms, a loop for a head and it goes down.

D: Some of the crosses have all the arms the same length.

S: This is not. (It sounded rather like an ankh, the Egyptian symbol of life.)

D: What does it symbolically stand for?

S: It is the symbol of salvation.

D: Can you explain that?

S: It is said that it shall be understood when the prophecies have been fulfilled.

D: Salvation to me indicates saving from something. What or who is to be saved?

S: It is somehow bound up with the fate of the Messiah. Of all this I am not sure.

CHAPTER 18

The Star of Bethlehem

There has been much discussion and controversy about the Star of Bethlehem. Many think it never existed, that it was merely a myth or legend. Others think it may have been an extremely rare conjunction of stars or planets. A conjunction occurs when two or more planets happen to cross paths in the sky and appear from our vantage point on Earth to have merged into one great star. This has occurred many times throughout history, but rarely of the magnitude described in the Bible. According to Werner Keller in his book, The Bible As History, many experts place the occurrence in 7 BC, when a conjunction of Saturn and Jupiter was observed in the constellation of Pisces. Chinese records also refer to a bright nova (a sudden burst of light from a distant exploding star that may take millions of years to reach us) being seen in 6 BC.

There are also old records of bright comets appearing about this time in the Mediterranean area: Halley's Comet, for example, visited in 12 BC. Many, many explanations have been presented, even that the star was really an alien spaceship. It is a known fact that Jesus was not born in I AD at the beginning of our Christian calendar because of many inaccuracies in the early dating system. The only thing certain about this controversy is that no one is certain about what the Star of Bethlehem was or when it occurred.

I was certainly not thinking about any of this and it was the last thing I expected to come forth while working with Katie. This episode occurred during our first session when we had just encountered Suddi and I was trying to find out more about who he was. I feel extremely honored that we were allowed to participate in such a glorious event. I had merely asked him to move forward to an important day in his life. This is a routine command to keep the subject from bogging down in the boring mundane things that compose everyone's life. Moving them to an important day is a way of moving the story of their life forward. What is important to one person is not necessarily important to another and this adds to the validity of the account. Thus this was the last thing I expected when I asked him to move to a day that he considered important, counted him there, and asked him what he was doing.

He said he was with his father and they were watching the stars. Not an unusual thing to be doing, but there was something different about her voice. A quiet excitement, a feeling of wonder and awe that alerted me to the fact that this was not a normal night.

He took several deep breaths and said, "It is the beginning of everything. To be able to see this for myself. It is all that I could ask. To know that the prophecy is being fulfilled." Katie (as Suddi) clasped her hands together in front of her and her body seemed alive with excitement. Suddi continued, "It is the coming together of the four tonight."

See Chapter 3. Suddi's father had told him there would be a sign in he heavens when the Messiah was coming. "It is said that from four corners that stars will rise together and when that they meet, it will be the time of his birth."

There were many of the Essenes with Suddi and they were watching from the "waiting point of the hills," which was probably above Qumran. He could hardly contain his excitement, "Never in my wildest hopes!" His voice contained so much awe it was almost a whisper. I asked him to describe what he was seeing.

S: It is like the heavens themselves have opened up and all of the light is just shining down upon us. It is like the sun of day! It is so bright! They are ... they come together. They have not met so that it is larger than it will be.

He formed a large ring with her thumbs and forefingers touching, to show how the stars appeared as they moved in to merge. It was clear that he was seeing something very unusual.

His excitement was contagious and his voice gave me goosebumps. This was only one of many times I wished I could see what she was seeing, but we would have to settle for the second-best of Suddi's eyewitness description. It seemed there were four stars coming in together to one point.

S: And it is said when that it becomes as one, in that moment he will take his first breath.
D: Do you know where he will be born?
S: He is in Bethlehem. It is of the prophecies.
D: How are the other people with you reacting?
S: They are all joyous. It is ... everyone is beside themselves. They are filled with joy and ... the energy that is coursing around us. It is as if the whole world holds its breath in expectation.

His voice was vibrating with emotion. There was no doubt in my mind that he was witnessing something extremely out of the ordinary.

D: What do you plan to do? Are you going to try to find the Messiah?

I assumed anyone at the time who would have knowledge of what this strange astral phenomenon meant, would naturally want to go and see him. It would really be a breakthrough to get that story. I didn't know at the time that there would be plenty of time later to learn of the Messiah.

S: We shall not. It shall be for them to come.
D: Do the prophecies say who will find him?

S: It is said that he shall be found by others and then they shall leave.

D: So you're not going to go to Bethlehem and see if you can find him?

S: No, for there will be dark years which shall come soon. Then he shall come to us. We shall be prepared for him.

D: This has been prophesied that he will come to your people?

S: Yes, it is known.

D: Will he learn from your people?

S: Not so much that he will learn from us, as to be awakened to what is inside.

D: And you have the ability to help awaken this?

S: We can but try.

This was the first indication that Suddi might be able to give us first-hand knowledge about Jesus. I fully realized the importance of this and intended to follow it wherever it led. She was taking big, deep breaths as Suddi watched the stars move closer together. I asked if he knew what time of the year it was.

S: It is the beginning of the year. The new ... year has just passed.

It is interesting to conjecture here that he maybe referring to Rosh Hashanah (or "Rosh Shofar," as he called it), the beginning of the Jewish New Year, which now occurs in the fall. The experts say there were three conjunctions of Saturn and Jupiter during 7 BC, and taking many other variables into consideration they think the Star may have been the conjunction that occurred on October 3rd, which would have been shortly after the beginning of their new year. Of course, when I was asking these questions I had no idea their year was any different from ours and I asked if it was during the season we call spring. He answered, "The season of growth is coming, yes.

D: What year of Herod is this now?

S: It is the twenty-seventh, I believe, I don't....

He seemed to wish we would stop talking and go away and leave him alone. He was so involved with what he was watching that he seemed perturbed by my questions. He showed his impatience, "You don't see it?! It is so ... beautiful!" There was so much emotion in those words. He seemed surprised that we couldn't see it also.

D: Are you going to do anything in particular whenever the stars all meet?

S: We will watch ... and give homage to him, for he is our king.

This could have taken quite a while, for the stars were obviously slow-moving, so I decided to speed things up by moving him ahead to when the stars had all come together and then I asked him what he was doing.

S: We give praise to Yahweh for his granting us that we be here. And we know that it is the great Ya (?) honor for we have lived in the time of the fulfillment of all prophecies. We are letting him know that we are striving to do our best, to be prepared. For this is a great honor that is being bestowed upon us. And, though we know we are unworthy, we hope to rise to the honor.

His hands were clasped, and the foregoing seemed like a prayer. I asked for another description of the stars now that they had all four come together.

S: There is a beam... it is like a tail. It comes down with all of the light. It is like a focus that drops straight from the star. And it is said that in this light shall he be born. (Or was the word 'bore'? There is an interesting difference in definition here and it opens up speculation.)

Suddi said they were within perhaps fifty miles from Bethlehem so they could not see the exact spot where the beam of light touched the earth.

D: Is it brighter now that they are all together?

S: It is like most of the light is being focused. In that it is no longer scattered about, but in a precise point. It is about the brightness of a very large, full moon.

I was preparing to ask him another question, when I noticed Katie's lips were moving quietly as though in prayer. I could almost see Suddi on his knees with his hands clasped toward the star and praying with an enormous heart-felt emotion.

D: You can say it aloud. We would like to share this moment with you.
S: *No! (Emphatically) Would I tell my soul to others? I tell my soul to Yahweh.*

I was quiet for a few moments in reverence and allowed him to continue until it looked as if he had finished. I was not rushing him to go on to another scene. This must have been such a dramatic moment, I wanted to let him savor every drop of it.

D: Has Elias also come again?
S: *He has been born also. It was a few months before. His father is known to its, for he is of us.*

Thus this prophecy had also been fulfilled. There are many references in the New Testament to this prophecy that verify that the people of the time accepted the fact that John the Baptist was the reincarnation of Elias. When Jesus was speaking of John to the multitude: Matthew 11: 10, 14, "For this is he, of whom it is written. Behold, I send my messenger before thy face, which shall prepare the way before thee... And if ye will receive it, this is Elias, which was for to come."

When the angel was telling Zacharias that he was to have a son named John, we see in Luke 1: 17: "And he shall go before him in the spirit and power of Elias, to turn the hearts of the fathers to the children, and the disobedient to the wisdom of the just, to make ready a people prepared for the Lord."

D: This must be a very exciting moment. I really thank you for sharing it with us. This is something that happens once in a lifetime, to see something as beautiful as this.

S: *It is more than a once in a lifetime, it is once in forever.*

D: That's true. And something we would never have been allowed to
   share if you hadn't talked to us about it.

It was such a tremendous experience I thought Katie would surely
bring the remembrance back with her. When I brought her forward to
the present time and awakened her, it was a bit sad that she had no
memory of what Suddi had seen. I had been very tempted to suggest
that she bring this memory forward. But we had decided in the
beginning of our work together that it would be advisable to allow
these experiences to stay in the past where they belonged. Can anyone
imagine how confusing it would be in your normal waking life to carry
around the conscious memories of so many different lives? I think it
would be extremely difficult to get on with the business of everyday
living. There had been times when Katie said she would later
remember fleeting glimpses of scenes. But these would be similar to
the fading fragments of dreams that we all experience upon awakening
from a night's sleep.

CHAPTER 19

The Magi and the Baby

We had gone forward in the life of Suddi and came to a time when he was visiting his cousins in Nazareth. He was sitting in the square watching the children play in the fountain. I wished to question him further about the phenomenon of the Star of Bethlehem in hopes of understanding it better. I also hoped to get more information about the birth of Jesus.

D: Before when I talked to you, you said you knew all the prophecies of the coming of the Messiah, and you were looking for him. Why is the Messiah so important?

S: *He is important because it is he who will bring light to the world. He will deliver and give hope to those who are without. He will show us and others how that we may gain our souls.*

D: Then he will be a very special person.

S: *He is a very special person, though he is but a child.*

D: Have you seen him?

S: *Once, when his parents came to us, asking us to help. For they knew of Herod's plans and they had to leave. They sheltered with us for many days while things were gathered so that they might make their journey in safety.*

D: Do you know what Herod's plan was?

S: *To slay all children born within a two year span. Because it was said that the Messiah had been born and he thought in this manner he would capture him in his net and rid himself of this worry.*

D: How did Herod know that the Messiah had been born?

S: *When the Magi came and stopped at the palace. They thought, mistakenly, that if a king was to have been born, surely it would have been born in the palace of the king. They spoke to Herod, and through them he learned that the Messiah had been born and he would be called King of the Jews. And this Herod could not hear. Therefore he, when the wise men had left, he ordered that this edict be followed. Because if there were a King of the Jews born, then being as he was known as King of the Jews, it would also follow that he would no longer he king.*

D: I imagine that if the Magi had known this, they probably wouldn't have gone to the palace.

S: *(Sigh) It was their destiny. For was it not written that this would occur? It was foreseen many many years ago and therefore everyone knew of it, so that we would be prepared for this. They were but following their destiny, as we must all follow our own.*

D: Some people have said that when the wise men came to Herod, it was a long time after the Messiah was born.

S: *No, for when that the Magi came to the Messiah, he was still at the place of his birth. He had not left.*

D: Do you know how many wise men came?

S: *There were three. They were men of Ur.*

D: Isn't that a city in Babylon?

S: *Barchavia (phonetic.) This is another name for, as you call, Babylon. Ur is more of a people than a country or anyplace. They are of Ur. This is their descent.*

D: I see. I have heard so many different stories. If you were there, you would know the truth.

S: *I was not with them when they spoke to Herod. But I have heard of this, and I know it to be true.*

D: How did the wise men know it was time to come?

S: *It was foretold in the heavens. It was the coming together of the planets and the stars, and they used this to guide them. They saw the star and knew it for what it was.*

D: Once when I talked to you, you said you saw the star on the night the Messiah was born.

S: *(Emotionally) Yes.*

D: Do you think the wise men saw the same star?

S: *All saw the same star!*

I attempted to find out, if possible, which celestial bodies were involved in the forming of the Star of Bethlehem. I thought he might possibly know the names of the various bodies.

S: *There are different names for them, and the different... (he searched for the right word) constellations have names. It is more that they are named in this manner than just individual stars to have names. It is said that each one of the stars that came together had a name, but I know it not. This is not my best study.*

D: Were they stars that are normally in the sky?

S: *Yes. It was just that they grew together. That their paths in the heavens crossed, as it were.*

D: Some people have said it may have been a strange star that had never been seen in the heavens (referring to the possible nova.)

S: *It was not one that was created in that instance for that, no. There are many who try to explain it in many different manners. They tried to say that it was a warning of the gods that Rome was about to fall. That it was a comet. It is said that there were points of light where the heavens opened up and shone through. They have many explanations for it. But it was God showing that this was his son, and giving us a way to know.*

There are many people who say that these things are impossible, and all things are impossible without faith. But when one believes, all things are possible. I cannot doubt it, for I saw it with my own eyes. All I know is that when it came together, that the light was great enough to cast shadows. And it was strong enough that you could not sit and stare at it for any length of time. It was something that had never in the known memory of man ever occurred before. Who am I to judge God's ways of doing things? The wise men - it is said that there was possibly a fourth. It is said that each of the wise men followed one of the stars, and at this point they met.

D: You mean they did not meet each other until they were in the area of Bethlehem?

S: *It was at least within a short traveling distance. Almost when the stars came together, the Magi met. All coming from directions, And it is said that one of them never made it, for there was one for each star.*

D: Do they know what might have happened to the fourth one?

S: *If they do, it is unknown to me.*

D: Do they think they came from four different countries?

S: *It could he said that they came from very distant lands, yes, four different points of origin.*

D: Do you know which countries?

S: *It was not spoken of, no.*

D: People have said that if the wise men saw the star in far away countries it would be hard to *see* the same star, and by the time they got to Bethlehem the star would have been gone.

This has been one of the arguments. If the star was one single bright light, it couldn't have been seen because of the curvature of the earth.

S: *This is true. The tales grow longer with each telling. But, they followed the stars who were growing together, for they knew what would occur. And they had been watching for hundreds and hundreds of years for this very happening. When that the star became one, it was seen ... everywhere.*

D: The magi must have known the prophecies, too, or at least knew how to read the stars.

S: *It is said that the men from Ur were the ones who gave us many of our prophecies. They also gave us Abraham.*

The original combined star was extremely bright on that night, and could still be seen in the sky for almost a month afterwards, but the light could not be seen during the day.

S: *It was only a focus for one night. It was... how do I explain this? The light was not quite the same. It was as if after they had initially come together, they were again separating and going their ways, so it grew less and less bright. It was perhaps a month for the light to be gone totally, yes.*

People have often wondered why Herod gave the order for all male children of two and under to be slain. Some say this is proof that it took the Wise Men that long to journey from their countries to Bethlehem. But according to Suddi's version, that could not have been true. He said the Wise Men found the Babe while he was still in the place of his birth.

I realize the Bible is open to many interpretations, but I think Herod waited for a while for the Wise Men to return to him with information of the child's whereabouts. Then I think he probably sent soldiers to find them. All this would have taken time. When he discovered the Magi had left the country, he angrily proclaimed that all the children within a two-year span be included so that the Child would not "escape his net."

D: What do you call the Messiah?
S: (He hesitated.) We call him not.
D: He has no name yet?
S: He has name, but to name him would be to name his death, and he must be protected.

This was unexpected. Apparently if people knew his name, word might leak back to Herod or his soldiers, and they would know whom to look for. It would seem that Herod would feel sure he had killed him in his slaughter of the children and he wouldn't have to worry about him anymore. But the Essenes thought he should remain anonymous until the time to reveal his identity arrived. This caution might present problems for my gathering of information. I asked if he had heard any stories of his birth, hoping to get something akin to the Bible version.

S: We know the story of his birth. He was born in Bethlehem, this is all that is needed to be known. It fulfilled the prophecy. At some later date he will again fulfill another prophecy in which, where he comes out of, it will be known. And an object of disbelief because of this. But to tell too much would be foolish.

He was apparently referring to the prophecy he had mentioned earlier about nothing good ever coming out of Nazareth. Still pressing for some sort of information, I thought Suddi may have heard of the Virgin Birth. Surely it would not endanger the Messiah if he told me of any unusual happenings connected with his birth.

S: He was born in a cave, if this is considered unusual.

This sounded strange but there are many references in the *Lost Books of the Bible* to Jesus' birthplace as a cave. The ancient Church of the Nativity in Bethlehem is built over the sacred grotto or cave that is recognized as the supposed birthplace. Caves were also used as stables in those days.

S: There are many stories about his birth. There will be many more in the years to come. But this is for a later time for this to be known, To know where he was born exactly would be to name

211

who his parents are. People are traceable. You may hunt for them and if you know enough about them, you will find them.

That, of course, made sense. I was still fishing when I assumed that if they had come to the Essenes for hiding, then they were probably not even in the country anymore. It would seem that the safest thing to do would be to leave the land of his birth, But he only parroted my remark, *"It would be a safe thing."* So, it was obvious I was not going to make him reveal any names. Maybe the next best would be to try for a description of the parents.

S: *His mother was but a child. She was maybe sixteen, no more. With such beauty and calmness, it was to be marveled at. The father was older, a very pious man. He loved his wife very much: you would see this in a glance. They had been together many times in other lives.*

D: Was there anything unusual about the baby?

S: *(His voice held so much adoration) His beautiful eyes. And the fact that he was the calmest child. He would look at you and it is like he knew all of the secrets of the universe and just gloried in them.*

D: Then he was different from the normal child?

S: *How would I know of normal children? (A natural answer, Suddi was a bachelor) They all cry and nurse and need their napkins changed. What can one say? It was as if he watched everything... to learn of it, to experience* all *at once.*

I assumed that if Suddi had seen him, it would have been such an emotional experience that he would have remembered every detail.

D: You said he had beautiful eyes. What color were they?

S: *They were never the same. One look they were gray, and the next time blue, maybe green . You were never sure.*

D: What color was his hair, or did he have any?

S: *What he had was a light shade of red, a very sandy red.*

This was a strange response that does not agree with the usual picture people have of the Christ Child. They always assume he was dark or at least brown-haired. However, this description agrees with the ones given by Taylor Caldwell in Jess Stearn's book, *Search For A Soul* and Edgar Cayce's writings about Jesus.

When the Messiah came to the Essenes for protection he was just a little baby, but Suddi knew it would be his destiny to see him again. This was another positive indication that we might get more of his story.

I changed tactics and decided to ask about John the Baptist. Maybe he would not be so protective of him and I could get information in a round-about way.

D: You told me about the prophecy of Elias returning and being born again a few months before the Messiah. You said that his father was known to you because he was one of you. (Suddi was nodding.) I have heard that his father was a priest, but I don't know of what religion.

S: *There are always the Roman religions, but it is said that the Romans believe in what is convenient. He was a priest of God. There is no other religion other than this. He was not a rabbi. He served at the temple.*

I was really unaware that there was a difference between the temple and the synagogue. In the Bible they are both referred to, but we are not taught that they could be different places and have different functions. I had always thought they referred to the same place. This is covered in Chapter 5 when Suddi explained the difference.

D: Can you tell me what happened to that child?

S: *The child and his mother are with us. He is in danger, for he also fits into the category that Herod wants slain. The father was killed. Unfortunately this edict occurred right after a census was taken, therefore they knew of the babes that had been born. And when they came to his house and asked, "Where is your child?" He told them, "I know not." And they believed him not.*

D: Was the baby there?

S: *No. The mother is very unhappy, for she feels that she should have been stronger with him, and to be sure that he had come. But he spoke to her and said, no, that he was an old man and would die in his duty to God. This was his wish.*

D: Did he know where she had gone?

S: *He knew to whom, he did not know to where.*

D: He probably wouldn't have told anyway.

213

S: No, he would have died, and did.

I assumed that the verification or the nullification of Katie's accounts would rest with the Bible since it is the most complete record we have of the life of Christ. But I was surprised to find many gaps and half-stories in the Biblical accounts. One case in point is this one about Zacharias. He is mentioned in the Bible as the father of John but the story of his fate is not. I found that the story of his murder is faithfully recorded in *The Aquarian Gospel of Jesus the Christ* and one of the apocryphal Lost Books of the Bible called *The Protevangelion,* supposedly written by James.

When I read in these stories that Elizabeth had taken the baby and fled to the hills, it was as though a bright light went on in my mind. "Of course she went to the hills," I thought. "What woman with a baby is going to be wandering around in the wilderness? She knew where she was going all the time. She was headed for the Essene community in the hills, where she knew she would be safe." It was utterly amazing how the story coming through Katie in deep trance made so much sense and was tying up so many loose ends that are left dangling in the Bible.

So far Suddi had mentioned no names except that this baby was the reincarnation of Elias. I asked if he knew the father's name. I said I wanted to know because I thought he was a very brave man.

S: The time is not now for it also to be known. Was it just not so that his child also was in danger? Therefore to name the father is to name the son.

A tinge of fear and secrecy always seemed to creep in when I got too close to forbidden topics. There were many things he felt honor-bound to protect. I was going to have to find ways to get him to release information. This protectiveness was very deeply ingrained, as witnessed in the earlier chapters. But now it became almost an obsession that he must protect the Messiah and John from any danger.

D: But they're not babies anymore, are they?
S: They are children. They have several years.
D: You said that this child (John) is with you. Does he seem to be

any different from the other children?

S: (Smiling) He is fierce like a lion. He is strong and lets everyone know exactly what he is thinking. They don't have to agree, but they are sure to know his point of view.

D: (I laughed.) Is he mischievous?

S: No, he is a good son. He looks much like his cousin (Jesus). Only he is perhaps of more blood and more like his father in strength. Whereas his cousin is calmer and finer.

D: Does he have the same color of hair?

S: His is definitely very, very red. It glows like fire around his head.

D: Some people think that those living in your country are dark-skinned with black hair.

S: Those who told you this, perhaps they have only met those who are from the south or maybe another area. But those who live here, (at Nazareth) for the most part they are light of skin and fair of hair and light of eye. There is much intermarriage with people from the south. Therefore, it is more and more being lost. There are fewer children that are born with red or yellow hair. There are more born with brown or dark.

D: Well, do you know, are there any other prophecies concerning what will happen to this child, the Messiah, in his life?

S: It is said that he shall spread the word and he shall take the suffering of the world upon his shoulders. And through his suffering we shall he saved.

We have heard this term, "we shall be saved," all our lives. But I wondered what it really meant, especially what it meant in Suddi's time. We shall be saved from what?

S. From ourselves. With the way that it is now, the way that it stands, one must always, through unstriving, say, gain the step up the ladder, as it were. Whereas, with divine intercession and asking for assistance or blessing, you may take the steps up the ladder easier. I'm not explaining this very well. My father explains much better.

D: Well, saved, up the ladder, does this have to do with reincarnation, rebirth?

S: To rebirth, yes. Of reaching the perfection of the soul, yes. For it says that a man must again be born. This is in some of the prophecies.

D: In order to attain perfection?

215

S: *To attain heaven.*

D: Well, let me tell you one thing that I have heard and you can tell me what you think. Some people say that when you're saved, it means you are saved from your sins and you will not go to Hell.

S: *(Interrupted) There is no Hell other than that that you create yourself. It is the image that you project, that you foresee. This has always to have been known. That the suffering that occurs, for the most part, is here. So that when you die, what you suffer is through your own need or desire to suffer. Why would God, who creates all things perfect, create something that was so horrid to him? This to me does not make sense.*

D: They say that he will send you to Hell to punish you.

S: *No one punishes you but yourself! You are your own judge. Does it not say, "Judge not others, lest ye yourself be judged"? It says, judge not others, it does not say self-judging. You are your own self's judge. (He seemed to feel very strongly about this.)*

D: Well, I've always believed that God was a good and loving God. He would not do things like that, but others don't agree with me.

St Mary's Well in Nazareth

CHAPTER 20

Jesus and John: Two Students at Qumran

During another session I came across Suddi while he was teaching. Again, this would not have been an unusual situation except that his hesitancy to answer alerted me that something special was going on. There was the same undercurrent of secrecy that was present so many times. The question was always how to get around this built-in guard. He admitted only that he had two students, and from his carefully worded answers I sensed who the students might be. I would have to proceed cautiously to find the answers. I asked him what he was teaching them.

S: *I teach the Law. (He paused and smiled tenderly.) This to me seems very odd. How can one teach the Law to someone who knows it better than I know it myself? (He gave a gentle laugh.)*
D: Are you speaking of your students?
S: *I am speaking of one of them, yes.*

Now I felt certain I knew whom he was teaching. But how to get him to admit it?

S: *They are both very intelligent. One is more of the fire temperament, and the other one just sits there and looks at you. And sometimes you feel so incredibly stupid because he puts a point across, and it is like you have been shown this for the first time. And you look at it with new light and new eyes.*

I told him I was surprised because I wondered what a child could teach a teacher.

S: *A child can teach many adults many things. How to love, how to be open, how to love others without considering perhaps what they will attain from the other person.*

I asked for an example of something he had shown him and Suddi gave me the following.

S: *He is very observant. He watches everything as if to learn from everything. He said that when a plant is growing, it knows when to put out new branches, and it knows when to blossom and when to seed. And it knows when to do all these things without any apparent guidance. It seems to know these things out of thin air, so to say. So, in the heart of things man can know things out of thin air, the way the plants do with the more basic things. Because man is a more advanced creature, he could know more advanced things out of thin air, and use these things for guiding his life and actions. I can not tell it the way he did. He has a beautiful way with words.*

D: Are these things that he has told you that you had not thought of by yourself?

S: *Not necessarily that hadn't been thought of. But it is like a breath of spring clearing the dust and the cobwebs away so that you may see it clearly. Perhaps for the first time.*

D: He must be an unusual child. Are your students very old?

S: *They are not yet to their Barmitzvahs. They are twelve and a half.*

Since I did not have knowledge of Jewish customs, I thought the Barmitzvah was celebrated when the boy reached the age of twelve, but Suddi said it was at thirteen. I wanted a little more information about what he was teaching them. By the law, did he mean the Torah?

S: *It is part of the Torah, but the Law is those laws given to us by Moses. The things that we must daily live by, in order to be considered holy and on the right path. These are guidelines, as it were. It is just part of the Torah. It is just one of the sections, as it were.*

D: Can you tell me, briefly, some of the laws that are important?

S: *There are all the dietary rules. There are the laws of... of course, the Commandments. The, Honor thy father and mother, and keep the Sabbath day holy, and do not commit adultery or sin, or steal or lust or any of those. Those are part of the Law. How you must treat those who work with you. How you must deal with... say, like if a husband dies, who then that the wife would become wife to. There are these laws. Everything about day-to-day existence is down in the law. Then there is the law that goes into... such as, how long that you may have a slave as part of your possession. The laws of slaves and freedmen and such useless things.*

D: What do you mean, useless things?

S: If there are no slaves, why should there be laws of them?

This was true. There were no slaves in Qumran. But Suddi said even though it was useless, it was tradition to learn these things. Of course, they would be important for someone living outside the walls to know. I asked him to explain the law of the slave and the freedman.

S: Well, after seven years the Hebrew is no longer a slave. You must be bound by law to set this slave free and make him a free man. Unless under certain circumstances. There are differences in this, but they are very few. It is very complicated and very involved, but this is the basis of it.

D: Are the Essene laws different from the Torah?

S: You would not consider them Essene laws. They are laws of nature. The law of manifestation. Where that, to desire and then to know that it shall be fulfilled, and the need shall be fulfilled. These laws are the basic laws of nature. This is what is also being taught, but there are others who would teach them this. How to utilize every part of oneself, for what is the purpose of one's life. What is the goal to ultimately reach. That goal, so that one may become fulfilled with this life.

D: These Essene beliefs are not found in the Torah?

S: It is not that it is not there. The laws are there for all to see. It is just that they are not paid any particular attention.

D: Well, to many people it's just words anyway. They don't really understand.

S: But these are the words of the Lord our God. I mean, they are holy, they must... it is beyond me how men, and there are many, go on in their day-to-day existence denying that God exists. For these I feel great sorrow, for they are going through life blinder than one born without eyes. For they have closed the eyes of their soul.

I thought I would try again to get the names of the students. He hesitated but finally answered, *"There is young Benjoseph and then there is Benzacharias."* Finally I had got through. He did not realize that I had tricked him. He could not tell me the names of the Messiah and the Way-preparer, but it was all right to reveal the names of his students since he thought I would not be able to associate the two. He could not be aware that these names would be enough for me to identify them. Apparently "Ben" in front of a name means "son of," and the names Joseph and Zacharias made it clear he was speaking of Jesus and John. He had no way of knowing that I knew the significance of their fathers' names, and that I would be able to put two and two together. Now I would have names to use that might elude the barrier of protectiveness. He could talk freely about his students without realizing he was giving anything away.

He said these were their fathers' names. They had two names: *"This is their second name, as you would word this, yes."* He still refused to give me their first names. That was all right. He did not realize he had told me enough already.

D: Have these students been studying with you very long?
S: *Since perhaps they were eight years old, about, yes. About five, four or five years.*

I now knew I could ask questions about Benjoseph and he would answer, unaware that I knew Benjoseph and the Messiah were one and the same. This method proved very effective.

D: Where did Benjoseph live before he came to you?
S: *For a while he sojourned in Egypt, and far off from there, to learn.*
D: Some people say that a child cannot think for themselves and learn anything when they are that young.
S: *This is because they are not treated as though they have any intelligence, therefore they have no need to show that they have powers of thought and assimilation. It is said that the first seven years of a child are what makes the man. He is a very unusual student. Therefore, yes, I would say they taught him. It is said that he went with his cousin to see many places farther away.*

*This I do not know, I have not questioned him upon this. I do not
feel it is my right.*

D: Do you know which cousin that was?

S: *It is one of his mother's cousins. I'm not sure, I believe it is his
cousin. His name is also Joseph.*

I was surprised that his mother would have allowed him to
go so far away, but Suddi said that she also went with them on these
journeys.

D: Is his mother living with you now?

S: *No, they live in their home. They did at one time live in the
community, but they have other children to take care of. And
there are many things that must be done in order to live day to
day. They felt that he will benefit from our knowledge and our
teachings. They come here quite frequently and visit. And he
goes home with as great a frequency. They live in Nazareth. It is
a few days journey. Maybe once a month they come to see him
and again then he goes and sees them. Therefore the contact has
not been broken.*

D: Is the Law the only thing that you teach these boys?

S: *Yes, but they study with all of the teachers here. They learn
mathematics, the study of the stars, the study of the prophecies,
the mysteries. Everything that we could possibly teach them.*

D: Do you think they are good students?

S: *Yes, I would say that they are.*

Every time he spoke of them, there was affection in his voice. They
were Suddi's only students. He had been devoting his time
exclusively to teaching them, thus the elders at Qumran must have
considered their education a very important project.

CHAPTER 21

Jesus and John:
Completion of Their Studies

When Jesus and John were fourteen years old I came across Suddi as he was writing a certificate for them. *"They must leave and this is to say that I have taught them and to have examined them and found them to have sufficient knowledge in Law to he considered first in Law. Well enough to themselves teach."*

At this point I got out a tablet and a marker I had procured and asked him to write for me some of what he was putting on the certificate. I especially wanted him to write the names of his students. But he said, *"The students will write their names in. It must be signed by them. "* He opened his eyes, took the marker and looked curiously at it. He took it with his right hand although Katie is normally left-handed. It was obviously a strange object to Suddi and he felt the point trying to figure out which end to use. He then wrote something from right to left across the paper, but to me it looked like scribbling. I asked what it said.

S: *It is just, basically, to anyone that it would be important to, that I have found that these students are first in Law. It goes on and on but that is part of it.*
D: Have they been good students?
S: *For the most part. There was some heated arguments at times. But for the most part they are very good children.*
D: Were these arguments between the boys or with you?
S: *A lot of this was between the two of them.*
D: They didn't agree with the teachings?

S: It was not that they did not agree with the teachings. Perhaps they did not agree with each other's interpretations (he had difficulty with that word) of the teachings.

D: Did you ever have any arguments with them?

S: None that I recall. (He smiled.) Benjoseph, he never had to argue. He just looked at you. If he felt that you weren't understanding, perhaps, his point of view on a certain thing, and he had gone over it several times, he would just look at you with those soulful eyes. And it was just like he was saying that, "Even though I know you do not understand, I forgive you anyway." And that would be the end of anything. Who would think of arguing then?

During all these years they were Suddi's only students. *"The classes are kept very small so that they will be sure to learn everything that has been taught. To have more would divide the attention too thinly."* Suddi had not made as many trips to Nazareth because his work with them had taken precedence over everything else. He was not going to have any more students after they left.

D: I thought you had to teach all the time?

S: No, there are times between students, yes. We are allowed time for further studies, other things to do. It is my time to go out for a while. To see what is going on in the world. It is time for a... break. I must go out and speak to others, so that they would know the great things that are happening. And give them hope and hopefully understanding of... maybe their lives and the whys of things.

D: Will you do this by going to people's homes or in a public place in the towns?

S: Sometimes both ways. We will become teachers to them. If there is only one, then you will teach the one, If there are many more who are willing to learn, then you will teach them... all that are willing.

Most of the teaching would be done by word of mouth since, *"Most of the people, they are unable to read any script or anything of this nature."* This sounded very similar to what Jesus told his disciples to do in the New Testament. This idea could very likely have come from this practice of the Essenes.

D: Are women also allowed to learn from you?

Jesus and the Essenes

S: Of course! This is understood by women as well as men. Why not?

D: Because I have heard that the Jews don't even allow the women in the synagogues.

S: They have a very narrow-minded look at existence.

D: Do Essene women ever go out to teach?

S: Usually they teach just in the school, unless it is perhaps to go to a community that they are as accepted in, as they would be here. Because it can be more dangerous for them to go out there than it would be for, say, myself

D: Do you expect to meet any opposition?

S: Yes. There are people who never return. The Romans will not like what I have to say. The people in power do not always like prophets. They are not very popular. To give hope to the masses is to perhaps break their link at control. And they feel they are losing control of the matter and this frightens them, and this is part of the problem.

D: Where are you going to go whenever you leave?

S: It has not been brought to my knowledge yet.

I asked for more information about Jesus, or Benjoseph, as Suddi called him.

D: Does Benjoseph have any brothers and sisters?

S: He has - let me think - six brothers and I think three sisters. He is the eldest.

D: Was he trained in any type of work besides his studies?

S: He is carpenter, as his father.

D: What type of carpentry is done in your community?

S: There are house people who erect the houses. There are those who build the furniture inside. There are those who would help build the temples. There are different types. The thing that he does the most is, he would build the furniture and he makes some very beautiful things. Many woods are available here. Then there are those things that must be brought in. It depends on what you wish to use it for. There is wood for furniture. There would not be wood for... say, building a temple out of it would not be done. It would be done with bricks or marbles.

D: What kind of personalities would you say the two boys have?

S: They are two very different personalities. Benzacharias is very exuberant, he is very much alive. He is very joyful with life, and the celebration of lift. Benjoseph is... he gets as much enjoyments

224

of life, but is perhaps in a quiet way. It's like comparing the tiger lily, which is wild and exotic and flashy. And comparing it to the lily, just the lily of the fields, they are very quiet and very small. But in their own way as beautiful as the tiger lily is in its exotic way.

I think it was significant that Suddi used this comparison, Jesus has been called the Lily of the Valley many times. I assume this was the small lily of the fields that Suddi referred to.

D: Does Benjoseph seem to be of a sad nature?
S: *No, he is a joyful child. He delights in everything. It is as if he sees with eyes that are just newly awakened and see the glory in all.*
D: Do you know if he knows of his destiny?
S: *(Sigh) He has knowledge. It is something that there is a very calm acceptance of. (A deeper sigh) But it is... how can one explain it? He knows perhaps what shall he to be, but his attitude is of a "Let's wait and see" and just living each day as it comes, so far.*
D: Then it doesn't bother him if he knows what might happen in the future?
S: *I am not his conscience, I cannot say if truly it bothers him.*

This topic seemed to bother Suddi, so I decided to try to get some information about where the boys would be going when they left Qumran.

S: *I'm not sure. They go on their journeys. Their pathway has been determined by the teachers. The elders know. They have knowledge of this, but it is for their path.*
D: Well, are they going to a different country or will they stay in this area?
S: *It is very possible that they shall travel to others.*
D: Do you think their parents will go with them?
S: *It is possible that Benjoseph's mother might, but it is very doubtful. Benzacharias' mother lives with us. But he will be travelling with his cousins. They will probably go again with Benjoseph's mother's cousin.*

This was the same person that Jesus had traveled with in his first journeys as a small child.

D: Will they be gone a long time?
S: Who can say? It is for Yahweh to decide.
D: Do you think you will ever see the boys again?
S: (Sadly) One I shall never see again. The other I shall see. Benzacharias, our paths shall not cross again. It has just made itself known to me. I feel a little sad, but he has his destiny and I have mine.

Maybe my question triggered the premonition. I was always hopeful we could follow the story of Jesus further, and not lose sight of him when he left the school. It now appeared that it would be possible since Suddi instinctively knew he would see him again.

CHAPTER 22

Jesus' Travels, and Mary

The next time that I found Suddi having any association with Jesus, he was around seventeen years old and was again being taught at Qumran. Benzacharias had not returned to the community but was with his cousins. I am not sure what that meant, it could be that he was staying with Mary and Joseph in Nazareth, for the brothers and sisters of Jesus were also his cousins. I thought that when Jesus received his certificate and left he would no longer have to take lessons from the Essenes.

S: *This is true, he does not* have *to. It is actually not so much teaching as it is discussing questions and talking about things. For several years he left and was on travels and has returned again. He desires instruction in certain questions that he has brought to us. There are questions as far as some of the prophecies, as to what their meanings are. Also, some of the interpretations. There are many laws which are very open to interpretations, and we are looking at different viewpoints of these things. Like, taking it one way and then looking at it and deciding if it could also be taken some other way. And what the ramifications of doing this would be.*

D: This is good, you are teaching him to think for himself

S: *And to question of things, yes. To never take something at face value. He said that in his travels he noticed that many of the teachers speak in ways that the people do not understand. He is concerned about this. He thinks there must be a way to speak to them so they will know of what you speak. By comparing the knowledge to things that they know and see about them in their day-to-day lives and in this way, perhaps they will understand the message. He watches nature and sees lessons in the simplest things, things that I could never see. (I asked for an example.) There is a plant that grows and increases in a strange way. The way it grows, it will shoot up a single plant from the roots and other plants can come up from the roots. And the branches that grow up will bend over and out, and when they contact the ground again, put down roots and start a new offspring plant. He said this was a good example of a man's cycle of lives. That the plant putting up new plants from the roots was like a man going through rebirths. And the branches tipping over and making new plants that way would be the man's family and his children descending that way while he comes back for new lives and starts new families. He uses circles in many of his examples of this. He used another plant as an example, a plant that is composed of many layers (similar to an onion). He said this would show the different planes of existence. He pointed out that, at the very center of the plant the layers are very thin and close together. If one could consider each layer as a different plane, one can see that at the center where it's the smallest and most limited, that is like the physical world. As one travels upward and outward in the planes, one's horizon of understanding would expand each time and you would see and understand more.*

Another example he came by from watching the water. He pointed out how a wave could come in from the sea and lap up on the shore, and pick up a bit of debris. And when this bit of debris is put back down it's almost at the same place that it was before, but moved over slightly. And so the piece of debris will gradually travel down the shore being picked up and placed back down by the waves. He said that this is like your cycle of lives. You go through your cycle of life, starting at one point and then when you die, it's like being picked up by the wave and then re-deposited in a life. Your spirit is re-deposited and it's a little bit further along the way of where you're meaning to go.

D: That would make sense. It would also show how slowly it happens.

S: *Yes, it is a very slow process. And one must have much patience and work on it diligently.*

Jesus' Travels, and Mary

It seemed as though Jesus was beginning to develop his concept of parables. I wonder if some of these were still too complicated for the average person of his day to understand. These are not mentioned in the Bible, most likely because of their reference to reincarnation which the early church strongly objected to. The parables that are included in the Bible show that he continued to simplify his teachings and often used things in nature as a reference.

D: Does he tend to stick to the letter of the Law or is he rather broad in his interpretation?

S: *He is broad in his interpretation in that he feels that love is the only law that one must abide by solely. And after that all the others pale into insignificance. We did not teach him this. He came by this conclusion through inner ... what do I say..? discussions with his soul, and deciding how he feels about certain things. Love cannot be taught. It is something that must just grow. And again, I am not explaining myself very clearly. The only restrictions he spoke of were those concerning harming other human beings and other living beings. To not physically harm other living beings and to try and to not mentally harm them either. He knows the power that thought has. If you think something strong enough, the vibrations sent out will cause it to come to pass, and he is aware of this. It is important not to think evil in your heart.*

D: Where did he go on his travels?

S: *Where did he* not *go? He traveled all over most of the world as we know it. It is said that Joseph (of Arimathaea), his uncle, went with him.*

Before, when I asked Suddi who accompanied Jesus as a child, he said it was his *cousin,* Joseph, although he did not seem too sure of the relationship. This may not be a contradiction, but an honest mistake. Suddi might not have been too sure how Joseph was related, except that he knew he was a relative of Mary's. He referred to him as Jesus' uncle from this point in the story onward.

D: Did his mother go with him?

S: *During part of the travels, but then she had to stay home with his sisters and brothers. His father stays and goes about his work. He is very much of* this *world, Joseph. He is a very good man, but he is very practical.*

229

D: That seems strange, to have such a difference between the mother and the father.

S: *Why is this strange? It gives a balanced look at things. You have one that is very much living in another dimension, and you have the one that lives in the here and now. It gives him a view of both sides.*

D: Are any of Benjoseph's brothers or sisters interested in the same things that he is?

S: *Perhaps not to the great extent that* he is. *They are, in the fact that they love their brother, and would be interested in the things that he is. But he has gone beyond them. Are not all brothers different from one another?*

In an earlier session Suddi had said that before the Messiah was born his mother was known to the Essenes. I wondered how they knew whom she was going to be.

S: *She was chosen by the elders to be instructed and for her destiny to be made known to her. It was known from her birth whom she would be. And her parents were of us.*

I had read in an Edgar Cayce book that Mary had been chosen from many other young girls. So I questioned with this in mind.

D: Did they choose her from others?

S: *How can we choose the mother of the Messiah? It is not up to us. That is up to Yahweh. But he allowed us to know, so that we might instruct her and perhaps guide her upon the path. The elders knew but they did not choose. It is said that there are others whose charts could possibly have fit, but there was study and it was decided that ... this was the only basic decision that I can think of was made. The chart was read and it was finally understood in what was meant. I am not explaining this very well.*

D: Oh, I think you are doing an excellent job of it. How is the chart made up?

S: *It is said that it has to do with the points at which the stars lie when you are born, and the path that they take while you live. But I do not create these, therefore I know very little about them. The master of this is Bengoliad (phonetic). I remember when that*

230

*we went to the classes they tried to teach me to follow the stars.
I'm not very good at this, it is not my field of study.*
D: But this was how she was chosen, from her chart?

He was becoming frustrated. We were having a communication
problem here understanding exactly what he meant.

*S: You still do not understand! We did not choose her. We were
allowed to have the knowledge in which to find out who she was,
in order that we might help her along this path. (Very
deliberately, as though talking to a child.) The only thing as far
as someone's decision, is about the interpretation of these charts.
There were several girls who were born at approximately the
same times that it was possible. And therefore the ultimate
interpretation came about. This was when that it was discovered
that she would be the mother of the Messiah.*

I thought I had better drop this topic, so I switched back to
Benjoseph.

D: Do you know what he will do with his life?
S: (Sadly) Yes. He is very special.
D: Can you share it?
S: It is not for me to share. It will be made known in time.
D: Do you think he will travel again?
*S: I have no way of knowing. For here he is now, he lives with us. He
said that his travels opened his eyes to many things that he was
heretofore blind of. And in this that it did great, great good.*
D: Why did he travel to the other countries?
*S: To learn of the people. It was told that they traded, which they
did. But they also did a lot of learning and speaking to people
and finding out their views on things and life.*
D: Do you think he might have gone to the religious leaders of the
countries?
S: It is not for me to say, I have not questioned him.

The next mention of Jesus was five years later when I spoke to Suddi
as he journeyed to see his sister in Bethesda prior to her death (see
Chapter 12).

D: Have you had any news lately of Benjoseph?

S: Not very recent, no. It is said that he travels. I do not know. If he returned, it was not for any length of time.

D: What about Benzacharias? Have you heard any news of him?

S: It is said that he has gone out into the world, and is gathering followers.

D: And he is supposed to be the way-shower or the preparer, am I correct?

He frowned deeply. It seemed to bother him that I knew this. *"I did not speak of this to you!"*

D: Well, someone did. You don't think you told me about it?

He quickly went on the defensive and answered coldly, "I *do not remember"*.

D: Well, I know it is supposed to be a secret, but we aren't going to tell anyone. I suppose he is not ready yet to let the people know?

S: No. He is gathering followers and knowledge and strength to prepare.

The Pool at Bethesda

CHAPTER 23

Jesus' Ministry Begins

I moved Suddi ahead again to another important day in his life. He had been staying for a while with his cousins in Nazareth. He had not been back to Qumran for many months. His voice seemed tired, *"I'm getting too old to travel everywhere."* He and his cousins were at the synagogue in Nazareth. I received a pleasant surprise when I asked if he had heard any news of Benjoseph. *"It is he who we are waiting to hear,"* Suddi announced. Jesus had been back from his travels for maybe six months, but Suddi had not yet heard where he had been. Since Suddi was just a member of the large congregation in the synagogue, he did not know if he would be able to speak with him or not. I asked him to describe what was happening.

S: *He's just reading of the Torah. And speaking of the Scriptures to (looking for the right word) define them in the terms which we can understand. He is reading about the promises that God made of the Saviour. He is reading also of Ezra and the promises that were made that Israel would again become a great nation.*

D: Has he been doing this before?

S: *It is done. From the time that you have reached your Barmitzvah, you are allowed to speak in synagogue, to read the Torah. But this is unusual. In the synagogue there are a lot of times great arguments that go on. Tonight there is no arguing. The people, they are very quiet. He has a beautiful voice that is very easy to listen to. He is also trying to explain a difficult concept about the different universes, and how all our lives are interconnected. He is using the example of a tapestry to simplify what he is talking about. The tapestry, you look on the back side and it's woven like a cloth. You look on the front side and there's pictures and action going on. The backside where it's woven like a cloth is like the structure of the universes. And the front side where you can see a pattern to it, that is our lives imposed upon the universes. He is trying to have them understand this, although some do and some do not.*

I was wondering when he started performing his miracles. I asked if the people had noticed anything unusual or different about this man.

S: Most of them just know that he is very gentle and calm. That if they have needs or problems, that they can go to him and he will listen.

Suddi's voice was very quiet as he spoke of this scene. Benjoseph was not aware that Suddi was there among the people. I could almost see the ageing teacher at the back or the side of the dimly lit synagogue, quietly listening with the others. And out of all the people there, only he perhaps, knew who this man was and what tremendous destiny lay before him as he began his ministry.

Jesus' physical description was that of a man with grey eyes, light reddish- yellow hair and a short beard. He was slightly taller than the average man of that time, very slender, "of a fine mold." He was wearing a light blue robe and the prayer robe, which is a long cloth that the Jewish men wear even today while in synagogue. It is draped about their head and shoulders like a shawl. *"His eyes are very piercing. They stare out of his face like something alive."*

D: What do you think of him?
S: (There was pride and love in his voice) I am very pleased. I think he is a good man. I think he will do well.
D: Do you think he learned well the lessons you taught him?
S: I taught him naught. I just opened his eyes to what was there.
D: Do you think he has changed since the last time you saw him?
S: He has grown more at peace. He is like a slow moving river that is very deep. You do not know what runs underneath the surface.

I thought perhaps now Suddi would tell me Benjoseph's other name. If he had gone out into the world, there would no longer be the need to protect him so closely.

S: Yeshua, this is his name.

I had him repeat it several times in order to get it correctly. It was phonetically "Yes-uah," with a strong accent on the first syllable.

D: Will you be talking to Yeshua before he leaves tonight?
S: (Softly) I think not. I think just knowing would be enough. I just wish to hear him speak words. He has grown well, and I can feel inside that perhaps I helped.

After I had finished writing this book, I came across a little known book called *The Archko Volume,* by Drs. McIntoch and Twyman, which was originally published in 1887. These men had found written reports in the Vatican Library that were sent to Rome during the time of Christ. They had them translated from their original language. One of these contained a description of Jesus that amazingly matches everything that Suddi had said about him.

"While he is nothing but a man, there is something about him that distinguishes him from every other man. He is the picture of his mother, only he has not her smooth, round face. His hair is a little more golden than hers, though it is as much from sunburn as anything else. He is tall, and his shoulders are a little dropped; his visage is thin and of a swarthy complexion, though this is from exposure. His eyes are large and a soft blue, and rather dull and heavy. The lashes are long, and his eyebrows very large. His nose is that of a Jew. In fact, he reminds me of an old-fashioned Jew in every sense of the word. He is not a great talker, unless there is something brought up about heaven and divine things, when his tongue moves glibly and his eyes light up with a peculiar brilliancy. Though there is this peculiarity about Jesus, he never argues a question; he never disputes. He will commence and state facts, and they are on such a solid basis that nobody will have the boldness to dispute with him. Though he has such mastership of judgement, he takes no pride in confuting his opponents, but always seems to be sorry for them. I have seen him attacked by the scribes and doctors of the Law, and they seemed like little children learning their lessons under a master."

When Jesus left the synagogue after the service he was going to go to his parents' house. Since Suddi was not planning on speaking with him, we probably would not have been able to learn much more. So I decided to move Suddi ahead another five years to an important day in his life. He was in Nazareth and was speaking with a friend.

S: *He says that he has heard of Yeshua and that he is beginning to preach to the others, and that the word is being spread. It is said that already in the few months that he has spoken, that great crowds come to listen to what he has to say, in hopes that he will perform a miracle. It is known that the powers are very strong that flow through him. It is said that he has cured a leper who but touched his robe. He said that it is the man's faith that made him whole. And that how could such a one, having so great a faith, be but part of a man. Therefore he would be whole. It is also said that there were the people who could not see, who could see. There are many miracles that have been said to have happened. The only one that I am sure of is the leper. A friend of mine saw this happen. He said that believing that just to touch the cloak would to make him whole, that his faith had done so.*

D: Was it because his faith was so great in Yeshua?

S: *That his faith was so great in God.*

D: Is that how you explain what happened, or *can* you explain it?

S: *I know how it is done, but to explain it is something else. The giving of the energy to heal... to be accepted is part of it. It must be accepted, and it is also said to be, to have faith in this. So therefore, the man's faith made it possible for him to be whole.*

D: It happened because the man was willing to accept the energy. Then you don't think it was anything that Yeshua, himself, did?

S: *He was a channel. I cannot explain it any better. He would often go into meditation with the person to be healed, and while there in a meditative state, he would transfer some of his energy to them. And sometimes people who were looking on could see the transferred energy.*

D: What did it look like when they saw it?

S: *It looked like a glow of light from, say, his hand to the affected part of the person's body. And their auras would start to glow brighter, to where people who ordinarily did not see the aura could see their auras.*

This would explain the halos shown around Jesus in old paintings. In the earliest ones, he is shown having a halo all over his body, and in later ones he is just shown with a halo around his head. This must have come from the stories of people seeing his aura brighten during these energy exchanges as he performed his miracles.

S: *This is why they would meditate first. The person would say they wanted to be healed, and they would get into a meditative state of mind so that they would be receptive to the energy. Because if they resisted, then it would not take place. I cannot explain it any better.*

D: Is Yeshua meeting any opposition?

S: *It is said that there are people who are unhappy because he goes around and preaches love. The Zealots are very unhappy. They wish him to say, "I am the Messiah. Follow me, I will be your King." And they would take up arms in a minute, at a moment's notice. But he shall never say this.*

D: You say that he preaches love? Love for each other, love for God?

S: *He speaks highly of love between your neighbours, love between your brothers and love towards strangers. To love someone, to share this with others is to share God with others. God is love. He is anything that fills a void that is inside. To share love with one another is the greatest thing that you can do, because it is sharing God. You are giving freely of yourself to another, without thought of return. This is part of the message. The people have accepted that the Lord God has a place in everyday existence. And they are learning to share this with one another, to grow closer, with this message.*

D: You said the people think he should just say, "I am the Messiah." Do you think he is the Messiah?

S: *(Emphatically) He is!*

D: Does he know this?

S: *Yes. This was taught to him since he was very young, who he was and what was to be. But to announce such would be they would be able to proclaim him crazy or a blasphemer. He tells them he is the Son of Man.*

D: What does that mean?

S: *He is, as we all are, sons of man and God. I cannot explain this very well. He is God's son as I am God's son, but his destiny is to*

237

bring light in a greater way than I could. He is closer to his final destiny than I am. I am so far off but he is almost to the point where we all strive. He is the next closest thing to perfection.

D: If we are all the sons of God and also the sons of Man, what is different about him?

S: He has learned his lessons and he has followed his path to its completion.

D: So you think this means he is perfect?

S: He shall be. It was his choice to come once again in order to give this light to people. He did not have to come back.

D: After this life would he ever return again?

S: So it has been said, but for what purpose I know not.

D: Do you have any news of Benzacharias?

S: It is said that he is at the Jordan and many people listen to him. And he is, as he says, a voice crying in the wilderness, perhaps to open the hearts and the ears of men to the news that the great one is here. There are many, like the Zealots, who find him very attractive, because he is so fierce. He is as a wild man. His pathway was different and I have not seen him for many, many years.

D: Do you think he has changed?

S: No, he was always very fierce.

He had been massaging his left elbow for quite a while as we talked and I asked him about it. He said his joint was giving him pain. *"I'm a very old man,"* he said with a sigh. *"They said that I have very little time left."* He said he was ill with the "coughing sickness" and had been staying with his cousins in Nazareth permanently. I gave him instructions that his arm would not really bother him and he would feel no physical discomfort.

D: Well, you have seen many things in your life. It was a great thing to be able to teach Benjoseph and Benzacharias.

S: Yes, it has been very good.

I asked who was the king at this time. He said the first King Herod had died and Herod Antipas was now king, but things were not any better. *"If anything he is very much worse."* He disliked speaking of either of them; the subject was distasteful to him.

238

Reference material refers to Archelaus as the successor to Herod, they do not mention Antipas. Suddi mentioned Philip as another brother, but he never mentioned Archelaus. I thought this conflicting and curious. Surely there would be something in the Bible about this. Both Harriet and I were reading the Bible more now than ever before, and getting a great deal more out of it as this history was being relived through Katie's remembrances. But, Antipas is not mentioned in the Bible, while Archelaus is said to be the successor of Herod. The king at the time of Christ's birth and the one at his death were both always called Herod. During the time of Christ the king is only called Herod, the tetrarch, in the Bible. Where did Katie ever come up with the name of Antipas? Again, research revealed that she was correct.

Herod the Great was Jewish by religion but a Roman citizen of Arabian blood, which may explain some of the resentment the people had to being ruled by him. As Suddi said, *"He cannot decide whether he wishes to be Greek or Jew, and therefore, he is not a very good one of either."* He also was extremely cruel. He became king in 36 BC, at the age of 37, and died in 4BC. He had murdered some of his own family, but out of those left alive, three of his sons were named to continue the rule. They were Archelaus, Antipas and Philip. It was decided by the Roman government that the country would be ruled by all three. They were to be what is called "tetrarchs."

Sometimes a Roman province would be broken up into sections, and a tetrarch or "petty king" would each rule a section. Archelaus, being the elder, was given the largest area of Judaea and appointed ethnarch or governor. Antipas and Philip were made tetrarchs over the remainder of the kingdom. But Archelaus displeased Rome, and in 6 AD he was banished from the country. Judaea then became a third-class Roman province to be directly administered by Roman procurators, (this was an official who managed the financial affairs or acted as a governor). The most famous of these was of course, Pontius Pilate. Philip was at this time ruling northern Palestine. Since he was not making waves, he was allowed to continue. After Archelaus was banished, Antipas took his place and became tetrarch over the largest part of Judaea. He adopted the name of Herod and he was the one in power at the time of the beheading of John and the death of Christ. It is amazing to me how Katie could have known these uncommon names involved with the history of the time - unless she was there.

Suddi sounded so old and tired and sad during the last part of this session. I was hoping that he would live during the entire lifetime of Jesus. I wanted to get more information about his life. How many times does a chance like this come along? But now it appeared that Suddi might die just as Jesus was beginning his ministry. I hoped to get the story of the crucifixion. But how? Suddi was in Nazareth, too ill to travel and Jesus was crucified in Jerusalem, quite a distance away. Even if Suddi lived, it looked very doubtful that he would have been able to travel there. So it appeared he would die on us before the story was finished. I hoped maybe there would be some way. But if not, we would just have to be grateful for what information we had received.

I had taken Suddi ahead in time to when he was about 50 years old. He was sitting off on the hills above Nazareth, probably not far from his cousins' house. His voice sounded so weary.

S: *(Sigh) I'm very old. I'm fifty-one ... something, fifty-two? I'm very tired. I am a very old man.*

It was hard for me to accept that age as old, but I suppose it was so in their culture. I told him I did not think of him as an old man.

S: *But it is! It is of an age where that many men have died sooner. I'm an old man. (Sigh)*
D: What are you doing up in the hills?
S: *It is not far. I could not walk far. I'm communing. Trying to bring myself into touch with the universe and meditate upon my life. Soon I will die. It is known to me. I have perhaps a year. I no longer am able to... take... air to breathe. My chest hurts... and I cough much. Thus I know because of this and the fact that I am just very tired.*
D: Does it bother you to think that your time is almost up?
S: *Why should it? This makes very little sense. This is foolishness. Why not pass on and learn from this experience and start another?*

He sounded so depressed that I wanted to change the subject, but I chose one that was also depressing to him.

D: Have you heard any news of Benzacharias?
S: *He has died. He was imprisoned by Herod... and beheaded. (He disliked talking of it.)*
D: Why was he put in prison?
S: *For preaching sedition.* (That was an unfamiliar word to me.) *He preached what they believed was wrong and against the prophets. It is like... treason against the state, only it is against God.*

She began to cough deeply. I gave her reassuring suggestions that she would feel no real physical discomfort.

D: I did not think that Herod was a religious man. Why would he be worried about what Benzacharias was preaching?
S: *Herod does not know what he believes. This is his faith and his trials.*
D: And this is why Herod had him imprisoned?
S: *That, and the fact that he was afraid of him, of what he would do. He had many followers.*
D: What exactly was he preaching?
S: *The things that he spoke of were of the Messiah, of his coming. That all sin must be faced. That they must confess to* themselves *that they were in wrong. Doing that is half of the battle toward freedom. It was Herod's idea to have him imprisoned so that he would speak with him, but it is said that it was his whore that had him beheaded.*
D: Why would a woman have anything to say about something that important?
S: *He preached the truth and the truth must eventually get through to others. (See the reference to Herodius in Chapter 6) It is said that Herod began to believe. And therefore since Benzacharias spoke so much out against her and her vileness and the life they led, she was afraid of losing power. For Herod to believe in what Benzacharias said, and to face that what he did was wrong. If he faced this, then would not he have set her aside? And thereby she would lose power.*

241

Katie paused. Suddi seemed to be having discomfort. *"There is great difficulty in ... breathing. Lack of air."* I decided to move Katie forward to relieve her of the physical symptoms.

Incidentally, I have never had a case where experiencing these physical reactions have caused any effect on the conscious personality. The subject always awakens feeling fine with no memory of any illness associated with their death in another life. All of that is left totally in the past with the other personality.

CHAPTER 24

Preparation for Crucifixion

I had moved Suddi ahead to relieve Katie of the distressing physical symptoms. When I finished counting she was smiling, and when she spoke his voice no longer sounded so tired and weary.

S: *I am among my friends. I am with my sister.*
D: Oh? Didn't your sister die?
S: *You speak of dying. There is no death. There is only other forms of existence.*
D: Where are you?
S: *I watch as they prepare my body.*

When I first began working with regressions and I found I was able to speak to someone after they had died, it was quite startling. But I have done this so many times since, it has now become commonplace, if something this strange can ever be called common. I have observed during the sessions that the hypnotized person does not become upset upon finding themselves dead. It usually bothered the observers in the room much more than the subject. The witnesses expect a violent reaction, a protesting against death, or at least a revulsion when the person sees their own dead body. Peaceful, natural deaths show no trauma at all. But the personality usually wants to hang around long enough to find out what happened to the body. You do become attached to the thing, after all. After they watch the burial or whatever, then they are ready to go on to something else.

It is also a surprise to observers that the personality continues intact after death with little change. I have become quite accustomed by now to talking with the dead after they have crossed over, but this is often hard for the other people in the room to understand. I have found you can obtain much information from the spirit. But the quality of that information depends upon the evolution or development of that spirit. Here again, they will tell you only what they know at that time.

Suddi was about fifty-three, fifty-four years old when he died in Nazareth while living with his cousins. I wondered why he had chosen to stay there with them instead of returning to his beloved Qumran.

S: *My duty had been discharged. I no longer had a great purpose to stay there. I had no family to keep me.*

I misunderstood his statement. I thought he meant there was no one to keep him, to take care of him. Surely, as humanitarian as the Essenes were, they would have provided for him in his last days.

S: *No, when I say no family to keep me, I mean my family was no longer there. Therefore, my ties were almost broken.*

This was true, his only sister had died. He had expended so much energy in the teaching of Jesus and John, maybe he had no desire to return and teach others.

S: *I traveled for a while. Talked with the people and listened to what they had to say about the prophecies. I let them know that the time had come that they had been preparing for all their lives. And hopefully, in the teachings that I did, I enlightened a few people. I left a few seeds, hopefully they gave growth..*
D: Well, sometimes that is all-you can hope for.

Earlier, when I asked Suddi what his illness was, he said he had the "coughing sickness." Now, after death, he was well aware what the trouble was.

S: *There was a cancerous growth in the lungs that had all but consumed them.*

This obviously would have caused a great deal of coughing, pain and difficulty in breathing, so he had defined it correctly in the terms of his day as the "coughing sickness."

D: Do you know what caused that?

S: *Who knows? The dust? It was... it had been chosen before that this would be the manner of my death. It was to help in my growth.*

D: Oh? To die in a certain way has an importance?

S: *Yes. To learn to deal with it on, a day-to-day basis. How to* live *with it as well as die with it.*

He had had much pain before he died but he had been able to control it *"by use of the mind and manipulation of the energies."*

D: This is good, you didn't have to suffer, because you knew how to do these things. Many people don't know how to use these mind processes.

S: *Most people do, deep within. They have just closed themselves off to this knowledge, and this is a great tragedy. It can be regained by the practicing of meditation. Of opening oneself up to the knowledge that is there. It is there just to* grasp, *but you have to open oneself up. You must start from within. That decision must be made that you* shall *be open, then it shall begin to come and it shall grow.*

D: In other words, they have to want it themselves?

S: *Yes, just as all healing must come from within. It has become time to pass on this knowledge. If people are ready for the seeds, they shall grow. It is up to them.*

He was watching as his body was being prepared. I asked what would be done with it.

S: *It shall be burned as I requested. It shall be burned outside the walls of Nazareth and my ashes shall be taken to the community. There they shall be scattered to the four winds.*

I was very disappointed that Suddi had died before our story was finished. Since he died before Jesus, did this mean our story was over? I sincerely wanted to know about the rest of the life of Christ. This had been a unique, once in a lifetime opportunity, but I was at a loss to figure out how to obtain more information. At least I could ask questions about what Suddi knew of him just prior to his death.

D: Did you have any news of Yeshua before you died?

S: *He was teaching, and he is still trying to shed light to the multitudes. There are many who are listening. He is ministering to the people. Speaking to them of love and hoping to pass the understanding upon to others.*

D: How are the people accepting this?

S: *There are always those who would believe anything, no matter what was spoken, just because it was spoken. And there are those who believe because they have considered. Then there are those who doubt because of who he is. And they say, "How is it to be that this man should have all this wisdom?" They speak of his family. That he is not a prince among men. That he is just a poor man, who has no possessions. They say, "Where are his fine robes?" And they have not come to the understanding that possessions do not make the man, but the man possessions. A man, he can have nothing, but if he has goodness and understanding and compassion toward others, he is richer than the man who has a country and has not of these things.*

D: But they don't know of his great education, do they?

S: *No. It shall not be known of how he was taught. Not taught, but showing that he was on the right pathway. Showing himself, giving himself faith in what he was doing.*

D: Why was that to be kept secret?

S: *(Sigh) We are of a people who* wished *that it remain secret, because of the problems with different religions and others. And the fact that he was* taught *was not important. The fact that was important was that he* knew. *He* has *this knowledge, this is what is important.*

D: Was he born with this knowledge or was this something he learned in his life as Yeshua?

S: *He was born wise, but he was not born with all of the knowledge that was amassed in his lifetime. He was taught in many schools. Among them, those known as the community of the Essenes. There were many lands and many teachers that he sat at their knees and listened and learned, He was shown many different ways and paths. And in turn he showed others the right ways upon their paths.*

Suddi had said earlier that Jesus had gone to all of the known world on travels with his uncle in his search for knowledge. I wanted to know more specifically which countries.

*S: There were trading outposts of the Phoenicians that they went to
in the North. There were those toward Cathay and those treks
that were traveled upon. He went to India and spoke with some
of their wise men. Egypt, to different countries of that area. He
also learned upon the shores of what is known as Britain. I do
not know if he went to others or not. He went to most of what is
known to man.*

Jesus' uncle, Joseph of Arimathea, was a trader of mostly tin and
other metals. Their group travelled under this guise, but they knew
Jesus went with them for another purpose. "*To gain understanding of
others, and also to give understanding to others.*" He was
sometimes accompanied by his mother on these journeys.

Suddi said she was called something similar to "Maria" in those
days. His father, Joseph, had been much older than she, and had died
when Yeshua was in his twenties. "*He had seen his son come to
manhood and this was his task.*"

Friends had asked me to inquire about the death of Joseph. They
wondered if maybe this was what delayed the ministry of Jesus. That
maybe he had to take the responsibility of helping Mary raise the
large family.

*S: Were there not his younger brothers and sisters? They were not
that much younger. At the time there was help by Joseph (the
uncle) and others. There were several helpers who were
carpenters, who kept the family business going, so that there was
an income. And, from time to time, Yeshua would come back and
help out.*

D: Do you know if his younger brothers and sisters ever felt
resentful that he wasn't there constantly?

*S: They were raised with the knowledge that he had much to do, and
not a great amount of time in which to accomplish this. How can
children raised by such understanding parents be
misunderstanding? They accepted. There was great love. One
could not know Yeshua and not love him. This was not possible.*

D: When Yeshua was traveling to all the other countries, why did he
come back to his own country to start his ministry there?

S: *Because, at the time, this was a meeting-place of halfway between the East and those of the West. Therefore the knowledge might be spread to a great many from this central point. And this was known.*

D: Did he have any followers in these other countries?

S: *It is said that he had a great many people who listened to his wiseness.*

D: Didn't he know that when he came back he would be in danger?

S: *Yes. He knew from a very young age how he will die. This is the hardest part to accept. Is knowing that even with this foreknowledge, that he would still love man so much, to give up of himself for them.*

D: Yes, it's one thing to not know what's going to happen to you. You don't have any control over it then. But he knows, and still is willing to do it anyway. That would be very difficult. You know, there are stories that he has done miracles. Are these stories true?

S: *Yes, miracles is the term that you would use. There are things that you would call miracles. They are not in a sense miraculous. For* everyone *has this ability, it is innate and inborn. One could develop this ability if one had the discipline and the time. To meditate and have the mental disciplines that one must do, so that one could do similar things. He was in tune with himself and with the spiritual planes as well as having great ability. And the combination of these helped him to work what are called 'miracles'. It is using the laws of nature and the universe. In his knowledge of these laws he was able to do things that others considered miraculous, but which all men have the power to do. But you must open yourself to be a channel of the power, so that these may be performed. You just must have the knowledge and the will to use it. He was just a very clear channel.*

D: Was he taught how to do these things?

S: *Yes, he was. That was part of the regimen of training when he was growing up. And since he was to be the great exemplar, he was able to develop these abilities to a very fine-tuned point. His teachers could do things, like raising objects or changing lead to gold. But he could do better things, like breathing life back into someone who was dead, changing water to wine or what-have-you. And he could, using his abilities on those who were sick, he could balance their energies to where they would be well again.*

D: I wonder how he could go about changing water to wine?

S: *It's hard to explain. It's like a combination of several abilities working together. Everything he did applied to the natural laws of the universe. It's just that some of them he applied on the earthly plane that usually apply to the spiritual plane. They can apply to the earthly plane but they have to have a medium, like a human being, to help and to channel it, yes.*

D: Have you heard of some of these so-called miracles that he has performed?

S: *He performed so many every day, that I would not be able to list all of them. But he did things, in general, like healing the deaf, the lame, the blind and things of this nature. You just must have the knowledge and the will to use it. He was just a very clear channel. He has drawn people back from this side, back into the existence, by just calling them. All things are possible with faith. One must just believe that one can do this.*

D: But once someone has left the body, wouldn't the body begin to deteriorate?

S: *After a certain time. You would not do this with someone who was six months. ... dead. But, in all of the cases that I have heard of this occurring, they had newly crossed over, and perhaps, by* mistake *had crossed over. It has not been unknown, that perhaps the body ceased to function at a time that it was not supposed to. He was not doing it to try to unbalance the cycles of their lives. But in those cases to where their life was cut short by an act of circumstance, and he could see that they had not worked out their debts yet. And it would be better if they could work out their debts at that time. He breathed life back into them so they could come back and work out that portion of their debts. Have you not heard of people who had died and then resurrected from the grave because it was not their time? He was just there to help guide them back.*

This sounded a great deal like the NDEs (near-death experiences) that are now being reported in ever increasing numbers. These are cases where people have been pronounced officially (medically) dead and then they miraculously revived. Often today this is due to our advanced medical care.

D: I thought it was an infallible, system. That you die when you're supposed to and there was never any chance of mistakes being made.

S: There are always chances of things to go awry. It is not very often. Sometimes it is also a lesson that must need to be learned. Therefore, they are let loose to the other sides, to awaken themselves to the knowledge that is here.

Suddi said Yeshua had called people back a few times and I asked for specific cases.

D: Were these people he knew or just strangers?

S: Sometimes he knew them and sometimes they were strangers. The centurion's daughter he did not know. This Roman commander's daughter was very ill. He heard that there was a prophet that could help her, so he sent a servant back to Yeshua, And it was two days' journey. And the servant says, "Please come, please hurry, she is very ill." And Yeshua says, "Wait a minute, I've got to finish what I'm doing here first." And Yeshua basically took his time getting back to the Roman commander's house. When he got there it was too late and the daughter was dead. And Yeshua saw that her life was not yet finished and she had more debts to work out. So he breathed life back into her body, telling the Roman commander, "Do not worry, she's only asleep now." Then he left. She slept a normal span of time and then she woke up and she was well. Then there was one who was his cousin, Lazarus. He was the only son of his widowed mother. He was called back. But it was not his time to die, he had much to do and Yeshua knew this.

D: I thought once he had been put into the tomb that he couldn't....

S: (Interrupted) He had not been sealed up. The seal had not been placed. All they do for preparation in this country is to anoint the body with oils. A few of them would burn them on pyres. But for the most part it is just anointed with oils and wrapped in linens and placed in the tombs or whatever.

D: How much time could elapse and they would still be able to come back into the body?

S: A few days. Maybe two at the most. After that it would require renewal of much more than just the spirit entering back.

D: One of the miracles that we have heard of- I don't know if you know of it or not - is where he fed a whole lot of people.

S: Where he fed them with just a few fish and loaves of bread? Yes, this is done through, again, the natural laws of bounty. If you have need and believe it will be there, it will be there.

It certainly didn't sound to me like a natural law to be able to divide up a few things among many people. Suddi was patient with me as he tried to explain.

S: *But you have got to believe that it shall happen, and it shall occur. He believed he could divide it and they all believed in him. I know not if it were an actual fish or if they believed in it and were sated.*

This brings up an interesting concept. If the people believed strongly enough in what Jesus was doing, it did not matter whether or not the food was solid three-dimensional physical food. It could have been an illusion. The main thing is that they believed they were being fed and thus their hunger was satisfied. That was the purpose even though it may have been accomplished by psychological means. There were many questions about Jesus' life that people have wondered about and this seemed to be a good opportunity to find out. I said, "Some people say that he had a very strange birth. Do you know anything about that?"

S: *Just that he was born in a cave and there was a star gathered overhead. This was the only unusual occurrence of his birth.*

The Biblical version mentions only that Christ was placed in a manger after his birth, it does not say where the manger was located. Even today caves around Bethlehem are used as animal stables. Suddi had not mentioned one important aspect of the birth and I had hoped he would tell me without probing. Since he did not, I decided to come right out with it.

D: Some people say that his mother was a virgin. Do you know what that means?
S: *This sounds very familiar, but this is not true. His mother was a woman like others, just like his father, he was a man.*
D: Well, the story we have is that the mother was a virgin and the father was not a human being, the father was God.
S: *We are all children of God. He was more open to this than others and it was the time for the knowledge to be brought forth.*
D: Why do you think people would tell a story like that if it were not true?

S: Why do people say anything, other than to just bring more attention to certain aspects?

I thought maybe I could find out something about his disciples.

D: Does he have any specific followers that are with him?
S: The number varies. There originally were approximately thirty in the central group, and more who are just followers. He is their teacher in hopes that they will learn from him. But some of them have many doubts, they are but human. His disciples can perform miracles, too, because they are studying under him. This is part of the studying, teaching several meditation exercises to help make one receptive to these things, and to develop these abilities. They spend much time alone up in the hills studying these things. There are both men and women followers, although there are at times slightly more women than men, because the female develops better. They are more receptive to things of this nature than the male.

It does not take much imagination to figure out why there is no mention of female disciples in church history. The early church was strictly male oriented and dominated.

D: Do these followers go with him everywhere?
S: Has he not sent them out to teach others what he has taught them? And they must go upon these paths.
D: What happened to the women disciples?
S: They are very active. When Yeshua split up his disciples, it was in pairs of two. And the women disciples were split up also. They have been sent all over the known world to spread his teachings and to have disciples of their own to help spread these abilities they have learned.
D: Isn't this dangerous for women to travel like that and to have these powers?
S: The way he split them up was generally male and female paired together.
D: Oh. Because you know the way the male dominated world is, they do not accept women doing these things.
S: Yes, he knew of this and he wanted to protect the women from those who did not understand. And so the disciples were sent out in pairs. Usually they are paired up according to their charts.

He has twelve that follow him most places. But he wants the disciples to be able to break away and develop on their own and be stronger by themselves, otherwise they would continue to depend on him. This was best for the disciples so they could develop to their full strength.

D: Do you know any of the names of these people?

S: *I'm familiar with a few... there is Simeon, who is called Peter. Ah... and there are Benzebedee, his two sons. There is Bartholomew and Mathias and Judas. There are several others, I cannot... I do not know them that well. We are learning here of what they will do. We are being shown somewhat.*

Benzebedee is mentioned in the Bible as Zebedee, the father of James and John. But the Bible says that James and John left their father in the fishing boat and became disciples. Zebedee is not mentioned after that. It is interesting that Suddi mentioned the father by name and not the more well-known sons. Bartholomew is one of the lesser known disciples. And Mathias is not even mentioned in the Bible until after the death of Christ. Peter is well known but Suddi called him by a name that was pronounced differently: "Simeon" instead of Simon. I find it significant that he mentioned these lesser known disciples. This adds validity to Suddi's account.

D: Do you think all of these followers will do as he taught them?

S: *(Sadly) No. There will be a few who will go out and speak. (Sigh) And there will be those who feel that because they have known him, that they are righteous and will live their lives believing that they have found the pathway. This is very sad, for this was not what he taught them... And then there is of course, Iscariot... He tends to be very moody and is not popular with the other disciples.*

Here again it is interesting that he called him Iscariot instead of Judas. He had already mentioned Judas as one of the disciples, but there were two Judases. He distinguished this one by calling him Iscariot. At other times the pronunciation of his name sounded like "Iscarot."

S: *He is known as the betrayer. For it is his destiny to be the tool of others, in the performance of this deed.*

D: Who will he betray?

I had to constantly pretend as though I knew nothing about the story, as if I were completely ignorant of the happenings. I felt in this way Suddi would tell the story in his own way without being unduly influenced. Even though Katie also knows the story (as everyone does) there are noticeable differences. And they are differences one would not consciously make.

S: *He shall betray Yeshua. He hopes to force him to let others know who he is. Because though they (the followers) believe that he is the chosen one, the Messiah, he has never spoken of this. Others spoke of it of him. And it is Iscariot's wish that he* declare *himself, which he shall not do. He shall always leave it to the judgement of others to decide whether or not he was a good man, and chosen of God to help lead others upon the pathway so that they,* too, *shall be one with God. Iscariot believes so truly, that he believes that truly Yeshua is a god. And that* being *a god, that he would say, "Command these mere mortals to stop," and therefore they* must.

It may have been possible that Iscariot was one of the Zealots that Suddi spoke of. This was definitely their line of thinking.

D: Do you think Iscariot is going to try to force the situation?
S: *It is his nature. He believes that this shall not occur. That Yeshua* must *declare himself But this is not what shall be.*
D: Will this betrayal be considered a bad thing for Iscariot to do?
S: *It is something that* has *to be. It is something that* shall *be. But the worst of it is, what he thinks to occur, will not. And in realizing this, he will then take his life. This is known with great sadness, for this is a great wrong.*

Apparently the suicide was a much worse deed than the betrayal of Christ.

D: Why do you think he will take his life?
S: *Because he will know that he has been part of slaying a man without* sin, *and this cannot be borne. But we do not condemn. It shall be his own judgement.*
D: Do you know how he is going to betray him?
S: *No, I do not know. But the day is dawning soon toward the end.*

Preparation for Crucifixion

Yeshua shall soon he here with us (in the after-death state). We know this, how can we but help but know it? (Sigh) Though it is ordained, it is still very hard to sit back and to watch this to occur... It brings much sorrow to know that this must happen in order to save. To show others that the way is possible. That it is open to them. I'm thinking about what is going to occur and weighing my life in the balance. I'm gathering my strength so that I... will be there. (Sadly and with difficulty) I, too, must learn lessons of this, as we all must. It is something that will be very difficult, but I hope to learn from this... If I but have the strength.

I breathed a sigh of relief and said a quick silent prayer of thanks. I thought if Suddi died before Christ was crucified, we would be unable to get the rest of the story. Now it looked as if it might be possible, if he was able to watch it from the other side. This was an unexpected but welcome development.

D: Will there be others in your spirit world who will observe?
S: *I think there will be multitudes who will. There will be a great lesson here. The lesson of selflessness, for this was his choice. We know this. To emulate this is to apply one's self to the pathway.*
D: I thought if you had followed him so closely through his life, that you might want to be there during his time of trial.
S: *It is not his trial, it is ours!*
D: You *speak as though you know what will* happen.
S: *He will die upon the cross.*
D: Wasn't the cross supposed to be for criminals, felons?
S: *He shall be treated as though he is a felon. And in their eyes he is, for he dares to make them question. He dares to make them look inside themselves, and to them this is a great crime. Because how many men can look at their souls and face what is there? Also, there are many who believe that he is who others say he is. That he is the Christ and the Messiah. They believe this, but they doubt because of his teaching love. He teaches that we must not hate. And that war is not the way that the kingdom shall be won. But they do not understand this. They are hoping that if he is pressed so hard, that he shall come out and say, "I am the Son of God and therefore you cannot do this." But they do not see that this has been told and retold for all of time, that this shall be his*

255

destiny. They cannot see this.

This was a very emotional speech, with much stress on the words. I thought the cross would be an awful way for such a gentle person to end his life.

S: *Many people end their lives in horrible manners, and people think not of it. Because it is not someone important, it is not someone they know, it is not their selves. In being someone who is without sin, who is without jealousy or hatred, who is just filled with love, this shall bring home to them that there are many that this happens to.*

D: Could he back out? Does he have a choice?

S: *He has always known that this was his destiny. The time was not now to do this, it was before (before coming into flesh). Once the decision was made, there was no turning back. He can ask for help in that he may have the strength to come through this. . . whole, and it shall be given.*

D: What does it mean when people call him the Christ?

S: *It means the Savior, the embodiment of living God that lives.*

D: But aren't we all the embodiment of living God?

S: *But are we all aware of this? How many of us are in touch with the deeper soul that is our self, that is our true self, while we inhabit the corporeal body? How many of us can go in a day-to-day existence living with the temptations thrown at him, and living with everything that he has? He could have said, "Stop, no, I refuse to go through this!"*

But he did not. Therefore, that is why he is different from us. I would not have the courage. He is what we all can be. What we all must strive for. It is possible. He said he is the Way. If we can but open our eyes and our hearts, we should see this. (A pause, then a deep sigh) But it will be difficult to watch. To know that someone without sins, without blemish, would give them self up for others of us, to show us the pathway to take. Is this always not hard to watch? To know that someone, even if they didn't know you, if they had never seen you before, would sacrifice themself, just because they loved all of mankind. And for oneself to know that you are not worthy. Is this not hard to take? Mankind has gone for aeons making the same mistakes. Going on from time to time, but never really changing. And he is showing us that it is possible to grow. That in order to escape and to attain the freedom and the knowledge of love, that you must grow. He is showing us this, and therefore it is within him to do this as it is within ourselves to do other things.

D: I'm afraid there are going to be many people who will never understand the reasons.

S: *They do not understand the totality of Yeshua. His totality is too much for them to grasp, so they try to limit him. But people will understand. Maybe not in the sense of earth embodiments, they might not understand in that form. But here, we know and we are learning.*

It appeared that we would be able to get the story of the crucifixion from Suddi's view on that side. But I believed this story was too important to rush. I intended to devote an entire session to it. I also did not want to run the risk of running out of tape or time. I intended to devote as much time as possible and go into as much detail as possible. I felt this was a great breakthrough, that we might have a rare chance to obtain an eye-witness account of perhaps the most memorable and controversial events in the history of mankind. Would his version match the version that has been handed down to us? We have already found in the earlier chapters that often Suddi's story differed from the accepted one.

CHAPTER 25

Crucifixion and Resurrection

The next week I had mixed feelings as we started the session. I was hopeful we would be able to obtain the crucifixion story; it would be the crowning jewel in this experiment. It would also be very important to many people. But I was apprehensive that maybe we would not be allowed to have it. The subconscious has a very effective protective device. It will not allow the subject to experience anything that it assumes will be harmful. It is a well-known fact in hypnosis that if someone sees or remembers something they cannot face, they will wake themselves up immediately, even though they are in a deep trance.

I have seen this happen. I had no idea how the subconscious would handle something as traumatic as watching a dear friend die in such a horrible way. I knew I could not override this protective system and I would not even want to try. I would have to rely on our long association together and the gradual build-up of trust that had grown between us, to convince the subconscious that all was safe. My foremost concern is the well-being of my subjects and their protection is always of the utmost importance.

Katie didn't sense any of this and was excited to find out what would happen. So I said the keyword and watched as she slid effortlessly into the state she had become so accustomed to and we began.

I took her backward in time to the life of Suddi and returned him to the spirit plane just after his death. And we resumed where we had left off the week before.

D: I'm going to count to three and we will move ahead to the time all this is to happen. If you are in a position to know, I want you to tell me what is happening. If it's possible, I would like you to watch it. I want you to share this knowledge with us. I think a great deal can be learned from this experience, if you have the strength to watch it and share it. 1, *2, 3*, it is the time when all this is to take place. Can you tell me what is happening?

I was not sure if Suddi would be in a position where he could witness the events. He said he would if he had the strength, so he knew how difficult it would be. Would he be able to go through it or would he back out? When I finished the count, there was no hesitancy, he seemed to just charge right in.

S: *There has been an offering, in which it is the custom of the Romans, upon each holiday to offer one prisoner his freedom. And Pontius Pilate does not believe Yeshua is the evil being that they say he is. He knows in his soul that this is wrong, a great wrong. Therefore he has offered him and Barabbas as the choice, knowing that as many men as Barabbas has slain that they, of course, will free Yeshua instead.*

I sensed that he felt if he didn't just charge right in, he might lose his nerve and not be able to tell about it.

D: Barabbas was a murderer?
S: *Yes.*
D: You talk as though Yeshua is imprisoned.
S: *Yes, he was taken. By the Sanhedrin (pronounced 'San-had-rin') And after they had questioned him and found him, in their eyes, guilty of blasphemy, they decided that it was up to Rome. For they could not slay someone who others said was the Messiah. For then this would bring the terror of the people down upon their heads. They would in exchange give him to the Romans for trying to start a revolution. In saying that he had incited his followers to do things against Rome.*

Apparently it was the politics of the time. Jesus was not a threat until he began to gather followers. Before that he could be dismissed as a radical or a crazy man.

D: Who were the ones that did that?

259

S: *Sanhedrin. (It was hard to understand because he pronounced that word so strangely.) The Sanhedrin. The body of lawgivers for Israel. (Israel was also pronounced differently.)*

D: They had the power to do that?

S: *Yes. It was one of the things that Rome law allowed them still.*

D: Earlier you said that Iscariot would betray him. Do you know if that happened?

S: *He went to the priests and told them where Yeshua would be. And sold him.*

D: Did he get anything for doing that?

S: *They say a bag of silver. I do not know.*

D: But at this time they are going to offer Yeshua and Barabbas to the people so they may choose who will go free?

S: *(This was very emotional for him) Yes. But the Sanhedrin have many people in the crowd who are being paid to speak the name of Barabbas.*

D: I see. They are going to try to keep the people from choosing Yeshua?

S: *There is no choice. They cannot, for it ... it is his destiny.*

D: These people, the Sanhedrin, are afraid of him?

S: *They are afraid that he might be who others say he is.*

D: They can't afford to let him go free? Is that what you mean?

S: *No, they cannot.*

D: Is this why they paid people to be in the crowd, to incite the crowd?

S: *To speak the name. It is said that the name that is spoken the loudest is the one who will go free.*

It was obvious Suddi was feeling this deeply. There was much emotion in his voice. I hoped he would be able to continue.

D: Okay, let's move ahead and find out what happens. I would really like you to tell us. Many people may gain a lot from this. If it bothers you too much, you may watch it as an objective observer.

I could tell it was already bothering him to watch what was happening to someone he loved so much. I was afraid it would be even more traumatic for him to watch the actual crucifixion. I could only hope that his desire to share this information with others would counteract any revulsions he might feel. I continued to give calming suggestions for Katie's well-being.

D: I will count to three and we will move ahead. 1, 2, 3, what is happening now?

S: *It has been decided ... that this, eventide shall he and two others be nailed ... to the cross to die in crucifixion. The traditional Roman style of killing felons and murderers and thieves.* (This was difficult, but he continued.)

D: It seems as though he would not belong in that category, would he?

S: *(A whisper) No. He has never done harm to another. But it is said that he shall bleed for all of the world.*

D: Are there any other people with you watching this?

S: *There are* many *who are here.*

In the Bible it speaks of the graves being opened and the spirits of the dead being seen by many at this time. Could they have seen the spirits that were with him watching from the other side? An event of this type of emotional magnitude could have heightened the psychic perceptions of the people.

S: *And there are many, hundreds, who are on the earthly plane, who watch... in* horror. *For they* love *him. They cannot believe that this would be done. That this could be let to happen.*

His voice was almost overwhelmed with emotion. He was close to the point of tears. He was feeling every bit of this, in spite of instructions that he could remain objective if he wished. I had to continue to remain detached so I could watch every movement very closely. If there was any sign that it was too much to handle, I would have brought Katie out of trance immediately. The story is never worth compromising the well-being of the subject.

I am usually so engrossed in monitoring the subject that the full emotional impact of the session is not evident to me until I play the tapes back later. Then I, too, feel the overwhelming emphasis of what was said.

D: Do you know how he feels at this time?

S: *He is very calm. He has secluded himself away from a lot of the pain. It helps somewhat to know that ... there is not* total *suffering.*

D: This is good that he has this ability. Does he have any feelings toward the people who are doing this to him?

S: *He feels great love, in knowing that they cannot know what they do. And he knows that many of them will, from* this *realize.*

He seemed on the verge of tears. There was not a single doubt in my mind that he was witnessing this.

D: Do you want to move ahead and tell us what happens? (I tried to be very gentle with him, I knew this was very hard.) If parts of it are hard to speak of, you can skip those parts. As I said, it is a very important event and the whole world should know about it. Don't you agree? (He responded with a very emotional *"Yes."*) I believe all of *time* should know about these things that happened.

S: *He carries the cross through the streets. And, it is very heavy and he falls. (This was spoken slowly, as though he was watching it occur step-by-step.) Several of the people along the side help him up. The soldiers tell one of them that he must help him to bear it, its weight.*

D: One of the soldiers or one of the people?

S: *One of the crowd is picked to do this.*

D: How does that person feel about it?

S: *He would do anything to lift the burden. There is a great deal of gladness knowing that he helped in some way.*

D: How does the crowd feel about this?

S: *They are in tears. There are a few who are jeering, saying, "Why not save yourself?" But for the most part they know that no matter who others say he is, this is a man who is ... very beautiful. (He took a deep breath.) Without human frailties. He is risen above the day-to-day problems that beset us... They have lain the cross and he has been laid upon this and his arms tied. And his legs. And spikes ... are . . . entering into the flesh. (Several deep breaths.) It seems as if the very world is being torn asunder. For the skies that were clear are very dark. And darkness is growing. (Deep breathing.) The cross is erected, along with the two others. It is central. From this point most of the city can see this. It is upon a rise outside of the city, so that all may see.*

D: Why have the clouds come and it is getting dark? Is it being caused from your side?

S: *It is as if the world cries out. That this must not be! (Deep, deep breaths.) He asks that ... our Father forgive him.*

D: Why? He has not done anything.

S: *(A long pause, then a whisper.) I know not. Then he asks that Abba forgive the others for doing this deed. For they know not. (A long pause as he breathed deeply.)*

D: The two that are on the other crosses, are they real felons?

S: *Yes. One spoke to him though. I know not truly what he said, but the other one reprimanded him. Asking him did he not know a truly good man? And Yeshua looked at him and said that he would be with him today... in his kingdom.*

D: What does that mean?

S: *He shall be* here. *I mean, this is not always so, but he - I believe that it has to do with ... even if it is at the last moments of his life, he has gained understanding of what is.*

D: Is there anything different about the body when it's on the cross? Does it have anything on it or on the cross?

I was remembering all the pictures and statues I have seen of Jesus.

S: *There is a crude placard that reads, 'This is the King of the Jews', above him. On the other ones, it gives their name and their crime.*

D: Can you see what theirs were?

S: *(Pause, he seemed to be reading.) I'm not sure of the name. The one to the right says ... that he was guilty of thievery, of stealing another man's articles. I'm not sure what. I think out of the home or something. But the other one was guilty of murder.*

D: Which is the one that he said would be with him?

S: *'Twas the thief.*

D: What about Yeshua's body? Is there anything different?

S: *There were - before he was nailed to the cross, there was a cloak that he had tossed over his shoulders ... and some woven thorns about his head. But these were removed when he was placed upon the cross.*

D: He doesn't have the crown of thorns on his head as he is on the cross? (It is always there in the pictures.)

S: *No ... And the soldiers are at the foot of the cross. They are gaming, they throw lots. Part of the custom is that the personal items of the felons are dealt with in this manner. Who wins the lots wins the articles of clothing or whatever. It is ... the sky is almost pitch though it is early in the day. But, himself. . . the strength of his soul shines out still. It is like the only spark of light around. It is one of these soldiers, knowing that it is Sabbath ... he tosses a spear into one of the thieves to make sure there is a death.*

D: What do you mean, knowing it is the Sabbath?

S: *The bodies of the felons are always taken down upon the Sabbath, no matter when they were put up. Therefore, to be crucified means to die upon the cross, which usually takes days. And they must make sure that they are dead before they are allowed to be taken down.*

D: Then they are killing them?

S: *Because the sky darkens and Sabbath begins at dusk.*

It was not really Sabbath yet because the sky was darkening earlier than usual.

D: I see. They have to kill them. The bodies cannot be left hanging on the Sabbath? Is that correct?

S: *Yes. (Suddenly) He is gone! He has left the body!*

D: What? Did the soldier have to kill him, too?

S: *No. The head fell forward at that instant, at the instant he left. They are curious now because they cannot believe that one could die so soon. So they have thrown also a spear at his side, and the blood slowly runs down.*

D: They want to be sure he really is dead?

S: *Yes.*

D: Does his spirit stay close to the physical body?

S: *He is standing with his mother as she is walking away. She is aware of him.*

D: Does she feel his presence or is she able to see him?

S: *I do not know, but she is aware.*

D: Will he remain on your level?

S: *For a while, not long. There are things that must be dealt with, and then he shall go on.*

D: What happens to the body?

S: *It still hangs as yet... It is said that the earth trembles, though I do not know. I know that there are people who are running in terror, for they know that something horrible has happened. And they say that the earth shakes.*

D: You wouldn't be able to feel it, would you? (He shook his head.)

Okay, move ahead and tell me what happens to the body. Can you see?

S: Joseph (pronounced 'Yoseph') *has requested of Herod that he be allowed to take this body. And Herod sent him to Pilate who gave his permission.*

D: Why wouldn't Herod give permission?

S: He told Yoseph that it was not his to give. Because he was slain by the Romans, it was theirs.

D: This is Joseph, his uncle?

S: Yes, and Pilate gives him permission to do this. And they take the body down and it is placed in the tomb.

D: Whose tomb is it put in?

S: It is Joseph's. He was having it prepared.

D: Was it for himself?

S: No, it was for Yeshua.

D: He knew then that this would happen? Do you think Yeshua ever told him?

S: It was not need to be told, for they all knew.

D: What do they do with the body?

S: They anoint it with the oils, and incense is lit, and it is wrapped in linen and laid. And the stone is rolled over the doorway.

D: Was the tomb sealed?

S: Yes.

The tremendous emotion was now gone. It seemed the hardest part was to watch his beloved friend being hurt, humiliated and slain. Now the voice had returned to normal.

D: Does anything else happen?

S: During the next three days, it shall be as no more. For it is not needed. Then it shall be gone.

D: The body will be gone, you mean?

S: Yes ... I know that there are ways of doing this, but I'm not familiar with the method.

D: What do you mean exactly? I thought you meant that the body was dead.

S: The body is dead, but since it is no longer needed, it is. There are ways of making it as if it had not been. I do not know the method. I cannot explain any better.

D: Oh? It is something you don't understand yourself?

S: It is known only to the masters.

D: You mean the body disappears, in other words?

S: *Yes, it is made as if... It is made of the dust that it was and it is no more.*

D: Do the masters on your side do this, or the masters on the earthly side?

S: *It is the masters on my side.*

D: Why would they do this? Why would the body have to disappear?

S: *Because it was foretold in the prophecies that he would rise upon the third day. And in order to rise, they must show that the place where he was laid is empty. And he cannot be taken away by normal means. That the body cannot be . . . they (his friends) cannot get to it to do anything. Therefore it must be done from this side.*

D: Yeshua did not do it himself? At the time that the body is no more, where is he?

S: *He is there with them, aiding them in doing this.*

D: His forces with the forces of the other masters?

S: *Yes, with the other masters.*

D: It would be very complicated. You would have to be very advanced to do that.

S: *It is done with the aid of the others also. I do not know this method. I'm not upon that level.*

D: And they made the body just disappear. Would that be a good word? (I was trying to understand.)

S: *To be as no more, yes.*

D: No more. Well, did Pilate or anyone take protection to make sure....

S: *(Interrupted) Yes, there were guards out, because they knew of this prophecy. And they knew that others spoke of him as being the Messiah and therefore there were guards there.*

This is something that apparently has been misinterpreted down through the ages. I think what they were trying to do was to show that even the physical body can be made to transcend time and space.

The tomb was sealed and guards placed so there was no chance of the body being stolen and taken away by normal means. It had to be shown that only abnormal, supernatural forces could have removed the body. This must be part of the lesson of the empty tomb, to prove that these higher forces do exist and that he was one of them.

D: You said the prophecy was that he would rise again. Will this happen?

S: *Yes! How* can *he not! He* is as *he* was *before. Is this not in essence a rising? For he is risen from the body which is made out of dust and clay, and is as he was.*

D: I think people think it means that the body itself will rise. You know, like Lazarus, when you talked about him.

S: *But then Lazarus was again a* human *entity and inhabited a* human *body. Whereas the Messiah, as he is called, is to show that there is continuance* afterwards. *Not just to say that we can go back into the body, for this has been shown before. But we must show that there is continuance. That there is existence after the human body ceases to exist.*

D: I think this is what people think the prophecy means, that the body would physically rise again.

S: *This is* why *it must be destroyed! So they must know by other* means.

D: What happens then? Do the people find out that the body is gone?

S: *You see, it is the custom of several days after, the body must again be anointed. And his mother and her cousin had come to do this. And it (the tomb) was again opened for this, with the guards being there. And they found that it was empty.*

D: But his *mother* was one that came with another woman?

The Bible does not mention that Jesus' mother was one of the women who came to the tomb. It speaks of Mary Magdalene, Mary, the mother of James and the "other" Mary, according to which version you read in the various chapters.

D: That would be hard to do, I think, to view the body after it had lain there for several days. It would be an act of love, wouldn't it?

S: *And who more willing to perform that act of love than a mother?*

D: But who opened the seal?

S: *The soldiers helped open the seal.*

D: What did they think when the body was gone?

S: *They, of course, said that someone had gotten past them and stolen the body. But what could be said? The linen was still there with the blood upon it. And everything was as had been left.*

D: And the seal had not been broken, had it?

S: No.

D: What did the mother feel when she found the body was gone?

S: *She knew that he had left and was being prepared to go on.*

D: Did Yeshua go on, or did he remain around there?

S: *For a while he remained, for he must go to the ones who believe in him and tell them, "Do not be dismayed. To know that everything as is, I have preached." He must let them know that he spoke of the truth. And to do this he must show that he exists ... to them.*

D: You sound as though he was talking with them. Could they see him and hear him?

S: *Yes, for they have this ability. All who open themselves have this ability and could have seen him. Many did.*

D: Do you think they saw him as a physical person?

S: *Yes, but one who is... different. Who is more like one of the beings of light than having an earthly body. It is not one you could perhaps reach out and to touch, for your hand would pass through.*

D: But they were able to see it?

S: *Yes. To know that it was true.*

D: Does he still have any marks on the spiritual body? (I was thinking of where they had driven the nails.)

S: *Yes, for a while it shall echo the things that have been done. Because this was a way of proving to them. The doubts that he perhaps was who he said he was.*

D: Did some doubt?

S: *How can there not be somewhat of doubt in man? For it is his nature.*

D: This is why he still carried the image, so to speak, of the marks? To prove who he was?

S: *Yes.*

D: And others saw him also? We have heard many stories. Some of them say that he appeared as his physical body and he walked the earth.

S: *It is him as he is truly, rather than as they knew him.*

D: And the physical body was just completely taken apart, so to speak.

S: *Reduced to dust and ash, yes.*

D: That makes more sense, reduced to ash.

It appears that the story of the angel and the stone rolled away may have been a cover-up invented later by the soldiers to save their own skins. In the stories circulated over the years, it seems that the real miracle of the resurrection has been obscured. In my opinion, this miracle was the disintegration of the physical body and the appearance of the spiritual body. Since it was seen by so many people, he hoped to prove the continuance of life after death, because his physical body was no more. This main point seems to have been clouded and confused in the religious dogma that has grown up around this issue over the years. Suddi was correct, hundreds of people have returned to their physical bodies after being declared dead. This phenomenon is not as unique as the churches have claimed. The masters apparently were also trying to show the unimportance of the physical body.

D: You mentioned the beings of light. What does this mean? Is this the nature of the person when they leave the physical body?

S: *It is those, some of its, who are beyond the need to return again. Who are the next step with being one with God again. They are those who come and help and guide us in many ways, in directing our path.*

D: What happened to Yeshua?

S: *He eventually went back to be with the others. To be with the masters and our God, as we know him.*

D: Did anyone watch this happen?

S: *It is said that his mother was there. And they saw that there was a blending of light, and then it was no more.*

D: As he went to the other plane. Would that be a way of saying it?

S: *Yes.*

D: Where is Yeshua now? Is he on the plane that you are on?

S: *He is with the masters. He is not here. I am not anywhere near that level.*

D: Do you know what level that is on?

S: *The ninth, at least. Very close to ten level.*

D: How many levels are there all together?

S: *Ten is perfection.*

D: If he is on that level, you would have no way of seeing him now. Is that correct?

S: *Unless he came to ours, no.*

D: I see... We've heard stories where people say they *have* seen him.

S: *I do not doubt.*

D: I mean many years after he had gone, left the earth.

S: *But to us a year is just an instant, therefore how is this not possible?*

D: Would he allow people on earth to see him then?

S: *If he wished to. Perhaps if there was something for this individual that must needs be done and they had still doubts. Would he not reveal himself to them? Letting them know that they believed in truth.*

D: According to their belief system, it would help them?

S: *(He was showing frustration trying to make us understand.) I'm finding great difficulty. If there was a great task for this person, such as to spread the word, that he* lived, *and to let others know of this, would he not reveal himself to them? So that they would know that what they believed is right.*

D: I thought that maybe he was busy on the other level. He would never come down to earth for things like that.

S: *If he had not care of man, he would not have come in the first place.*

D: Can you tell us the reasons for his death by crucifixion? In our time or where we're looking at it from, it is said that he died for our sins. There is some disagreement about this. Are we not responsible for our own actions?

S: *(Sigh) This is a very weighty question.*

D: It has many answers, I suppose.

S: *There are many influences upon those answers. He was to be crucified to be ridiculed by others. To show that when he again lived, that he was able to rise above this and that we, too, are able to rise above this. This is something that he needed to go through for his own lessons as well as the other meanings. That he was not as perfect, is not as perfect as others would possibly want to assume. That* he *was willing to pay the penalties and show that we should not be afraid of them also. And, in paying for what we have done, then we can rise above that, This is part of the reasoning behind that. Is to show that it can be done* by man, *that man can do such things.*

D: Then when they say that he died for the sins of all the people in the world, does that make sense?

S: *How can he die for someone else's sins? You must all pay for your own. If not this time around, then perhaps the next, or even the next. But ultimately, you must endure what you have made others endure because of you.*

D: Then his life, his dying will not wipe out the other people's sins?

S: *There is a law of grace that will exist. But it is not because he paid for your sins, but because you would accept him as being worthy and perhaps a messenger of God. And the law of grace deals with God's love for you, not because he died for the sins.*

D: Well, then people are misinterpreting this, aren't they?

S: *It is very possible. Man misinterprets many things.*

D: We should try to be like him. But this does not necessarily mean that we have to follow him in such a way that we worship *him*. It is the way that he has shown us that we need to emulate. Is this correct?

S: *This is correct. He is a point of almost worship, because he could do it. And he showed that it could be done. Therefore he is to be marveled at, but not to be worshiped. Not to be defied, because we all are part of God.*

D: Do you think he wants to be worshiped?

S: *He wants to be remembered, but perhaps not in the way that many shall remember him. Basically, what he had in mind was a concept similar to a guide, a spirit guide to guide people to greater enlightenment, to help them achieve greater power. To help them become more spiritual in their perceptions. He mainly considered himself as a helper, a guide, an example, like a good friend who is helping you with advice.*

D: There are many people that will think of him as a God in his own right. It is hard to think of him as a human being.

S: *We are all part of God. Some of us are more aware of this than others. I would say that he is one of these such people. But to consider him and deify him in his own right, and separately, this is wrong.*

D: This is what I am afraid people will do in the future. Deify him and also deify his mother, because she *was* the mother.

S: *If this means that in so doing they will* live *like them, this is good. But if this means that instead they shall make them into gods and then say, "Because they are so wise, they will forgive me for anything I do." And go ahead and do it anyway, this is a great wrong. He was just* aware, *and she was also aware in many ways, of what is possible for all of us. It just takes much struggle to attain.*

D: Would he be a person who would encourage people to think for themselves, or rather to follow blindly?

S: *Never to follow blindly! Always to question. To think things out for oneself is to make the decision all the greater. Because it was made rather than just handed. If one does not question, one does*

271

not have faith. Because you cannot be thinking about some things if you do not question them and look at them from all angles. And then *when one has done this, if you believe, if you find it good,* then *it is worth believing in.*

D: Some people say that whenever you question, this is the work of the Devil... if you have a Devil in your society.

S: *(Sigh) There is no Devil! (Gently, but firmly, as though talking to a stubborn child.) Inside oneself, there are two parts. There is the questioning part, which* can *be brought to bring about wrong. But it also is a very* good *part, in that it* makes *you think about things and* makes *you think about people. Because all people are not good. Would you accept a person at face value if they smiled at you but had the knife sticking in your back? You* must *question things, but you must also have faith. It has been* shown *that this is true. You* can *have faith in things. This sounds like a paradox, but it is* not... *truly.*

He was getting frustrated. He felt so strongly about this and was trying so *hard* to make us understand.

D: I understand. You're doing a beautiful job ... But, how do we know when we find new knowledge, if it is the truth? How can we tell?

S: *(Sigh) Truth... it might make you sad. But somewhere deep inside of you, you know that it is truth. If you can but open yourself up, you know when things are true and when that they are not. For this as available to you.*

D: Sometimes when we discover new knowledge, people tell us this is bad.

S. *Does it* hurt *anyone in any way? Is it harmful? This is not to say that it does not make you sad. But if it* hurts *someone, it cannot* truly *be good. If it brings no harm, take it and study it. And find the truth. Find out what is* good *about it.*

D: Isn't it true that during your lifetime, in the synagogues and the different religions, several of them said, "Don't question, just accept?"

S: *Most of them said this, yes. It was stated.*

D: *Your* people were different, weren't they? The Essenes, they liked to question.

S: *Yes.*

D: Can you tell us if the Christ will return to earth at some future time?

S: *Yes, he shall return.*

D: Will people be aware of his coming beforehand, as you were aware this time, or will he come suddenly?

S: *There will be those who will know.*

This session appeared very difficult for Katie. She was very tense and emotional while watching the crucifixion, as though it was extremely painful. Of course, when she was brought forward and awakened, she had no memory of anything she had seen and felt fine. I realize this session will open up a great deal of controversy. But I think it should be looked at and examined for what it is, an alternative view of some of the most important events in our culture.

What amazes me in this account is not the inaccuracy, but the accuracy, That the version we have in our Bible could come down through two thousand years and be as intact as it is, is truly remarkable. That it was able to pass through the Dark Ages when such a tremendous amount of irreplaceable knowledge was lost, and endure despite various scribes, translators and deliberate exclusions and inclusions, is truly a miracle. No rational, thinking human could expect it to be the literal word-for-word truth when our own recent history books contain many contradictions. Even modern news stories vary according to the reporter's viewpoint. We should not quibble over differences, but be thankful that we have the story. The fact that the Bible has survived at all is truly a gift from God.

CHAPTER 26

The Purpose of the Crucifixion and Resurrection

I realize volumes have been written on this subject and many more shall be in the future. I want to see what interpretation I can gain from the information that was brought forth about Jesus in the regressions. In order to do that I would have to wipe out all the church and dogma training I have been exposed to since childhood, I would have to look at him with fresh eyes, seeing and hearing his story for the first time. This would be very difficult. The "brain-washing" begins very early and is deeply ingrained. I hope to make an attempt to find out what Jesus had to say to mankind.

What was he really trying to communicate to the world through his crucifixion? What was the real message behind the resurrection? These are deep and ponderous questions, and I am not a philosopher. But I wish to present what I got out of the story and what lessons I learned. Someone else might see much more than I can, and another person might see something totally different. Everyone has their own viewpoint colored by their life experiences, and people will never be able to agree on something as deep and personal as religious beliefs. But my interpretation may help someone who is groping in the darkness of confusion.

We were all created at the same moment and are all children of God in this sense. When we came to earth to experience life, we became

274

entrapped in the physical. We forgot from whence we came. At least we forgot on the conscious level. Deep inside a spark still remembered and longed to return "home," to the loving Father who made us. He, was waiting patiently, because he knows no such thing as time; waiting for his children to uncover once again their true potential and destiny. But humanity enjoyed life and became absorbed in the ways of the world, making mistake after mistake, further entrenching itself through the law of karma. Was there any way out? The more lives humans lived the more karma they created for themselves. We could not return to God until we are once again perfect, having atoned for all the wrongs we have done our fellow man.

It seems hopeless. For each mistake we repaid we made two more. We are on a wheel going round and round and getting nowhere, because we do not understand what we have to do to get off. How could humanity climb upward if it is constantly going round in circles? This was what Jesus came to "save" humanity from. Humanity needed an example, someone to show him the "Way." Humankind had gotten itself into the mess it was in through the use of free will. God did not punish, he loved his children too much for that. He allowed them to make their own mistakes and hopefully they would eventually learn from them and see "the light" and find the pathway to take them "home." Since God will not interfere, (he can only help and guide) he decided to send someone to be an example.

I believe Jesus or Yeshua was a master of the tenth level. This means that after countless numbers of lives filled with human frailties, he had at last attained perfection and had returned to the side of God from whence he had come. Only this type of entity could possibly resist being sucked down into the murk and mire of human existence. Even for a master it was dangerous, for the lure of the flesh is very tempting, and he might forget his purpose in coming.

It was important that he come, as we all must come into a human, physical body and be exposed to all the trials man must face. He had to show that he could rise above it. If he could do it, humankind could also. He had to be taught all the knowledge of the world, so he could understand the time he lived in. He had to be trained in the complete use of the mind, in order to show its marvelous capabilities. To show that a human was not merely an animal body, but a supreme spiritual creation.

He never claimed to perform miracles, but told people they could also do these things, and things even more wonderful. He had to learn meditation so he could remain close to the source from which he came. In this way he could keep his goal ever in sight and not be swayed from it. His goal was to show humanity through his example how they should live. That the greatest lesson to be learned was to love their fellow creatures on earth. If love was present, no further negative karma could be created. If love was present, there would be no more wars and suffering. Humanity could get off the wheel of karma and begin to progress up the ladder again. Jesus was the perfect example of what each person had within them and what they were capable of attaining. But still they didn't understand. His perfection frightened and confused them. They feared him because he was different, and their only solution was to kill him.

I believe the purpose of the crucifixion was to show by vivid contrast what humanity had become, the depths to which it had sunk. I believe God was offering people a choice: stay on your present course and become like these vile and debased creatures with no consciences, who think only of their worldly, mundane existences; or try to pattern your lives after his beautiful example and you can rise above the chaos of the world and attain perfection.

He had gained understanding of the mind and thus did not have to suffer extremely on the cross. He was able to leave the body at will and died sooner than was normal. Long, prolonged suffering was not the point, the example and the contrast were. In this way, he truly died for all mankind. If he had not lived, Man would still be groping in the dark without the shining example of his perfect life.

I believe the purpose of the resurrection has also been lost and muddled by people's thinking. God meant to show that the physical world is not all, that man was more. An eternal soul, a spirit that could not be snuffed out. That the spirit had continuance and could exist after the body ceased to function. To enter again into the body would not have proved the point the masters were trying to make. It would only show that it was possible to continue in the physical. Thus the earthly body of Jesus had to completely disappear.

The body had been sealed in the tomb. Both Roman and Jewish guards had been posted outside the tomb. Neither trusted the other and they wanted to be sure no one could get past and steal the body. With the tomb sealed and guarded, the masters went to work with the help of Jesus to disintegrate the body, break it down to the atoms and turn it back into dust. It was as if the natural process of decay and decomposition had been speeded up to become almost instantaneous. The linen wrappings were left to show that the body had not been physically removed. When the guards opened the tomb themselves and found the body missing, it was evident there was no possible way it could have been taken. It could have only been accomplished from the other side, the spiritual side.

Later, when the figure of Christ was seen by so many people, they had to know that this was the part of man that survived everything and was eternal. That the spirit was the true nature of man and there was something beyond the mere earthly existence man clung to so fiercely. They would have to believe this, because the body could not possibly return, it had been completely destroyed.

But somehow, down through the ages this has all become jumbled and confused. The soldiers were ordered under threat of death to guard the tomb. The Sanhedrin and the Romans knew of the predictions that the resurrection would take place. They must not let anything happen to that body. When they opened the tomb and found the body missing, the soldiers feared for their lives. I can imagine that in order to save their own necks, they came up with the story of the angel rolling away the stone and Christ walking out.

It is a known fact that the Sanhedrin later paid the Jewish soldiers to say that someone slipped past them in the night and stole the body. These stories have been accepted and passed down through the centuries because they were easier to understand. The real purpose behind the resurrection was apparently too complicated and obscure for their minds. There also may have been other reasons for denying the true story. Fear does strange things to people.

If you will examine the Biblical accounts, you will find there are many references of Jesus after death appearing and disappearing suddenly from among groups of people. These stories are more representative of the spirit than the human body.

The story of Jesus' life is so beautiful in itself as an example of perfect love that he left with us. I cannot understand the need for the supernatural trappings that have been heaped upon it. Why the story that he was born of a virgin? Larson says in his book, The Essene Heritage, that this comes from the ancient Egyptian beliefs that a god must always have unnatural beginnings. There are many learned theologians that do not believe in the concept of the virgin birth. Why was it necessary? He was transformed into a god by people who did not understand the reasons behind his coming. He did not want to be a god, he never intended to be worshiped. That was Man's doing. What better way to honor and remember him than by trying to live like him?

Of course, this is only my own interpretation and opinion. But what a terrible thing if he had lived and died and the real meaning of it all was to be lost in obscurity.

No explanation will suffice to account for a normal young girl living in the Twentieth Century being able to bring forth enough information about a lost civilization to fill this entire book. One thing for certain, it was done by paranormal means. There will undoubtedly be countless arguments over this phenomenon, whether it is reincarnation, spirit possession or many other explanations. I, personally, prefer the reincarnation theory. But to me it no longer matters. During the three months I worked with him, Suddi

Benzahmare emerged as a very real person. No one can ever convince me he did not live.

By itself, there is nothing truly remarkable or exciting about the life of Suddi. He was a quiet, peaceful man filled with innate goodness and understanding, who devoted his life to the preservation and teaching of knowledge. During his infrequent journeys into the outside world he seemed to be disappointed by the human condition. The uniqueness of his life came from the people he dwelled among and the fact that he was able to become so closely acquainted with perhaps the greatest human that ever lived. This seemed to bring him joy, to have lived in the time of the fulfilling of the prophecies and to have been some help in the teaching (or opening-up) of the Messiah.

This crossing of their paths at Qumran is important for it describes an unknown area in Jesus' life. It allowed us to see the very human side of a man whose deification has blown his image all out of proportion. After this experience, he is no longer a face in a picture, a cold statue or a limp figure hanging from a crucifix. He lives, he loves, and cares for all mankind. Suddi's association with him illuminated me in a way I never thought possible.

The story of Suddi's life is also valuable because of the wonderful knowledge he has passed down to us through two thousand years. For this sharing, we shall be eternally grateful. He has shown us a side of the ancient mind we never knew existed.

To Suddi I can only say, "I'm glad you lived. I'm glad you chose to speak to us. I thank you from the depths of my being for sharing this information. I shall never forget you."

ADDENDUM ADDED IN 2001

After "Jesus and the Essenes" was printed in England in 1992 1 began to travel and lecture about the book. Most notably, I spoke at the Essene Network Summer School in Dorset for several years. During one of the first lectures, a man in the audience asked a question that made me think. I was talking about Jesus' travels with his uncle, Joseph of Arimathea, and that he was a rich merchant trading tin and cloth. The man asked, "Where did Joseph get the tin?" I replied that I didn't know, I hadn't thought about it. Then the audience said there were many old legends in that part of England about the tin mines, and that Joseph came there. I had heard of his connection with Glastonbury and the Chalice Well, but I had not heard about the tin mines. They said the local people there still sing a song "Joseph was a tin man." I found this fascinating because it was verifying yet another part of the story we had received. I told the audience I would certainly like to know more about these legends. As a result in the next few years I received books and pamphlets from my readers in England. The research done by the authors seem to be based on solid records and history. I decided that if this book was ever printed in the U.S. that I would add an addendum that would include this research. It is utterly amazing how the entire story continues to hold up under scrutiny, and pieces continue to be added.

* * *

THE DRAMA OF THE LOST DISCIPLES, By George F. Jowett, 1993, Covenant Publishing Co. Ltd., London. This book is highly recommended as the most complete history I have read. It was probably the inspiration of the others. While the other books hinted that the entire story of Joseph in England might be a myth or legend, this book quotes from ancient historical records dating back to Roman times and before. His sources cannot be disputed. It is a forgotten story of the founding of the Christian religion that needs to be retold and brought back to our time, even though it will probably upset many who are entrenched in church dogma. It is a privilege and a God-given right to think for oneself and to constantly search for knowledge. This is the only way to find the answers, no matter how distasteful they may seem. We must constantly strive to restore "lost" history, and to preserve it for our posterity. To this aim my work is devoted.

* * *

Joseph of Arimathea is given only a passing mention in the Bible. He is referred to as the rich man who claimed the body of Christ, and gave up his tomb for the burial after the Crucifixion. According to both Jewish and Roman law, unless the body of an executed criminal was immediately claimed by the next of kin the body was cast into a common pit with others where all physical record of them was completely obliterated. Joseph, the family guardian, personally went to Pilate for permission to claim the body, remove it from the cross and prepare it for burial in his private sepulcher on his estate. However, there is much, much more to his story that has been forgotten and "lost" down through time. The story is glorious and needs to be brought back to the people of our generation.

First the story as it relates to the information uncovered through hypnotic regression that is reported in this book. Joseph of Arimathea was indeed Jesus' uncle, related to Mary. He was the younger brother of her father. He was one of the wealthiest men in the world, not just in Jerusalem. He was a metal magnate controlling the tin and lead industry. Tin was as valuable as gold in those days, the chief metal used in the production of bronze. It was an ultimate necessity in all countries and in great demand by the warrring Romans. Joseph's world control of tin and lead was due to his vast holdings in the ancient tin mines of Britain. He had acquired and developed this trade many years before Jesus began his ministry. The world's major portion of tin was mined in Cornwall, smelted into ingots and exported throughout the civilized world, chiefly in Joseph's ships. He owned one of the largest private merchant shipping fleets afloat that traded in all the ports of the known world.

Joseph was also an influential member of the Sanhedrin, and a legislative member of the provincial Roman senate. He owned a palatial home in the holy city and a fine country residence just outside Jerusalem. Several miles north he possessed another spacious estate at Arimathea, located on the populous caravan route between Nazareth and Jerusalem. He was a man of importance and influence within both the Jewish and Roman hierarchies.

After Joseph, the father of Jesus, died when Jesus was quite young, Joseph of Arimathea was appointed legal guardian of the family as next of kin. This explains Jesus' association with his uncle from an early age, and his ability to travel with him on his voyages.

There are many legends in England that say when Joseph came to the islands to obtain the tin he often brought his nephew Jesus with him. Less often Mary, the mother of Jesus, accompanied them, especially when Jesus was younger. This would seem only an interesting sidelight, except that we know from the story in this book that Jesus went with Joseph to all the countries of the known world under the disguise of merely traveling on the trading missions. He actually was being taken to study with the various wise teachers, and to study the mysteries of the ancient teachings. This fit very well with the stories of Jesus and Joseph visiting England to transport the valuable tin. For many centuries Britain was the only country in the world where tin was mined and refined, and was called "The Tin Island." In the making of bronze, tin was the main alloy. Thus it can be safely said that the Bronze Age had its inception in Britain. The tin trade existed as early as 1500 BC, and was the source of the world's supply. The Phoenicians were the original inhabitants of Britain and the miners of lead and tin. Many ancient writers say that the Phoenicians first came to Cornwall for tin over 4000 years before the birth of Christ. They had the monopoly on the tin trade and jealously guarded the secret of where the tin mines were located. Later when the Romans tried to follow their ships to find the location, the Phoenicians would deliberately wreck their vessel.

The Phoenicians were a mysterious race. They were tall men with red hair and blue eyes -- not a Mediterranean people. Scholars have had great difficulty tracing their origin, because Phoenician means "red headed men", and was not what they called themselves. They were known by various names in different parts of the world. In early Biblical records they are referred to as the people of Tarshish. There are some who believe they were the inhabitants of the lost continent of Atlantis! One thing for certain, whatever name they went by, they were connected with the tin trade from Britain. Another mystery is how, four thousand years before the birth of Christ, they knew there was tin in Cornwall. How were they able to sail unknown seas, find a land they did not know existed, and then dig for a metal which they knew nothing about? Then they found that mixing this new metal with copper would make bronze? Many scholars believe, and there is much evidence to support this theory, that before the great flood there lived in Britain a very advanced civilization, with great practical knowledge of Science, and which knew more about metallurgy than we do today. Thus the claim that they did not sail to Britain from Europe, but were originally inhabitants of Atlantis, and that part of Britain is the surviving remnant of that lost continent. These facts are not crucial to our story of Jesus and Joseph of Arimathea, but they are a mystery and an interesting sideline.

Glastonbury, where the bulk of the history abounds, was also the cultural center of the Druids. Druidism was nationally organized since 1800 BC. The Romans later tried to make people think there were only barbarians living in the British Isles at that time, and they started the vicious rumors that the Druids conducted human sacrifice during their religious ceremonies. Both of these claims have proven false. The Romans considered anyone who was not Roman to be barbaric. The truth was that there were large cities, cultural centers, libraries, and forty huge universities (containing at times as many as 60,000 students) in England that would rival anything we have today, as far as knowledge and education is concerned. London was founded 270 years before Rome in 1020 BC.

The Druids had beliefs that were remarkably similar to the Judaic beliefs, and are believed to have a common root. They had been looking for a Savior, a Messiah, and they even called him Yesu, the only recorded mention of the name. This can be explained because the Druids are believed to have been an offshoot of Jews that settled in the British Isles in ancient times. They naturally would have some of-the same beliefs. They had a mystery school steeped in the Kaballah (among other subjects, such as: natural philosophy, astronomy, arithmetic, geometry, jurisprudence, medicine, poetry and oratory). It normally would take twenty years to complete all of the studies, but we know that Jesus was not the normal student. He had the capacity and the ability to absorb information at an incredibly fast rate. This was evident in the short amount of time he spent studying with the Essenes. By the time he returned to Jerusalem to begin his ministry, he had already been taught by all the wise teachers in all the mystery schools in the world. There are many other stories and legends from many countries to confirm this. So this was a missing piece of the puzzle, why he spent so much time in England.

Yet there is much, much more to the remarkable story of Joseph of Arimathea, and what he accomplished after the death of Christ. This, as Paul Harvey says, is "the rest of the story." After the Crucifixion the disciples and followers of Jesus feared for their lives. The Romans were afraid that, even though they had disposed of the main instigator (Jesus), his followers might still have the ability to spread revolt through their dramatically different teachings. Many followers were hunted down and killed. Joseph was the protector of the small band of disciples during the perilous years following the Crucifixion, the head of the Christian underground in Judea, and the guardian of Christ's mother, Mary. Joseph was too rich and powerful to be killed outright, so a unique method of disposal was devised for him and his accomplices. He and his group were put in an open ship without sails, oars or rudder, and set adrift in the Mediterranean. A sure sentence of death, under normal circumstances, but nothing in the story of Jesus was ever considered normal.

Various existing records agree that among the occupants of the castaway boat were: Joseph of Arimathea and his family and servants. On the list were: the three Marys (Mary, mother of Jesus, Mary Magdalene, and the other Mary, the wife of Cleopas), Martha, two servants: Marcella and the black maid Sarah, and twelve disciples (including some of the originals). Also among the group were Lazarus, Jesus' cousin whom He raised from the dead, and Maximin the man whose sight Jesus restored. Some other names listed were: Salome, the wife of Zebedee, and mother of James and John. Eutropius, Trophimus, Martial, Clean, Sidonius (Restitutus), and Saturninus. Marcella probably went along in her old capacity of handmaiden to the Bethany sisters, and not one of the missionary band. Joseph of Arimathea was Mary's guardian until her death. As she was under his protection he would not have left her in Jerusalem where she would have been in extreme danger. She was definitely accompanying him, even though the sea voyage had been designed to kill them all.

The Romans thought this was a unique way of getting rid of these trouble-makers, because there was no way they could survive in the open sea in a boat that could not be maneuvered. But a current caught the boat and brought them safely ashore on the coast of France. The location is now called Saintes Maries de la Mer or Saint Marys of the Sea. Here Lazarus and some of the others settled, and eventually founded the first church of France (then called "Gaul"). The rest of the group continued on (in a much more seaworthy boat) to Britain. Their friends, the Druids, were there, and Joseph had connections with the ruling families of Britain (his daughter Anna was married to the King's youngest brother). They returned to Glastonbury, where they had been many times before and were given land by the King of Britain. Here Joseph established the first Christian Church in the world, within three years after the death of Christ. It was not called "Christian" until hundreds of years later in 250 AD. In those early days the religion was known as "The Way", and they were known as the "Followers of the Way," because Jesus had said, "I am The Way." They referred to Christ and his spiritual philosophy as "The Way."

Joseph sent the disciples out to spread the teachings of Jesus, and through Lazarus and the other disciples established on the continent, succeeded in spreading Christianity throughout Britain, France and Spain. There were always twelve, and whenever one died another took his place in order to keep the number constant at twelve. Joseph lived 50 years after the Crucifixion, and his contributions to Jesus were called "The Golden Age of Christianity." Mary lived at Glastonbury until her death, and she is buried where the old church stood. When Joseph died he was also buried there, and eventually all of the disciples. The epitaph on Joseph's gave read: "I came to the Britons after I buried Christ. I taught. I rest." This sacred ground is called "the holiest ground on Earth." John was the last apostle to die and be interred there. He lived to be 101.

Their descendants even established the first church in Rome hundreds of years before the Vatican even existed. Another remarkable fact: all of the royal line of British kings and queens, down to the present Queen Elizabeth 11, have descended directly from Joseph of Arimathea. Thus they are all related through a long unbroken line of ancestry to Jesus.

There is much, much more to this story, but it is too long for this addendum. At that period in history Britain was the only free country in the world. The Romans never conquered England. In 120 AD Britain was incorporated (by treaty - not conquest). There were many bloody wars as Rome tried unsuccessfully to take over the birthplace of Christianity, and many false tales spread when Rome finally was converted three hundred years later. They tried to topple Britain as being the first country to accept the teachings of Christ.

Many years later in the 1400s there was a big debate with the Vatican over which was the oldest church or the first church. Was it England, France or Spain? They were all founded during the same time period within three years after the crucifixion of Christ. It was finally agreed, and became part of the Vatican record, that the church at Glastonbury was the first church. They tried to deny all the wonderful work that Joseph of Arimathea and the apostles did to spread the teachings, in the way Jesus wanted, immediately after his death.

The story of Joseph's accomplishments were held in such great importance that immediately after the invention of printing, when books were so scare, his story was printed. (1516 and 1520).

Joseph should be remembered and honored for following Jesus' example when he build the first Christian church in the world. It was hundreds of years before the rest of the world caught up, while Joseph and his band of 12 disciples were establishing the beginnings of Christianity. Today few people know this remarkable story, and accept the Roman Catholic version of the origins of Christianity. For the entire narrative, based on solid historical documents, I suggest reading "The Drama of the Lost Disciples," by George F. Jowett. It will open many eyes to the "rest of the story."

Bibliography

Allegro, John, *The Treasure of the Copper Scroll,* Doubleday Pub., New York, 1960. Revised edition, Anchor Books, Garden City, N.J., 1982.

Allegro, John, *Dead Sea Scrolls,* Penguin Books, Middlesex, 1956.

Allegro, John, *Dead Sea Scrolls: A Reappraisal,* Penguin Books, Middlesex, 1964.

Allegro, John, *Dead Sea Scrolls: The Mystery* of *the Dead Sea Scrolls Revealed,* Gramercy Pub., New York, 1981.

Allegro, John, *Dead Sea Scrolls and the Christian Myth,* Prometheus Books, Buffalo, N.Y., 1984.

Dupont-Sommer, A., *The Jewish Sect of Qumran and the Essenes.* Macmillan Co., New York, 1956.

Fritsch, Charles T., *The Qumran Community. Its History and Scrolls,* Macmillan Co., New York, 1956.

Ginsburg, Christian D., *The Essenes: Their History and Doctrines,* Routledge & Kegan Paul Ltd, London, 19Z.

Heline, Theodore, *The Dead Sea Scrolls,* New Age Bible and Philosophy Center, Santa Barbara, 1957. (An interesting Theosophical approach)

Howlett, Duncan, *The Essenes and Christianity,* Harper & Brothers, New York, 1957.

Larson, Martin A., *The Essene Heritage,* Philosophical Library. New York, 1967.

McIntosh and Twyman, Drs., *The Archko Volume,* originally printed 1887. Reprinted Keats Publishing Inc., New Canaan, Connecticut, 1975.

Szekely, Edmond Bordeaux, *The Gospel of Peace* of *Jesus Christ,* C.W Daniel, Saffron Walden, 1937.

Szekely, Edmond Bordeaux, *Guide to the Essene Way of Biogeni Living,* International Biogenic Society, Box 205, Matsqui, B.C. VOX 205, Canada, 1977.

Szekely, Edmond Bordeaux, *The Gospel of the Essenes, C.W.* Daniel. Saffron Walden, 1978.

Szekely, Edmond Bordeaux, *The Teachings of the Essenes jrom Enoch to the Dead Sea Scrolls, C.W.* Daniel, Saffron Walden, 1978.

Tushingham, A. Douglas, "The Men Who Hid the Dead Sea Scrolls," *National Geographic, pp.* 785-808, December 1958.

There are many others that I read while doing my research, but many of these repeated each other and did not offer anything new. Also there were many references in magazines and encyclopedias. I highly recommend John Allegro's work because he was banned from the committee for revealing too much information too soon. Another fresh approach is Martin Larson's *The Essene Heritage.* He was not bound by any religious organization in his reports. I have not used Szekely's books. His sources are quite controversial. I have included his titles mostly because they are well regarded in England. Many of the other authors adhered strictly to religious dogma, and were afraid to deviate in their thinking. However, they do offer interesting historical insights.

Index

About the Author

Dolores Cannon, a regressive hypnotherapist and psychic researcher who records "Lost" knowledge, was born in 1931 in St. Louis, Missouri. She was educated and lived in Missouri until her marriage in 1951 to a career Navy man. She spent the next 20 years traveling all over the world as a typical Navy wife and raising her family.

In 1968 she had her first exposure to reincarnation via regressive hypnosis when her husband, an amateur hypnotist, stumbled across a past life while working with a woman who had a weight problem. At that time the "past life" subject was unorthodox and very few people were experimenting in the field. It sparked her interest, but had to be put aside as the demands of family life took precedence.

In 1970 her husband was discharged as a disabled veteran, and they retired to the hills of Arkansas. She then started her writing career and began selling her articles to various magazines and newspapers. When her children began lives of their own, her interest in regressive hypnosis and reincarnation was reawakened. She studied the various hypnosis methods and thus developed her own unique technique which enabled her to gain the most efficient release of information from her subjects. Since 1979 she has regressed and cataloged information gained from hundreds of volunteers. In 1986 she expanded her investigations into the UFO field. She has done on-site studies of suspected UFO landings, and has investigated the Crop Circles in England. The majority of her work in this field has been the accumulation of evidence from suspected abductees through hypnosis.

Her published books include: *Conversations with Nostradamus Volumes I,II,III - Jesus and the Essenes - They Walked with Jesus - Between Death and Life - A Soul Remembers Hiroshima - Keepers of the Garden - Legacy from the Stars - The Legend of Starcrash - The Custodians - The Convoluted Universe, Books I, II, III - Five Lives Remembered.*

Several of her books are now available in different languages.

Dolores has four children and many grandchildren who keep her solidly balanced between the "real" world of her family and the "unseen" world of her work.

If you wish to correspond with Ozark Mountain Publishing, Inc. about her work, you may write to the following address. (Please enclose a self addressed stamped envelope for the reply.) You may also correspond through our Web Site.

Ozark Mountain Publishing, Inc.
P.O. Box 754
Huntsville, AR 72740
WWW.OZARKMT.COM

Dolores Cannon, who transitioned from this world on October 18, 2014, left behind incredible accomplishments in the fields of alternative healing, hypnosis, metaphysics and past life regression, but most impressive of all was her innate understanding that the most important thing she could do was to share information. To reveal hidden or undiscovered knowledge vital to the enlightenment of humanity and our lessons here on Earth. Sharing information and knowledge is what mattered most to Dolores. That is why her books, lectures and unique QHHT® method of hypnosis continue to amaze, guide and inform so many people around the world. Dolores explored all these possibilities and more while taking us along for the ride of our lives. She wanted fellow travelers to share her journeys into the unknown.

THE STORY OF THE COVER PAINTING

The picture on the cover is a detail from the gigantic (195 ft. x 45 ft.) painting, The Crucifixion, by the noted Polish artist, Jan Styka. It was painted in Poland in 1894 and through a remarkable series of events it ended up in the United States where it languished for many years in a warehouse, because there was no building large enough to accommodate the mural's enormous size. It was acquired by Dr. Hubert Eaton in the 1940's for Forest Lawn Memorial Park in Glendale, California, where it is permanently on exhibition.

When Leila Sherman, a sculptor, first viewed the mural she was frustrated because she was unable to discern even a suggestion of the features of Jesus (the central figure of the mural). This was because of the great distance that separated viewers from the gigantic painting. She became determined to see the face closer. After years of frustration, "red tape" and disappointment, in 1955 Leila Sherman was given special permission to photograph the detail of the figure of Jesus with a telephoto lens from a balcony opposite the painting, (at a distance of approximately 75 ft.).

Although Forest Lawn holds the copyright for the mural, they granted Miss Sherman sole rights to the publishing and distribution of her picture. Miss Sherman has given us permission to share with the world this practically unknown portrayal of Jesus by a great artist. There is a video tape that documents the entire remarkable story of the painting of the mural, and Miss Sherman's steadfast determination to a passionate dream and the attainment of her goal.

For ordering information of copies of the picture, and the video, contact:

Lori Brigham
1O17 O'Donnell Dr.
Bozeman, UT, 59715
406- 86-0784
www.christpicture.com email:
info@christpicture.com

Other Books by Ozark Mountain Publishing, Inc.

Dolores Cannon
A Soul Remembers Hiroshima
Between Death and Life
Conversations with Nostradamus,
    Volume I, II, III
The Convoluted Universe -Book One,
    Two, Three, Four, Five
The Custodians
Five Lives Remembered
Jesus and the Essenes
Keepers of the Garden
Legacy from the Stars
The Legend of Starcrash
The Search for Hidden Sacred
Knowledge
They Walked with Jesus
The Three Waves of Volunteers and the
    New Earth
Aron Abrahamsen
Holiday in Heaven
Out of the Archives – Earth Changes
James Ream Adams
Little Steps
Justine Alessi & M. E. McMillan
Rebirth of the Oracle
Kathryn/Patrick Andries
Naked in Public
Kathryn Andries
The Big Desire
Dream Doctor
Soul Choices: Six Paths to Find Your
Life
    Purpose
Soul Choices: Six Paths to Fulfilling
    Relationships
Patrick Andries
Owners Manual for the Mind
Cat Baldwin
Divine Gifts of Healing
Dan Bird
Finding Your Way in the Spiritual Age
Waking Up in the Spiritual Age
Julia Cannon
Soul Speak – The Language of Your
Body
Ronald Chapman
Seeing True
Albert Cheung
The Emperor's Stargate
Jack Churchward
Lifting the Veil on the Lost Continent of
    Mu
The Stone Tablets of Mu

Sherri Cortland
Guide Group Fridays
Raising Our Vibrations for the New Age
Spiritual Tool Box
Windows of Opportunity
Patrick De Haan
The Alien Handbook
Paulinne Delcour-Min
Spiritual Gold
Holly Ice
Divine Fire
Joanne DiMaggio
Edgar Cayce and the Unfulfilled
Destiny
    of Thomas Jefferson Reborn
Anthony DeNino
The Power of Giving and Gratitude
Michael Dennis
Morning Coffee with God
God's Many Mansions
Carolyn Greer Daly
Opening to Fullness of Spirit
Anita Holmes
Twidders
Aaron Hoopes
Reconnecting to the Earth
Victoria Hunt
Kiss the Wind
Patricia Irvine
In Light and In Shade
Kevin Killen
Ghosts and Me
Diane Lewis
From Psychic to Soul
Donna Lynn
From Fear to Love
Maureen McGill
Baby It's You
Maureen McGill & Nola Davis
Live from the Other Side
Curt Melliger
Heaven Here on Earth
Henry Michaelson
And Jesus Said – A Conversation
Dennis Milner
Kosmos
Andy Myers
Not Your Average Angel Book
Guy Needler
Avoiding Karma
Beyond the Source – Book 1, Book 2
The Anne Dialogues

For more information about any of the above titles, soon to be released titles,
or other items in our catalog, write, phone or visit our website: www.ozarkmt.com
PO Box 754, Huntsville, AR 72740, 479-738-2348/800-935-0045

Other Books by Ozark Mountain Publishing, Inc.

The Curators
The History of God
The Origin Speaks
James Nussbaumer
And Then I Knew My Abundance
The Master of Everything
Mastering Your Own Spiritual Freedom
Living Your Dram, Not Someone Else's
Sherry O'Brian
Peaks and Valleys
Riet Okken
The Liberating Power of Emotions
Gabrielle Orr
Akashic Records: One True Love
Let Miracles Happen
Victor Parachin
Sit a Bit
Nikki Pattillo
A Spiritual Evolution
Children of the Stars
Rev. Grant H. Pealer
A Funny Thing Happened on the
    Way to Heaven
Worlds Beyond Death
Victoria Pendragon
Born Healers
Feng Shui from the Inside, Out
Sleep Magic
The Sleeping Phoenix
Being In A Body
Michael Perlin
Fantastic Adventures in Metaphysics
Walter Pullen
Evolution of the Spirit
Debra Rayburn
Let's Get Natural with Herbs
Charmian Redwood
A New Earth Rising
Coming Home to Lemuria
David Rivinus
Always Dreaming
Richard Rowe
Imagining the Unimaginable
Exploring the Divine Library
M. Don Schorn
Elder Gods of Antiquity
Legacy of the Elder Gods
Gardens of the Elder Gods
Reincarnation...Stepping Stones of Life
Garnet Schulhauser

Dance of Eternal Rapture
Dance of Heavenly Bliss
Dancing Forever with Spirit
Dancing on a Stamp
Manuella Stoerzer
Headless Chicken
Annie Stillwater Gray
Education of a Guardian Angel
The Dawn Book
Work of a Guardian Angel
Joys of a Guardian Angel
Blair Styra
Don't Change the Channel
Who Catharted
Natalie Sudman
Application of Impossible Things
L.R. Sumpter
Judy's Story
The Old is New
We Are the Creators
Artur Tradevosyan
Croton
Jim Thomas
Tales from the Trance
Jolene and Jason Tierney
A Quest of Transcendence
Paul Travers
Dancing with the Mountains
Nicholas Vesey
Living the Life-Force
Janie Wells
Embracing the Human Journey
Payment for Passage
Dennis Wheatley/ Maria Wheatley
The Essential Dowsing Guide
Maria Wheatley
Druidic Soul Star Astrology
Jacquelyn Wiersma
The Zodiac Recipe
Sherry Wilde
The Forgotten Promise
Lyn Willmott
A Small Book of Comfort
Beyond all Boundaries Book 1
Stuart Wilson & Joanna Prentis
Atlantis and the New Consciousness
Beyond Limitations
The Essenes -Children of the Light
The Magdalene Version
Power of the Magdalene
Robert Winterhalter
The Healing Christ

For more information about any of the above titles, soon to be released titles,
or other items in our catalog, write, phone or visit our website: www.ozarkmt.com
PO Box 754, Huntsville, AR 72740, 479-738-2348/800-935-0045